Diana Wynne Jones

Children's Literature and Culture

Jack Zipes, *Series Editor*

Diana Wynne Jones: Children's Literature and the Fantastic Tradition

Farah Mendlesohn

Routledge
Taylor & Francis Group
New York   London

Children's Literature and Culture, volume 36

Published in 2005 by
Routledge
Taylor & Francis Group
270 Madison Avenue
New York, NY 10016

Published in Great Britain by
Routledge
Taylor & Francis Group
2 Park Square
Milton Park, Abingdon
Oxon OX14 4RN

© 2005 by Taylor & Francis Group, LLC
Routledge is an imprint of Taylor & Francis Group

Printed in the United States of America on acid-free paper
10 9 8 7 6 5 4 3 2 1

International Standard Book Number-10: 0-415-97023-7 (Hardcover)
International Standard Book Number-13: 978-0-415-97023-5 (Hardcover)
Library of Congress Card Number 2005003668

Library of Congress Cataloging-in-Publication Data

Mendlesohn, Farah.
    Diana Wynne Jones : children's literature and the fantastic tradition / Farah Mendlesohn.
        p. cm. -- (Children's literature and culture ; v. 36)
    Includes bibliographical references and index.
    ISBN 0-415-97023-7 (hardcover : acid-free paper)
    1. Jones, Diana Wynne--Criticism and interpretation. 2. Children's stories, English--History and criticism. 3. Fantasy fiction, English--History and criticism. I. Title. II. Series: Children's literature and culture ; 36.

PR6060.O497Z76 2005
823'.914--dc22   2005003668

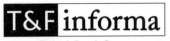

Taylor & Francis Group
is the Academic Division of T&F Informa plc.

Visit the Taylor & Francis Web site at
http://www.taylorandfrancis.com

and the Routledge Web site at
http://www.routledge-ny.com

For Carole Wale, nee Peart, and Marion Peel, nee McFall:
Because I read history instead

CONTENTS

SERIES EDITOR'S FOREWORD

Dedicated to furthering original research in children's literature and culture, the Children's Literature and Culture series includes monographs on individual authors and illustrators, historical examinations of different periods, literary analyses of genres, and comparative studies on literature and the mass media. The series is international in scope and is intended to encourage innovative research in children's literature with a focus on interdisciplinary methodology.

Children's literature and culture are understood in the broadest sense of the term "children" to encompass the period of childhood up through adolescence. Owing to the fact that the notion of childhood has changed so much since the origination of children's literature, this Routledge series is particularly concerned with transformations in children's culture and how they have affected the representation and socialization of children. While the emphasis of the series is on children's literature, all types of studies that deal with children's radio, film, television, and art are included in an endeavor to grasp the aesthetics and values of children's culture. Not only have there been momentous changes in children's culture in the last fifty years, but there have been radical shifts in the scholarship that deals with these changes. In this regard, the goal of the Children's Literature and Culture series is to enhance research in this field and, at the same time, point to new directions that bring together the best scholarly work throughout the world.

Jack Zipes

ACKNOWLEDGMENTS

This book would not have existed without the confidence and encouragement of Michael M. Levy.

In addition, thanks are due to the following people who all read and commented or assisted on some part of this manuscript. Any faults are of course my own.

Diana Wynne Jones, who very generously checked the first draft, but who even more generously refused to have anything to do with it until then.

Edward James who is, as always, the angel at my hearth; Jack Zipes, for commissioning this book; Chris Bell, Elizabeth Billinger; Mary Harris Russell; Maureen Kincaid Speller; Merja Makkinen; Chris Hill and Penny Hill; Pat Pinsent; John Clute; Ken MacLeod; Brian Ameringen; Alice Jenkins; N.M. Browne; Greer Gilman; Brian Attebery; Sandra Lindow; David Langford; Rowan Dalglish; Gary K. Wolfe; and particularly Charles Butler, who responded to the news that someone else was writing on Diana Wynne Jones with an offer to be my writing buddy. His year-long support has been invaluable.

Also Mike Houghton, Roz Trudgon, and Claude Pehrson for more general support; Judith Clute for peace, quiet, and pistachios; and to the staff of the British Library who eased the final few weeks of this project.

Penultimately to those people who have maintained Diana Wynne Jones fan sites that have made far easier the task of gathering together Jones's statements and self-reflection: Deborah Kaplan of *Chrestomanci*

Castle; and Meredith McArdle and Helen Scott of *The Diana Wynne Jones Fansite*.

Acknowledging pets may be sentimental, but cats hold a special place in the work of Jones and many other fantasy writers. My beloved Siamese cat Hubble died just as I was completing this book. He is much missed. To him and Potchka I owe much, for love, distraction and entertainment.

INTRODUCTION:
THE CRITICAL FICTIONS OF DIANA
WYNNE JONES

Diana Wynne Jones is a writer of children's books. Nicholas Tucker has described her as "the most consistently creative author writing fantasy stories for children during the past 30 years."[1] That Jones chooses to write for children is important, because an author's intended audience is always important, but Jones also writes for fantasy readers of all ages, and this is the audience of which I am a part. Within the field of fantasy, as Suzanne Rahn asserted, "Diana Wynne Jones sends seismic quivers through the foundations."[2] It is both legitimate and essential to explore the conventions and techniques of Jones's work in these terms, to discuss her not as a children's writer but as a fantasy writer. Readers of fantasy are notoriously uninterested in the adult–child divide.[3] It is perhaps the last group of readers to maintain what Beverly Lyon Clark has referred to as the category of "family" reading.[4]

What I hope to do here is to explore not so much what Jones writes about, or for whom she writes, but *how* she writes about it. My thesis is that Jones is both a fiction writer and a critic and that her fiction can be viewed as a sustained metafictional critical response to the fantastic. It argues against any sort of special treatment for children's books, as exemplified by Peter Hunt's statement, that "If we judge children's books … by the same value systems as we use for adult books—where they are *bound by definition* to emerge as *lesser*—then we give ourselves unnecessary problems."[5] It is not that I wish to make the argument that all (or some) children's books have the same "value" as all (or some) adult books,[6] but many critics of adult literary fiction would likely elevate the work of, say, Alan Garner over the work of an acclaimed science fiction writer such as Neal Stephenson, because Garner emphasizes a primary desirable "quality" of "lit-fic," psychological characterization, while Stephenson does not, because it is not a major criterion for the people for whom he writes. The issue is not about justifying children's literature or its study but about querying, as Robert Leeson has, why one set of literary values has been allowed to gain dominance.[7]

This book explores why a writer of fiction for children is so important to critics of the fantastic. Jones has "since the start of her publishing career, [been] thinking and rethinking the fantasy form."[8] She has published forty-five books to date (*Conrad's Fate* was published from Collins in 2005) and twenty-three stories. In Carolyn Cushman's list of best all-time fantasy in *Locus*, the trade magazine of science fiction and fantasy, both Jones's Dalemark and Chrestomanci series are listed (eight books in total; only Joan Aiken is listed with more).[9] She won the 1977 Guardian Award for Children's Books (for *Charmed Life*) and has been nominated for many others. Jones has written for children of age five years (the picture book *Yes, Dear*)[10] and produced books marketed to adults, with a book for teenagers appearing as a sequel to an adult book. A rough rule of thumb is that the more recent the novel, the older the age group for which it is marketed. I have used the word *marketed* rather than *intended* because Jones is one of the writers whose work seems to have a lasting appeal for its readers.

What do I mean by fantasy? Kathryn Hume, almost inevitably, invokes the hoary cliché of the blind men describing an elephant: "Each observation is accurate for what part of the whole to which it applies, but none can stand as a description for the entire beast."[11] Jones's own work illustrates this. Some novels—*Fire and Hemlock* and *Time of the Ghost*—can be approached in terms of Tzvetan Todorov's famous moment of hesitation between the *marvelous* (works that resolve into the impossible) and the *uncanny* (works whose events are explainable but shocking or unnerving).[12] Such ambivalence may however, be a central tool of the fantastic, and in this critique Todorov's categories are subsumed in a larger one called *liminal fantasy*. Eric Rabkin's argument that in fantasy "the perspectives enforced by the ground rules of the narrative world must be diametrically contradicted" might work for Jones's *The Merlin Conspiracy* and *Eight Days of Luke*.[13] Brian Attebery adds "… fantasy treats these impossibilities without hesitation: where science fiction would rationalize them, and mimetic fiction insist they were metaphor"; a paradigm we will see exploited to the utmost in *The Magicians of Caprona*.[14]

Faced with a multiplicity of definitions to apply to a writer who has sought to stretch what fantasy can do, none of the above seems terribly satisfactory. Gary K. Wolfe provides a more interesting route and one that better encapsulates the possibilities of the fantastic. Seeking to distinguish three different but related genres whose narrative markers in this field are unstable, Wolfe has written, "The genres of the fantastic … are more readily described as collective world-views than as patterns of repetitive action"; the collective worldview of science fiction is "the geography of reason" of horror "the geography of anxiety; of fantasy, the geography of desire."[15] For myself, if science fiction is the literature that wants the universe to be rational, then fantasy desperately wants to make it *moral*. Both of these approaches come closer to the passionate response to a confused universe, expressed in much of Jones's work.

What all of these critics, and many writers of fantasy from George MacDonald and David Lindsay to J.R.R. Tolkien, have in common is an insistence that fantasy is not allegory, something that frequently places them at loggerheads with criticism of fantasy by many children's literature critics, which tends to assume allegory and to search for metaphoric meaning. If we look at Jones's article for *Foundation*, "Answers to Some Questions," we see that Jones makes her own stance clear: "At its *simplest*, magic can be considered as metaphor … but I hope it goes on to be more. … It should then become a way of saying 'Think this through.'"[16] Fantasy—like science fiction—provides the playground for thought-experiment. This is not the same as metaphor. As chapter 2 argues, careful study of Jones's novels makes it clear that the human issues are almost always resolved *before* magic is invoked, and that frequently—as is demonstrated most blatantly in *The Ogre Downstairs*—the entire point of the story is to persuade the child reader to question the value of metaphors and fairy tales as paradigms for life. Magic is not a solution to real-world problems.

Where Jones Fits

Jones is recognized as a fantasy writer, but as Teya Rosenberg and Karina Hill have pointed out, she slips effortlessly between the boundaries of science fiction and fantasy. Given that these are famously permeable boundaries (endless words have been wasted in trying to assert a clear dividing line), there is a consistent emphasis from Jones that what is perceived as fantastic is contextual. The wizard-geneticist Derk in *Dark Lord of Derkholm* appears to have been written with Sir Arthur C. Clarke's Third Law in mind: "Any sufficiently advanced technology is indistinguishable from magic."[17]

Science fiction is a notoriously blended genre: there is no such thing as a science fiction plot, only an attitude toward the plots that science fiction steals with abandon from everyone and everywhere else.[18] Jones is a happy inheritor of this tradition, and moves fluidly from the treasure hunt (*Hexwood*) to the thriller (*Time of the Ghost; A Sudden Wild Magic*), the crime story (*The Lives of Christopher Chant*), the school story (*Witch Week*), and the romance (*Fire and Hemlock*). One suspects there is a western in there if one looks hard enough. Jones is quick to express impatience with "talk of genres":

> It doesn't seem to me that genres are, *per se,* necessary. There's no reason why you shouldn't mix them up a bit and change them around and make something new. This is what I like to do. This is what you can do with children. I don't see that much difference between science fiction and fantasy. You want to get from A to B by a very swift means not available at the present day. If you're writing science fiction, you go by spaceship, and if you're writing fantasy you go by magic carpet.[19]

As a fantasy writer, Jones is descended from those Victorians who used fantasy to survey conditions in the real world.[20] As a child Jones read very little children's fiction, and there is little sense of direct inspiration, but she does share a recognizable sensibility with two writers, Joan Aiken and Edith Nesbit.

Joan Aiken is another of the children's fantasy writers to be held in very high esteem by fantasy writers and critics. There are strong similarities between Jones's magic of the absurd and Aiken's ironic short stories. In Jones's 2004 collection *Unexpected Magic,* the short story "The Plague of Peacocks," in which a small child inflicts a plague of peacocks on awkward incomers,[21] could have come straight from the pen of Aiken. It is told sparsely, with the minimum of elaboration, and the assumption that whatever else might be fabulous, the actual magic wrought within its pages is not.[22] The newcomers seem more like fabulous beasts than does the child.

Jones might admire Nesbit, but she did not read most of Nesbit's work until she was an adult with children of her own. The influence, if it is there, is conscious, not subconscious.[23] She does remember that as a child she argued with her sister that Nesbit's *The Railway Children* was a "Goddy book" in which children came together "to Do Good."[24] But Francis J. Molson points out that it was Nesbit who first insisted that her audience was intelligent and perceptive, an argument Jones makes throughout her work.[25] Natasha Walter's discussion of Nesbit reminds us also that one of the gifts Nesbit granted to fantasy was realism—not merely the idea that the fantastic could take place in the real world but also the realistic sense of cringing embarrassment that would be felt when it did. Diana Wynne Jones's Goon in the Town Hall is a descendant of Nesbit's Babylonian Queen in London, and of C.S. Lewis's Queen Jadis of Charn. The children in all three incidents try to explain the reality of conventional life, only to see it smashed, and like children everywhere, they are, at bottom, conventional.[26]

What we might be seeing in Jones is less a direct influence of forms than similar conclusions about the relationship of the individual to the world from women who, for very different reasons, are living or have been brought up at crossways to the world and who understand the absurdity of convention. As Jones has written, she knew she would write fantasy "because I was not able to believe in most people's version of a normal life."[27] The same might be said of the bohemian Nesbit, who lurched from one bill to another and lived her entire adult life contrary to acceptable morality.[28]

What Jones Wants to Do: Jones as Critic

Jones has provided hard evidence of her critical sensibility well beyond the pages of her fiction. In addition to the interviews Jones has given, she has since 1983 written four extended critical papers in which she actively embraces the role of critic. "The Shape of the Narrative in *The Lord of the Rings*" (1983) is a structuralist consideration of *Lord of the Rings;* "The

Heroic Ideal—A Personal Odyssey" (1989) is an early discussion of how a Jones book is created; "The Profession of Science Fiction: Answers to Some Questions" (1997) addresses the questions Jones feels never get proper answers; and "Birthing a Book" (2004)[29] reconsiders some of the comments made in "The Heroic Ideal."

Jones's essay "The Shape of the Narrative in *The Lord of the Rings*," written for Robert Giddings's collection *J.R.R. Tolkien: This Far Land*,[30] is something relatively rare in criticism of the fantastic: a critical consideration of a text that is concerned not with content, theme, or the role of metaphor but with the organization of the book. It understands Tolkien's narrative in terms of building blocks, but it escapes the clunkiness of much structuralist analysis by using musical terms to describe how the text functions.

> *The Lord of the Rings* is organized in movements, just like a symphony, but with this difference: each movement has an extension, or coda, which reflects partly back on the movement just completed, and partly forwards to what is to come.[31]

From here Jones plots how long each movement lasts. Jones does not overlook the problems with Tolkien's narrative—the unnerving switches from the domestic to the epic—but she argues that these shifts are deliberate and operate as musical themes, one of which is dominant at any given time while the others remain present almost subliminally. Discussing Frodo's delayed start on his journey, Jones writes:

> The lingering ensures that as Frodo and his companions set off, autumn is coming on, with all that can imply. We are meant to take the point that local changes of season are cosmic in origin, but attention is on the domestic landscape through which the hobbits journey. This is so solidly persuasive that Tolkien is able to introduce the Ringwraiths with the lightest of touches. A few words and they are spine-chilling.[32]

Jones sees Tolkien, by the end of the novel, using his pattern of lingering themes, of repeated codas, to take us not backward but into the future, and juxtaposes his themes to reveal unexpected meaning: "Although it is odd that the positive side of the action is compounded of killing and politics, and the negative of love, endurance and courage, this is how it seems to be. Tolkien insists that the first is valueless without the second."[33] But the lesson Jones takes away with her is that juxtaposition and reflection are very powerful tools if used with rhythm and care. She clearly views Tolkien as a narratologist, and *The Lord of the Rings* as his thesis on narrative.

Following this article, Jones wrote three pieces in which she addressed her own work with the same conviction. The first piece was "The Heroic Ideal—A Personal Odyssey," published in the journal *The Lion and the Unicorn* in June 1989. This is the most frequently cited of Jones's self-analyses because it is the article in which she discusses her desire to create a female hero, and specifically a female hero who was more than a boy with breasts, and about whom boys would be willing to read. But the article also offers a fascinating insight into Jones's creative process. This is particularly evident in her comments on Chaucer:

> I found a man writing who was more subtle than Odysseus, *playing* with the kind of narratives I had previously enjoyed, telling them in different styles, delicately deflating the hero.[34]

Jones—as she herself points out—was not the first to notice Chaucer's subversion of the hero narrative. But what is interesting is the degree to which she was attracted to this position. As Jones came to reconstruct the hero in the form of Polly Whittaker, in her own novel *Fire and Hemlock*, she did so by creating Polly within the context of an ironic world that no longer believes in heroism and tying that into a curse that renders real but ironic Polly's imagination. Polly's initial conceptualization of the hero is pre-Chaucerian, and Laurel's curse can therefore undermine it. But as Polly becomes part of the ironic age, her more ironic heroism, when inverted, regains its purity. This is how Jones puts it:

> …people *do* lose sight of their ideals quite often in adolescence and young adulthood; they tend to see life as far too complex and then come up with the idea that things are only real and valid if they are unpleasant or boring.[35]

But the ending of *Fire and Hemlock* is a complex restatement of ideals in which Polly gives up her image of herself as Tom's white knight. This is both a revision of the construction of the hero and a revision of her relationship with the tales she has read: simply copying their endings is not enough—she needs to synthesize and re-vision them. Polly needs to be a critic. The antagonistic relationship with ideas that Jones presents in *Fire and Hemlock* is, I think, crucial.

In 1997 Jones wrote a piece for *Foundation: the Review of Science Fiction* as part of its "Professions" series, in which writers are given carte blanche to write about themselves *as writers*. Jones chose to approach the matter differently: she interviewed herself, setting out to answer the most commonly asked questions. In response to "Where do you get your ideas, or do you think of them yourself?" she wrote,

> Very shrewdly put, because some part of an idea, if it is going to start a book developing, has to relate to something outside me, even if I don't exactly *get* it from this outside thing. It has to be a creative mix of interior and exterior notions.[36]

Jones begins "Birthing a Book" with a discussion she had with one of her editors about the earlier article "The Heroic Ideal." This article, as I have already said, is most frequently cited because of its statement about the female hero. It also saves the critic in search of intertextual references an awful lot of work with that fiendishly complex text *Fire and Hemlock*. The article is far less commonly discussed as an exercise in self-reflection, but in these terms it is very interesting indeed, because in "The Heroic Ideal" Jones depicts *Fire and Hemlock* as a book planned with architectural detail, Escher-like in its moebius-strip connections. But in her "Professions" piece, she asks the question, "Do you plan your book out before you start it?" and responds "No: that kills it dead."[37] Some contradiction here perhaps? "Birthing a Book" sets out to clear this up. Terribly excited about the analysis she had produced, Jones passed the "The Heroic Ideal" to her editor.

> Libby, one of the editors—a wonderful wise lady with a voice like a sack of gravel being shaken ... looked up from it and shook gravel at me: "Very nice, Diana, but writers don't work like that."[38]

So Jones set out to work out how she did write, by writing a story about it, the *Künstlerroman* (a tale of the growth of an artist) "Carol Oneir's Hundredth Dream."[39] This story, discussed in much greater detail in chapter 7, stands as an analysis of the stories we tell about creativity. Carol Oneir, a child prodigy Dreamer (someone who "writes" dreams), is blocked. In the process of becoming unblocked, she has to submit to some very searching questions from the nine-lived enchanter Chrestomanci. Chrestomanci refuses to let Carol take refuge in the writer's rehearsed tales (where she writes, what pillow she uses, and so on), and Carol is forced to confront some uncomfortable truths: that her characters are her imaginary friends, that she has been using the same characters until they have no more sides of their personality to give, that she has ceased to look outward for inspiration, and that she is now expecting her creativity to work with very limited material. Carol learns what Jones learned in a childhood confusion of Germans and Germs (so that she thought, when she was very small, that Germs came from Twyford):[40] creativity is a process of mixing one's internal self with external stimuli. There is no such thing as imagination, in and of itself. Imagination is dialectic: it is not about copying the world but about arguing with it.

Jones is critically self-aware and embeds in her work a continual know-ingness. One of the central themes in her self-reflective writing is the hero. Although it is unclear whether Jones has actually read Joseph Campbell's discussion of the monomyth, she is clearly aware of story as a process of accretion (she often mentions the sixteen versions of a story about a Princess), and, as Alice Mills has argued very effectively, she is clearly aware of Jungian archetypes.[41] Jones's heroes are defined initially by Campbell's list of challenges and processes. But Jones builds on Camp-bell's ideas and looks in addition toward the stated and demonstrable role of heroes, finding her role model in the tennis stars at Wimbledon:

> For a start, they all had that larger-than-life quality. They stood out among other people even if you didn't know that one was the star. ... And though they defeated the villain on the opposite side of the net, they didn't save the world, they simply won a tennis match. It is very unidiomatic to consider that a hero saves the world. What gives a hero his/her universality is the fact that the gods or God, or the Fates, or some other supernatural agency is on their side. And tennis stars have that too. If one of them is in trouble in a match, their ball is sure to start just flipping the net and rolling down the other side, or they get a lucky call—or it rains.[42]

So heroes are heroes because the gods and the fates *and we* take notice of them. And we—and the gods and the fates—take notice because these people ignore the demarcations between polite society and the way we really and truly want to act. Heroes get to do what we *want* do to, without subtlety, without symbolism: "They sulk, they stamp, they throw racquets and they insult the umpires and the linesmen."[43] They even cheat. Whereas Campbell's ideas about heroes are about following the rules of a moral narrative, Jones argues "No." The thing about heroes is that they will not follow the rules. If they cannot stamp and shout their way to glory, they will be cunning or slithery or devious. And as Jones points out, we love them for this breach of acceptable behavior. What this means is that heroes are not something to emulate but "a scapegoat, to be blamed for doing exactly what you would do yourself."[44]

Jones, having studied the outside of the hero and finding something rather different from Campbell's ideas, then turns to the inside and offers this: when the hero goes to battle it is not her enemy against whom she fights but herself. The tennis star wins because she has won the battle with her own insecurities. In fiction, Jones compared this to Christopher in *The Lives of Christopher Chant*, a child who even comes equipped with "tennis parents" who have dumped on him the burden of expectations until he is on the edge of suicide. Christopher's desire to be "normal" (to deny his heroic potential), allows his Uncle Ralph and the Last Governess to dig their way into his private worlds, into "the centre of his personality." The moment of heroic recognition in this book is less his recognition of what is happening in the story than his realization that he is going to enjoy being Chrestomanci and that his own bumptious personality is a good thing. In thinking about who he actually is and throwing himself into bad behavior to deal with the Dright (the ruler of a very strange world), Christopher raises his game in order to be a hero. Repeatedly Jones tells us that in our bad behavior—such as the child she saw in the school who had hit the bully, only to suffer the punishment for fighting—we find both ourselves and heroism.

The confrontations of the hero are still all there in Jones's work. What she has done is to comment on them, and in doing so create an entire new layer of possibilities; but more, Jones has shown us that the process of spinning possibilities is at the center of a worldview: one should question not just received wisdom but also the premises of received wisdom.

In *Year of the Griffin* Jones wrote this as fiction: a group of students set out to study the work of the long-dead mage Policant. Elda (a griffin) finds herself questioning the questions Policant poses: "Before long she was wondering if Policant might not be asking the wrong questions on purpose, to make you notice the right ones."[45] This is one of the threads that can be traced through Jones's novels. In *Power of Three*, the gift of Sight Asked is a blessing only if the correct question is chosen. Otherwise it is positively a curse because it brings with it complacency. In *Deep Secret*, Rupert Venables lets himself be distracted by the desire to anticipate the answer. Repeatedly Jones shows us that learning (and criticism) are about questioning the premises. From there, students must begin the process of developing their own paradigms. Felim and Ruskin, also students in *Year of the Griffin*, adopt a method of beginning with one spell and then working out what spells can derive from it, to produce a systematic experimentation that results in geometric expansion of learning—much like the "sixteen versions of the same Persian folktale"[46] that Jones remembered reading when she was eleven, or the narrative developments Tolkien mapped for his students and to which she, as a student in his lectures, listened riveted.[47] Another student, Claudia, goes one better and produces a pullout chart of spells and their expansions and complications, "the last page folded out into a huge family tree."[48] There is a moment of realization here: all of Jones's novels are like Claudia's family trees or Ruskin's chart explosions. They begin with a simple arrangement of notes and expand to produce apparently endless variations.

What Jones Wants Us to Know: Remixing

Generally I agree with Sue Walsh's comment that "biographically informed narratives have a way of limiting the interpretation of children's literature to this supposed personal story."[49] In her article in *Foundation,* Jones rejects the idea that her work is a looking back to childhood in any sentimental way, but it is impossible to ignore the degree to which she uses her life as raw material.[50] Jones herself celebrates some of the ways in which her art is informed by life, accepting that the chaos of the war, her experience of evacuation, and the unsettled atmosphere of her childhood is played out repeatedly in her work. More specific, some of the incidents—Christopher's broken neck (*The Lives of Christopher Chant*) or Claudia's travel jinx (*Year of the Griffin*)—are unashamedly drawn from life.[51] The carnivalesque screwball comedy structures, she has said, are drawn from the way her life frequently seems to magnify small incidents until they end, as in "The Girl Jones" (in *Unexpected Magic*), with a small band of previously neat children naked and covered in mud.[52]

When Jones does mine her own childhood, it is rarely to reminisce, although there are one or two moments: Jones's Yorkshire Granny—"five feet of Yorkshire commonsense ... so superstitious that she kept a set of worthless china to break when she happened to break something good, on the grounds that breakages always come in threes and it was as well to get it over"[53]—is recognizable in *Fire and Hemlock,* as is the Welsh grandfather who has to wait until 2004 for his literary memorial in *The Merlin Conspiracy.* But most of the time Jones is more interested in memory as a tool of analysis. *The Time of the Ghost* is her novel most often acknowledged in these terms, and it is one of the books that leaves the adult reader wondering who the intended audience is. For a child, it is a horror story of parental neglect and an attempt at empowerment that goes badly wrong. Read by an adult, it is a rather penetrating consideration of childhood responses to adult ideology.

Jones's parents, and Thaxted, the village in which they lived, were a 1940s remnant of Bohemia and the folk and arts and crafts movements. The atmosphere of these enclaves was bewildering, because the mood of experimentalism ensured that everything was carried on at a high pitch of passionate commitment. My favorite anecdote is one of Jones's mildest: "The vicar of Thaxted was a communist and people used to come from Great Dunmow in hobnailed boots specially to walk out noisily during his sermons."[54] This resonates with my own childhood memories, because it encapsulates a sense of a world in which, however mad, everything matters *enormously.*

Although the sons and daughters of Bohemia interviewed by Virginia Nicholson generally remembered their childhoods favorably, it is all too easy to understand how in the hands of adults who did not particularly like children bohemian theories of childhood could legitimize neglect.[55] In Jones's work adults are very rarely directly cruel, but over and over again they justify neglect and disparagement within a paradigm of their own deservingness. Laurel and Ivy in *Fire and Hemlock* are the most extreme versions, but we can see the pattern repeating. Alice Mills has offered a detailed analysis of the role of the unpleasant mother in Jones's work,[56] and Jones admitted to Maureen Kincaid Speller that her mother is "in all of them, actually, and she's always a villain. And, so far, she's not managed to recognize herself at all."[57] Since *A Sudden Wild Magic,* Jones's mother has steadily retreated, and she is absent from *The Dark Lord of Derkholm.* But the parents in *Time of the Ghost* appear in more complex disguises. The organizational competence of Brid (*Cart and Cwidder*) is as much Jones's mother as is the snobbish Hildy in *The Crown of Dalemark* (see the description in *Something About the Author*),[58] while both parents manifest considerably kindlier guises in *The Merlin Conspiracy*. But Jones also points out that most of her characters are only one side of a person, and that to find the composite you might have to look in many places. Howl (*Howl's Moving Castle*) and the keeper of the Silver Casket in *A Tale of Time City* are built from the same person.[59] Jones's remixing is positively recursive.

Remixing myths is a strategy common to fantasy; as Brian Attebery has argued, "The materials of fantasy ... are partly individual invention and partly communal property."[60] In this, fantasy is no different from mimetic literature, but there does seem to be a higher expectation of originality of invention placed on fantasists even though many of the best fantasists— Angela Carter, Alan Garner, Robin McKinley, J.R.R. Tolkien—reserve their imagination for *reworking* the common stock rather than inventing new props. In contrast are the works of J.K. Rowling, whose use of prior materials is less coherent and systematic than that of other writers. Attempts to enumerate Rowling's influences result in compendiums of allusions that "only reveal the inconsistency and indiscriminateness of the allusive strategy."[61] I am including Gupta's comment on Rowling, only because an attempt to create a compendium of Jones's use of myths results in a very similar feeling, but for very different reasons.

Two of the articles in the collection of papers on Diana Wynne Jones, *An Exciting and Exacting Wisdom* (the first sustained critique of Jones, published in 2002), demonstrate what I mean. Karina Hill's essay "Dragons and Quantum Foam" explores the raid Jones has undertaken on the stock-cupboard of science fiction, from starships, to world gates, to time travel.[62] Sharon Scapple's "Transformation of Myth in *A Tale of Time City*" looks for physical clues to connect Dr. Wilander and his limp to Faber John and the Greek god Hephaestos and deconstructs in very literal terms how Jones has built her characters.[63] This results in lists in which each character or trope stands for more than one reference, which in turn "widens her readers' points of knowing and understanding."[64] Such an approach kills the tale, because in Jones's work, myths or legacy texts must first be seen as themselves[65]—as in *Eight Days of Luke*, in which Jones wanted to "try to express how the ancient and chthonic things are in fact nearly always present to everyone"[66]—and then as dialogic, interacting with each other as well as with the reader in order to create not a route to origins but a route into something that is more than the sum of its parts. Furthermore, with an author as forthright as Jones, the pleasure in reference spotting is weak. As she says, in an article that acknowledges T.H. White, Malory, Chaucer, Gothic Romance, and *Sir Orfeo,*

> It seemed extraordinary to me that anyone could think that one could write anything without being heavily indebted to things that had gone before—and not know it. What I want to say is, yes, I do know really where I'm getting it from and it is intentional and very grateful I am too.[67]

The difficulty, as Daniella Caselli points out, is that "few critics pause to think about what allusions and quotations *do* in the text."[68]

In her self-reflective criticism, Jones does precisely this. Of Bristol and its role in *The Homeward Bounders,* she writes "I think it is because there are an enormous number of triangular towers and curious places, and you seem to go from the ancient to the modern in two easy steps."[69] Although Jones plunders British landscapes (see Charles Butler's chapter "Applied Archaeology"),[70] landscape is not about the places themselves—she regards it as unfair to tease children with places they have never seen[71]—but about the possibilities of those places (what if the mountain spine of England belonged to a dragon, as in *The Merlin Conspiracy*?). The point is that places are not landmarks: they are routes, patterns worked out by people. They are not static either; places are continually being rebuilt, and this construction creates a sense of place as process—something that becomes crucial to the denouement of *The Crown of Dalemark.*

Jones regards her own work as a process of translating, converting historical moments into analogous modern situations.[72] The most vivid display of this can be found at the "Diana Wynne Jones Fansite." On the left-hand side is a link to "Old Irish Hymn." Here Jones has taken a song reputedly sung by a Celtic prince from Spain and turned it first into a villanelle and then into a sestina. In the process the poem simultaneously changes in meaning and retains its original meaning, so that in the original poem the speaker claims godhead, while in the final version, the speaker claims the power of words, the power of a writer, which is a kind of godliness.[73] A similar transfiguration takes place in *The Spellcoats*, which is, at heart, a creation myth.

Jones's use of myths, legends, folktales, and fairy tales, as well as recognizable images from late nineteenth-century and early twentieth-century children's classics, can be encompassed by Zipes's term "postmodern montage."[74] Take, for example, Jones's *Dogsbody*, which, as Alice Mills points out, questions the ending of the Beauty–Beast narrative, leaving the Beast realizing what audiences have long known, that it is as Beast that Sirius's Beauty loved him.[75] Or consider *Castle in the Air*, which Maria Nikolajeva suggests is inspired by *The Arabian Nights*,[76] but in which Grimm's *The Twelve Dancing Princesses* is also clearly recognizable[77]—and in which Gili Bar-Hillel has convincingly argued we can find not only the markers of *The Wonderful Wizard of Oz* (the Witch of the Waste/West, the dog companion, the scarecrow, etc.) but a wider homage in which Sophie's leaving home parallels Dorothy's: "Dorothy has a blue-and-white dress, because she was previously described as the only spot of color in her grey surroundings. Sophie is just the opposite: the only patch of grey in the multi-colored May Day celebrations of Market Chipping."[78]

But Jones does not set out to retell traditional stories or liberate the reader from classic versions of the text.[79] Instead she combines an argument that in the texts themselves are planted the seeds of reader liberation, with what Christine Wilkie described as "identifiable, shared, clusters of codes and literary conventions grouped together in recognisable patterns" that emerge from the kinds of myths and fairy tales that are themselves collaged.[80] The resulting montage assumes foreknowledge, and when a text is written for children, it is a puzzle. Writers such as Susan Cooper and Lloyd Alexander resolved the problem by divorcing their sources from their product. In *The Dark Is Rising* sequence, children are told what they need to know about Arthur. Alan Garner's *The Owl Service* proceeded the same way, although by *Thursbitch* Garner had decided that it did not matter if readers picked up only shards of legend. Lloyd Alexander's Prydain quintet simply ignored the existence of the Mabinogian in all but the afterword and interwove the stories of this myth cycle into the narrative as if told for the first time.

Jones seems to take delight in the awareness that the reader's intersubjective knowledge cannot be assumed. *Eight Days of Luke* is the first and paradigmatic example of this approach. The novel not only demands acceptance on its own terms but also insists that it can be read with or without knowledge of the Norse myths that underpin the adventure. The book's resonance is about structure as well as content—Jones has written that it was an attempt to recreate the medieval sense of story time, sometimes in ways that pass the reader by. No one but Jones seems to have noticed that *Charmed Life* is "a Gothic reversed—young heroine defenseless in frowning Cornish castle ruled by a flinty-hearted macho lord—only in this case the young heroine is a sort of fifth column for an attack on the castle and most people are defenseless before her."[81] Knowledge of these issues neither enhances nor destroys the text; rather, there are two texts to be read: one written to tempt the ignorant, the other to create delicious collusion with the knowledgeable. Both readings are equally demanding, as I argue in chapter 7, and the reader is expected to move from one position to the next.

Dogsbody is relatively casual with its allusions (Herne the Hunter appears as a character but is fundamental only in emphasizing the unchangeability of innate qualities), but it contains an internal *mise en abyme* in which each of the two stories, one of a child Dogsbody, the other of a star in a dog's body, serves as metaphor for the other story. This is a technique that runs through Jones's work at a variety of levels, some superficial and flippant, others providing the ur-narrative for the whole. The apotheosis of this strategy is *Fire and Hemlock,* a novel clearly designed for the reader, the child or adult for whom rereading is a compulsion. These readers revel in Barthes's "circular memory of reading"[82] and particularly treasure authors whose texts are sufficiently polyphonous and multilayered and whose intertexts and hyperlinks are sufficiently multidimensional that the process of rereading is not one of recapturing the sense of wonder that is the first reading but a continual process of "first reading." [83] Of those writers whose work is marketed for children, Alan Garner's more recent fiction and the fiction of Terry Pratchett (most of whose work is not marketed for children, but they love it anyway) operate in comparable ways.

Thus, some of the remixing is done by the reader. Teya Rosenberg recalls first reading *Howl's Moving Castle* while a graduate student, and in addition to the fairy tales and romance "made funnier" there were also "all the graduate school roommates, everyone frantically busy with something and the house in a state just as with Howl's castle,"[84] so that the listener became also a storyteller, "a receiver and giver of counsel."[85] This tendency for the reader to identify intimately is one reason why this book of mine cannot help but be inadequate—there is simply no chance that I will have picked up on every reader's favorite moment in Jones's work.

Organization of This Book

Each of Jones's books can be open to multiple interpretations. In this book there are three distinct interpretations of *Fire and Hemlock*. Jones's wordplay opens out into a complex matrix that can be endlessly unpicked. There are essays to be written on the narrative implications of Jones's parallel worlds, on the political and cultural concerns that repeat in the novels, on her construction of masculinity (given that this is a feminist writer, with three sons, who wanted to get boys to read about girls), on her orientalism, on cats, on Victorianism and medievalism, on belief—the list goes on. Many themes and moments I wanted to comment on have fallen by the wayside. This study focuses, therefore, less on what Jones writes about than on how she writes about what she writes. Its argument, as Jones herself has said, is that fantasy is less the subject matter than the tool.[86]

One consequence is that this book is not structured thematically. The book begins with a consideration of Jones's second published novel, *Wilkins' Tooth*. (Her first novel, *Changeover*, published in 1970, was an enjoyable but unremarkable Evelyn Waugh–style satire on liberation in a Ruritanian African country.) *Wilkins' Tooth* (*Witch's Business* in the United States) was written after Jones had already written *Eight Days of Luke* and *The Ogre Downstairs*, but she had been unable to secure a publisher for them: it was a very conscious attempt to write a book that Macmillan would accept.[87] *Wilkins' Tooth* is a book that does not quite work, but in the ways in which it does not work are the hints of Jones's critical eye.

One challenge for critics of Jones's work has been to find workable groupings of the texts. Teya Rosenberg's suggestions in *An Exciting and Exacting Wisdom* offer an approach that is essentially series-oriented but that seems to limit the questions that can be asked and to restrict the overall consideration of Jones's work as a forty-five-volume (so far) thesis on fantasy. In response, each of the chapters of this book represents an attempt to make a different grouping. The result is that chapters overlap. Books appear and reappear. If some receive more attention than others, it does not mean they are better, just that they had things to contribute to the discussion at hand.

Chapter 2 considers the relationship that Jones posits between magic and empowerment, and the growth of the individual into agency, frequently in opposition to others who construct games and rules to control them. Chapter 3 moves us into the heart of the book with a discussion of time travel in Jones's work. A major element of my argument here is that Jones's texts are metafictive and metacritical. In discussing how Jones has written time travel, I intend to demonstrate how she has woven time narratives into the body of her text: she does not simply write about time travel but uses words to construct the movement.

Chapters 4, 5, and 6 are rather different. They move decisively into a consideration of the rhetorical strategies that Jones uses to construct her worlds. Early in this introduction I offered several definitions of what fantasy is. But once we get beyond definitions, there are many ways to create the fantastic. Conventional classifications of fantasy literature tend to fall into three camps. The first camp is the thematic: urban fantasy, indigenous fantasy, medieval fantasy—all label the tales according to what we might call the landscape of the text. Although this has produced some productive comparative studies, a cursory consideration of the consequences of these categories quickly reveals some difficulties. Some texts fit into too many categories; Terry Pratchett's *The Colour of Magic*, for instance is an urban, neomedieval, and heroic fantasy (and a satire on all three). Any consideration of just one aspect, although interesting, misses the fullness of the novel. Such categorizations also permit bizarre comparisons. *The Colour of Magic* is an urban fantasy, but so is Mervyn Peake's *Titus Groan*, Samuel R. Delany's *Dhalgren*, and Diana Wynne Jones *Archer's Goon*. These novels could not be less alike.

The second most common form of categorization has been through the cast of fantasy. This is seen most clearly in bookshops, where supernatural fiction has been categorized, at least in part by the presence of ghosts, werewolves, and other creatures of the night, and placed on the shelves marked horror, whereas the presence of "other peoples," either those of an elvish–dwarfish persuasion or exotic orientals, will send a book to the fantasy shelves. The difficulties can be seen in the random placements of authors such as Laurell K. Hamilton, some of whose work has all the accoutrements and cast of the supernatural fantasy, but includes elves for good measure.

The third category is the most traditional: High and Low fantasy. High fantasy is traditionally a fully built world, with epic adventure, and almost always some kind of pseudohistorical setting. Low fantasy is "this world" fantasy, often with an urban background.[88] I have come to find this categorization rather unhelpful. Many of Jones's secondary worlds are not medieval and do not contain earth-shattering conflict. Many of her real worlds—supposedly Low fantasy—"contain supernatural intrusions into the 'real world,' "[89] which are accepted by all participants as natural, rather than unnatural, as, for example, the chemistry sets in *The Ogre Downstairs*. When the children explain their nature to the Ogre, he does not question the children's veracity. Any consideration of the narrative strategies of different fantasies needs to focus on three basic but critical questions: how the texts become fantastic, what the consequences of the text's becoming fantastic are for the position of the reader within the text, and what the consequences are for the construction of that text in terms of the language used and the political consequences of the telling of the story. By applying these arguments in Chapters 4, 5, and 6 to Jones's work, I intend to demonstrate the degree to which Jones is both an innovative writer within the field as well as the degree to which her work functions as much as analysis as it does the analyzed.

If we categorize fantasy fiction by its narrative and rhetorical strategies (and the consequences of those strategies) it is possible to see four very rough (and not wholly mutually exclusive) ways of writing the fantastic. It is perfectly possible for a story to make the transition from one structure to another, but when it does, the mode of telling is usually transfigured.

The most apparently straightforward form of fantasy, and that best known to those unfamiliar with the sheer range of the field, is the portal–quest fantasy. This term is an apparent conflation of two forms of the fantastic: the portal fantasy, in which the protagonists travel from one world to another, and the quest fantasy, in which the protagonists move through a fully imagined fantasy world with no "otherworld" in existence in search of something. I have conflated the two for two reasons. First, there are very few portal fantasies in which the transition to another world is not succeeded by a quest (even time travel narratives such as *Charlotte Sometimes* feature a quest to "find out" something or sometimes to change the future), and, second, in both portal and quest fantasies the protagonist moves from the mundane world to the magical, describing the world in detail but restricting the reader's position to that of a forced companion. The protagonist in portal and quest fantasies is always an explorer of an unknown land, and this shapes the way in which the world and the story are told. One consequence can be that only one reading is available because the protagonist is usually isolated from the world and dependent on what he is shown for his knowledge by someone who also has a very restricted view (although David Lindsay's *Voyage to Arcturus* manipulates this to keep the reader and protagonist permanently destabilized). And it is with this category, the portal-quest fantasy, which we will begin in Chapter 4 to consider how Jones critiques and reworks the narrative strategies of the fantastic.

In immersed fantasies, the magic just is. It is all around us, the protagonist is competent, and we ride invisible, picking up hints and clues. These fantasies depend on a form of ironic mimesis to achieve their affects. Chapter 5 will discuss the ways in which Jones builds her worlds using an awareness of politics and political economy to construct an economy of style that conveys more than it actually tells.

Chapter 6 will discuss Jones's use of liminality to command the attention of her readers. Liminal fantasies are the most complex; they rely most heavily on Todorov's ideas about hesitation and uncertainty, and they maintain their sense of the fantastic through equipoise, irony, and a dependency on the knowingness of the reader and the understandings of the conventions of genre. Unfulfilled expectation underpins their dynamic.

In addition, although it is rarely used by Jones, it is helpful to be aware of the fourth category. Intrusion fantasies begin with rupture: the fantastic intrudes into the everyday world (although sometimes this is the everyday world of the immersed fantasy) and the story arc usually involves a negotiation with or defeat of the fantastic. Such tales are dependent on a studied naïveté—the reader is required to enter each text as a naïf—and on the creation of awe or amazement, often through a forced mimetic style. This form appears to be the most moral of the fantastic narratives but does not seem to be a favored form for Jones. *Dogsbody, Eight Days of Luke,* and *Time of the Ghost* are intrusion fantasies, but Jones does not appear to attempt to subvert the form in the way she does with the other three categories.

In much of her work, Jones deliberately addresses the narrative strategies that I have associated with specific categories of fantasy—teasing, challenging, and twisting to subvert the expectations of the reader. That this is intentional is demonstrated by the 1996 publication of *The Tough Guide to Fantasyland* and its fictional sibling *The Dark Lord of Derkholm*

(1998), which together form a devastating and extremely funny critique of the clichés of genre fantasy which is almost always a form of quest fantasy. Yet although quest fantasies dominate the bookstores, they are by no means "all" of what fantasy is.

My final chapter, chapter 7, will bring together the ways in which Jones has written fantasy to consider more directly Jones as a critic and teacher of how to read and how to write. This is the chapter most directly concerned with Jones as a producer of metafictions and as a writer who takes enormous pleasure in the power of the written word. Finally, the epilogue will consider who Jones's readers are, suggesting that Jones's writing offers some challenges to the usual critical construction of the figure of the child reader.

CHAPTER 1
WILKINS' TOOTH

Diana Wynne Jones's first novel, *Changeover* (1970), was aimed at adults. Her career as a children's novelist began with *Wilkins' Tooth*, a curiously hybrid novel that resonates with the conscientious multiculturalism of the 1970s and the concern to focus children's fiction on relevant issues,[1] yet which is placed alongside a fairy-tale and fantasy structure whose tropes intensify the metaphorical understanding of the text. Parallel to this dual structure runs a third strand that subverts the expectations nourished by both traditions. The result is an astonishingly complex novel that almost collapses under the weight of meaning it is intended to carry. This might well explain its almost complete invisibility. Although *Wilkins' Tooth* has recently been reprinted (Collins 2001), the novel had only limited availability (there was a 1984 Puffin edition) for almost twenty years. It is omitted from the entry on Jones in the *Oxford Companion to Children's Literature*, and, perhaps more significant, Jones glosses over it. Jones has written that *Wilkins' Tooth* was a very deliberately contrived novel designed to break into the children's market. *Eight Days of Luke* was still being considered but was regarded as too radical: "While they ummed and ahhed, I decided I would write a book with all the current shibboleths accounted for … [but] … would slide in doing my own thing." The consequence was that Jones "never, for this reason, regarded *WT* as really one of my books."[2] But *Wilkins' Tooth* is flawed in very precise ways that suggest that from the very beginning of her career Jones's writing was as much an

1

act of genre criticism as any academic paper. In this context *Wilkins'*
Tooth, although a minor and marginalized work, demands close attention.

Each of the strands—the realist and the fabulous—that I have
described intertwines with the others to create a layered resonance. For
each incident there are three potential readings. The first we can describe
as an "issues" understanding—something relating to the social context of
the story and the political sensibilities of 1970s children's fiction. The
second is an interpretation drawn from the world of fantasy and fairy tale
that exists first in hints and allusions and is only gradually brought to the
fore to become the focus of the novel. Each of these understandings brings
with it a weight of tradition in terms of the cast of a novel, of their
assigned roles, and of the meaning of certain actions. But the third strand
of the novel, the critical strand, works consistently to manipulate the
signifiers and to subvert the apparent structures of status, of internal hierarchies, and of morality.

Wilkins' Tooth is a continual negotiation: ideas and patterns are worked
out within the interstices of the conflicting literary cultures represented
here. In later works, the result of these critical decisions is not a rejection
of these elements but a blending to create a characteristically layered and
heavily referential work. In *Wilkins' Tooth*, however, the ingredients and
layers are unblended, still there for the literary archaeologist to uncover. In
this first chapter I will attempt to demonstrate how these three elements
not only combine—creating a much richer text than is at first apparent—
but also distort the novel, creating something that is neither one thing nor
another while generating a precursor text, already alive to many of the
possibilities that will emerge in future novels.

Issues books emerged in the late 1960s as a way to tackle the perceived
divorce of children's literature from real life. They were powered by new
ideas about ways to portray class, by the American civil rights movement,
and by changing ideas about the way to depict girls. In addition, they were
ostentatiously concerned with a new way of socializing children and
explored such issues as bereavement, divorce, and bullying. They rejected
what Alison Lurie has described as the "pastoral" assumptions of children's
fiction, "that the world of childhood is simpler and more natural than that
of adults."[3] Their sometimes strident ideological stance can seem like a
break from the past; of course it is not. Those who complained, and
claimed for children's literature an ideological neutrality, were championing
books such as *The Water Babies* and *The Lion, the Witch and the Wardrobe*,[4]
with their evangelical messages, the pastoral and child-centered idylls of

Five Children and It and *Swallows and Amazons,* and the many novels of Enid Blyton, with their clear belief that a very particular kind of middle-class existence was the norm for which children should strive.[5] Even in the work of a writer such as Philippa Pearce, conscious of class and willing to make a working-class boy her protagonist, the assumptions of a book such as *Minnow on the Say* continually effaced difference in such a way that the emotional focus of the book was on the upper-class friend,[6] whereas Eve Garnett's *The Family from One End Street,* an early attempt to go beyond the middle-class family (1937) and a Carnegie medal winner, was a rather patronizing attempt to show the life of a working-class family. In this context, *Wilkins' Tooth* is a rather weak example of the new form. It is multi-cultural and multiclass and has the same number of girls as it has boys. From the beginning Jones makes class a driver of the plot. The assembling of the cast caters to the expectations of the socially conscious novel and shapes the adventure on the mimetic level while, as we shall see, immediately creating a metaphoric resonance that could (but does not) alert us to a potentially fantastic scenario. But although divorce and bullying drive the initial narrative, they rapidly recede into the background, while Jones moves in the direction mapped by Edith Nesbit and brings the fantastic into the urban and ordinary environment.

The novel begins with Frank and Jess, brother and sister, who are mourning the loss of their pocket money after an accident in which they have broken a chair. The opening is conventional—loss of pocket money is a standard mise-en-scène of children's comic book fiction—but here its loss is compounded by their father's insistence that they not undertake to earn money (running errands) to replace that loss. In the lexicon of the issues novels of the period, pocket money is an indicator of social class, at least in urban England. Frank and Jess receive pocket money to make sure they stay middle class (in English terms), which means that they stay children.[7] Unlike middle-class American children, they are not supposed to work and gain independence; consequently the punishment is not precisely about paying for the chair, it is about restricting possibilities. When Frank seeks to get a newspaper round ("route" in the United States) it is made clear that there is a distinction between his need—for sweets and to pay a debt—and that of Vernon Wilkins, who needs the money for reasons unspecified but implied. Immediately we are introduced to a multiclass world, distinct from the cozy middle-class fiction of the 1950s and 1960s and from the often ostensibly class-neutral world of the children's fantasy novel, but one that does not present poverty as tragic.

Frank and Jess must deal with the denial of independence and agency by their own (loving) parent: the route to independence—work—is posited as illegitimate. The structure is patently unfair and as such establishes one of the paradigms of this book: that fairness is a matter of balance, but fairness cannot be expected in the adult world. The restrictiveness of the specifically middle-class response, that children must be protected from independence (which would grow stronger as children's fiction became more realistic during the next decade), constructs the initial setup of the novel, which then follows the trajectory of a *Famous Five* or *Secret Seven* Enid Blyton adventure (children leave home and deal with villain) that were still extremely popular at this time but that were increasingly out of step with ideas about appropriate levels of independence for the young.

But the issue of pocket money and the children's efforts to circumvent parental control can also be read within the context of the fantastic. If their actions are read metaphorically, Frank and Jess have committed a transgression—the breaking of the chair, the decision to avoid the punishment—and wander "into the woods" away from home into the wild world of bargains, debts, and exchanges that structure the traditional fairy tale. The mistakes they make in the real world are paralleled by consequences in the fantastical world that shadows and then intrudes. And in this transgression, they offend a witch. The further into the woods of a multiclass, multiracial world they wander, the stronger will be the structures of fairy tale. Although this part of the book has a fairy-tale structure, it is all metaphoric; that is, this part of the book (except for the hint about the rainbow) is entirely realistic.

In response to their father's edict, Frank and Jess decide to set up in business illegitimately, and they erect a notice facing the river path advertising "Own Back Ltd." The "Ltd" (a term indicating a limited liability company), they assure themselves in that peculiarly literal understanding common to children, is their get-out should a job prove too hard. Their first job, offered by Buster the local gang leader (a precursor of Ginger Hind in *Archer's Goon*), seems very much of the real world: to exact vengeance for Buster's lost tooth by securing one from the offender, Vernon. Their payment will be ten pence, the amount Frank owes him. The susceptibility of the text to a dual interpretation strengthens. On one hand, this is the exchange bargaining common to the playground, morally dangerous because by taking the job, Frank and Jess have made themselves complicit in Buster's bullying. But the situation also carries with it the fairy-tale ethic of balance. Balance in the mimetic world—canceling the debt to Buster—is paralleled by balance in the fantastical world—assuaging the "giant" or other villain through service. And the complicity implied in the first turns out to be equally entangled with the second.

Buster, the bane of Frank and Jess's life, is the leader of the local gang. It is almost impossible not to relate this gang to the British comic strip the "Bash Street Kids" (in *The Beano,* published by D.C. Thomson & Company Ltd, Dundee). It is a large group, distinguished as individuals through physical characteristics such as a squeaky voice. They are obviously working class and, despite Frank and Jess's assumptions, loud rather than evil. They use bad language, a matter over which Jones reaches an uneasy compromise substituting "blank," "blanketty," and the names of various colors for swear words (as in the euphemism, "colorful language"). As the terms "crimson nig" and "Take a blanking look at this! ... Blanketty Own Back!" indicate, the result is possibly worse in implication than the use of contemporary swear words (such as "bloody") might have been, but writers of children's books did not use real swear words in 1973 (neither did many writers for adults) and playground language—substitutes for swearing—was common.[8] Language is indicative of the gang's appearance as the villain, and the language conditions the expectations of the reader, creating a presumption of the morality of the gang novel: Frank and Jess will form their own group of friends who will, in the end, defeat Buster and his friends.

Frank and Jess's difficulties begin because the symbolism, which runs alongside the practical, everyday world is ignored. Buster's demand for his own back—a tooth to match the one he lost—ignores the symmetry already created with the scratch on Vernon's arm. Because this is fairy tale, and with the morality of a fairy tale, Own Back is thus *fated* to create consequences because it offers not vengeance but feud. The spiral is established early, preceded by the discussion of the biblical injunction to take an eye for an eye. Unknown at first to Frank and Jess, their attempt to secure Vernon's tooth for Buster has already exceeded the biblical directive that limits vengeance. When they do learn that Vernon knocked out Buster's tooth as retribution for the long and rather nasty scratch he received (and Buster's lost tooth is a milk tooth so it is also a temporary wound), Frank and Jess understand that they cannot legitimately extract vengeance. However, fear of Buster leads them to accede to a suggestion from Vernon that sets them on the next turn of the spiral. Vernon points out that they have been asked for "Wilkins' tooth" and Vernon's younger brother Silas Wilkins is about to lose one. In a moment, the deal is done. Frank and Jess take the tooth to Buster to wipe out the debt Frank owes of ten pence while agreeing to pay Silas five pence for his tooth.[9]

There are a number of elements here that are susceptible to the interpretation of the fantastic: the exchange bargaining that we have already seen moves into the second stage of fairy tale in which debts are shifted from one party to another (e.g., the ant that helps the prince in return for assistance it has received), the exchange is reciprocal and creates a network of interdependence; in addition, Vernon's status is challenged. Although a minor character, he makes here a significant decision that, according to the rules of fairy tale, involves him in the action. The decision will also influence the role he is to play, something to which I will return. The mimetic role of this action is confusion; it is the fulcrum on which a comedy of errors turns and is a pattern that extends throughout Jones's work from *Changeover* in 1970 to the most recent novel, *Conrad's Fate* (2005). The third element is the importance of true and accurate naming, something that is a constant theme in fairy tale and fantasy. In *Wilkins' Tooth* Biddy Iremonger's name links her directly to the Baba Yaga. Biddy is a name frequently used for hens, (and "old biddy" is a common term of abuse for elderly women), and her surname invites dissection: she is a purveyor of rage and resentment, limited to truth by her very nomenclature. This particular link is never really emphasized, and there is no indication that the meaning of the chosen names is in itself significant—although giving the one black child a Norman name is a nice touch—but the point is made: in terms of the fantastical the significance of this scene in *Wilkins' Tooth* is that the truth of Names and the power of Truth, have been ignored—this is the real world, after all. In the period of contemplation immediately after this second exchange, Jess suspects that she might have done something wrong, demonstrating a knowingness that is important for the fantastical element of this book. This short aside in the text also functions as an indication that Jess might be coming to the fore. As if to confirm her worries about witch doctors, Jess and Frank next meet the Adams sisters, Frances (usually known as Frankie) and Jenny.

The naming of Frances Adams has to be a deliberate statement. Apart from its riff on the popular song, "Frankie and Johnny", Jones also allows Frank to comment on how confusing it is to have two people with the same name. Even here we are allowed parallel readings: one suspects that this an early sign of Jones's critical inclinations, pointing out how absurd it is that in any given novel no two people ever have the same first name—despite the ubiquity of Janes and Johns in the world. More significant, the resonance of names runs as an undercurrent through the book, hinting at connections between characters, bonds that must be worked through. There are similarities between Frank and Frankie—their willingness to believe the bad in others and to act on impulse—that suggest that both are expected to learn about themselves from each other.

Frankie and Jenny Adams want revenge on Biddy Iremonger, who they believe is a witch who ensured that the family had to leave its house and put the evil eye on Jenny so that she is now lame. Frankie is vindictive; Jenny is a follower. The final entry into the series of bargains is Martin Taylor, who now lives in the house that Frankie and Jenny vacated. He wants Frank and Jess to prevent Frankie and Jenny from teasing him—he is not allowed to hit them. Frankie and Jenny cannot afford to pay but are persuaded to desist from teasing as their payment for assistance in defeating Biddy.

With the cast assembled, the plot can proceed. This is relatively simple: the children must get the tooth back from Biddy, tame or recruit Buster's gang, and learn the value of solidarity. Forced to face a very real witch, Jess uses her knowledge of folktales and fairy tales to understand the tools to hand—some material, others human—to hold out against Biddy and eventually to defeat her. Buster's conversion to the side of good, although amusingly depicted, is a bit too easy and obvious. The real interest in this novel lies in the shift Jones makes between the mimetic and the fantastical and the way each interpretative world supports the other through to the denouement of the book. The paralleling is of both deeds and physical context: at the same time that the mimetic landscape is constructed in front of our eyes, Jones develops an alternative cartography of fantasy. As early as page 11, Mr. Carter, noting the offer to search for treasure on the children's advert, mentions the appearance of a rainbow in Biddy Iremonger's yard. A fairy-tale clue has been dropped; because this is structured initially as an issues book, we will be slow to pick it up, but the hidden magic is already intruding into the text, and from here on the children demonstrate that they know how magic works.

Jess's concern with the identity of the tooth's owner can resonate only if magic exists. Frankie and Jenny's appearance, and insistence that their losses are due to magic, forces Jess, at least, to confront the existence of magic. If Frank and Jess are to heal Jenny's leg, they must consider the dynamic of magic and whether the death of Biddy will offer release. Jess knows that death might prevent the lifting of a spell. When Silas is spell-cast (his face swollen as if he had mumps), the children discuss what they know about spells. This is where Jones is already departing from the Nesbit convention. Fantasy has not intruded into our world. Instead, and without noticing, we have moved through a portal to a different world where magic is real, where "My Mum's heard some, and there's books in the Library that maybe tell us."[10]

Jones produces two tricks here. Vernon's mother's Caribbean origins are communicated in what she knows, not in her color: she is from another culture, one in which witchcraft is understood, and this is casual-ized, placed on a par with the contents of the local library.[11] On the level of the issues novel, it is a relief that it is not rendered exotic,[12] but its casu-alization is unusual in terms of the fantastic also. It is reasonable to suggest that we may have moved into another world because there is no astonishment and no wonder: where Frank and Jess have doubted that Biddy is a witch, this piece of information is simply absorbed. Jones is already developing the casual segue into the fantastic, which we will see elsewhere.

The ways of knowing that the children exhibit are vital to the way the novel is constructed, and this extends to both the magical world and the mundane. The children negotiate two sets of relationships, that of chil-dren to adults and that of the real world to the fantastical: the two illumi-nate and inform each other. The first discovery is that adults see the world very differently. Frank and Jess's father defines an accident as deliberate destruction. Mr. Taylor assumes that any fight must have wrong on both sides. When Buster's gang chases the children through the Home's lawns, the Guests do not take much notice or realize there is an incident. It is children's business, not theirs. Similarly, the logic of the adult world passes the children by. Intervention is perceived as disrupting the balance of fairness. The arbitrariness of the adult world possesses a signifier of its own: in Jones's later work the unfair adult and his or her affect on children recurs (in *Time of the Ghost* and *Deep Secret*) but so too does the Fool, an undirected, apparently vague adult who possesses a secret (Andrew in *Deep Secret*, Tom in *Fire and Hemlock*, Anthony Green in *Black Maria*). In *Wilkins' Tooth* the Fool is Mr. Adams, Frankie and Jenny's father. Mr. Adams wanders through the action, disturbing events and breaking up the conflicts between the children. A seemingly marginal figure, he is actually crucial: he is the lost King, the amnesiac who must be restored if the Land is to be healed. He is one of the earliest examples of Jones's layered characters, one who must be peeled back by the protagonists. In this case the layering is rather shallow, but the deception is still there. As with their opinions of their peers, Frank and Jess must learn not to judge adults by superficialities.

By the time Frank and Jess make their first visit to Biddy, they have transgressed into the metaphorical woods and crossed the borderland into the portal that is Biddy's hut (they cross through into an otherworld only briefly, when trapped there at the end of the book).

> Biddy Iremonger's hut was under a big hollow tree beyond a clump of brambles. It looked as if it might have been a boathouse once. It was wooden, and settled slopingly down the river bank. In front of it was a patch of bare earth, and, heaped carefully around that, were petrol drums and paint-tins, to make a sort of wall. ...
>
> Biddy Iremonger's black cockerel flew up to the roof of the hut when it saw them coming.[13]

To someone schooled in fairy tales, the hut clearly belongs to the Baba Yaga,[14] even if it does not have the feet of a chicken. The text is layered even here, dependent for full resonance on a child's understanding of the legacy texts. In 1973 it was still a safe bet that a (British) reading child might have encountered the fairy-tale collections of Andrew Lang and Ruth Manning-Sanders, as well as of Roald Dahl. She or he would know what real witches were. Whether this would have the same kind of resonance for a modern child, whose knowledge of witches is from American Halloween decorations, *Sabrina the Teenage Witch*, and Harry Potter novels, is uncertain.[15] But even given these intertextual references within *Wilkins' Tooth*, Jones continues to set up dissonances between what the children have been taught and what they know, in this case, with regard to the character of Biddy.

> The oddest thing about Biddy Iremonger was that she was educated. She had a sharp, learned voice, rather like Jess's school teacher, which, when she spoke, made it very difficult to imagine her putting the Evil Eye on people—or, indeed, doing anything that was not just harmless and a little odd.[16]

As with Buster, who turns out to be a much nicer child than is indicated by his language, language is meaningful, must be used with care, and is deceptive. But because of this trichotomy, language is powerful, and Biddy respects this. In *The Spellcoats, Power of Three,* and *Witch Week,* language is something to manipulate, but for now, challenged over whether she is attacking the Adams family, it is enough that Biddy appears unable to speak anything but the truth.

> Biddy nodded again. "Yes, my dear. She's quite right. I did. I have it in for that family, you know."
>
> Jess's head came up. Frank went suddenly from hot and fat to cold and thin with horror, that anyone could talk as calmly and cheerfully as Biddy about a thing like that.[17]

Nowhere in this novel does Biddy ever lie. As is traditional in both the fairy tale and the mystery adventure, she drops the clues that the children need to defeat her: riddled, convoluted, and defracted, but unlike in the realist novel where the children must see through lies, here they must use what they know about the way magic works and do so truthfully.

The magic is no longer in question. We are now thoroughly involved with what will become a classic Jones trope in her early novels: the casual intrusion of the magical into the normal world. From here on *Wilkins' Tooth* conforms to the structure of an intrusion fantasy: the protagonists must accept, understand, analyze, and either defeat or negotiate with the fantastical that has disrupted their world. The process includes discovery of the rules of magic embedded in the realization that Biddy's Nine Tailors, the price paid for her vengeance, is the ownership of Buster's gang, in body and soul. The understanding that they are in a world of literal truth will color the rest of the tale: Buster and the gang are now dogs because they act as such. Metaphor is made real. Intentions become realities. To win, Frank and Jess will have to be very clear what it is they are seeking and why they are using the methods they chose.

Frank and Jess have made a bargain. Frances and Jenny are now their business and they cannot back down. Because they have usurped the witch's business—vengeance—they have transferred the witch's interest to them (an idea repeated in *Howl's Moving Castle*). Magic contaminates; it reaches out to encompass, and involvement once initiated cannot be withdrawn. Jess and Frank, and Biddy, are now bound by a morality that says the game must be finished—Frank and Jess must because they have made the deal, and Biddy must because she must "mind her business"; that is, take care of and ensure that her plans come to fruition, and they have moved in on it. The difference between "mind her business" and "mind your own business," a common playground taunt, is one of the more subversive themes in this novel, because it forces children to consider where the line of privacy is drawn—is someone else's pain your business?

Although the children are at risk from Biddy in a purely practical sense, the novel is also structured to demonstrate their moral risk. Own Back Ltd starts as a game. It becomes something more not only as the stakes escalate but also as the nature of what they set out to do is made clearer to Frank and Jess simply by its association with Biddy. If vengeance is something that a witch takes delight in, that brings into question the moral probity of such a course of action. Jones starts from the point that Vigen Guroian argues is the natural state of all children, a clear-cut understanding of Right and Wrong, Fair and Unfair.[18] But whereas a fantasist such as C.S. Lewis (Narnia) or Susan Cooper (*The Dark Is Rising* sequence) builds on this, Jones unexpectedly cuts across it. The children must learn not what is right or wrong but the ambivalence that surrounds actions and the extent to which intent distorts. Jones extends this idea in later novels. In *Charmed Life*, Cat learns that being horrified by Gwendolyn's actions without intervening makes him culpable, even though there is little he could do. Jones makes the same point about culpability in *Dogsbody*. In Jones's works, being good of heart and intention is not enough.

To make this point in *Wilkins' Tooth* Jones introduces a good fairy, a rather mysterious character, a young lady, vague and pretty, who is a Guest at the residential home run by Martin's parents. The lady, who turns out to be Frankie and Jenny's mother, is an amnesiac and is surrounded by amnesia; Mr. Adams, her husband, does not remember who she is until the spell has been lifted. She is an oracle, a speaker of moral truth. Taking on the fairy-tale role of catalyst-wise woman, she observes, "You've been meddling with people's worse natures, haven't you?" Denial brings the following analysis:

> Everyone knows how to do that. We may disguise it from ourselves by calling it a kindness to someone else—as I did—or telling ourselves that it's only fair to do whatever it is, but the fact remains that we've done a bad act disguised as a good one. And I have a feeling that's just what you've done.[19]

Own Back Ltd is now on dubious moral ground in two ways: the kind of people who exact vengeance are rendered morally suspect, and good intentions as justification for the unjustifiable are dismissed. From this point on, Frank and Jess are no longer seeking vengeance but trying to rectify their original mistakes. Once enlightened, they also can acknowledge the context in which they are moving: magic now makes sense, and if magic makes sense they can begin to deploy what they have and what they know, beginning with the lady's gifts of the eye pendants. As is traditional in fairy tales, the trick with magical gifts is not knowing that they are magical but knowing how to use them. The girl who throws her comb over her shoulder to create a magical forest must know (or be told) that this is the right way to do it. However, magical gifts in Jones's work, whether abilities or objects, are never unencumbered. Their possession demands bravery. Jones departs from the convention in that the children neither know instinctively nor are told what to do with their eye pendants (except wear them). It is Jess who is the tactician and realizes that the pendants deflect evil and that they can be used proactively. Instead of merely protecting them from Buster's gang, now officially allied with Biddy, Jess uses the force field they create around them to herd Buster's gang back. We have had hints before this that it is Jess in control of the adventure, but this is the first clear indication. It is also clear that it is Jess who learns the lessons that are taught: when Kevin, a very young member of the gang, asks for his Own Back—in the sense that he wants his brothers back from Biddy—Jess realizes that she cannot take payment for this.

Wilkins' tooth is eventually found with the aid of Buster and his gang, who change sides when Biddy begins to torture them. When they find it, the tooth is hanging from a string over a poorly described altar. The tooth hurts those who touch it, and it captures those who do—a combination of the golden goose and the many cases in fairy tale (and in the Tam Lin and Thomas the Rhymer ballads Jones uses in *Fire and Hemlock*) where that which is touched brings pain. The message of these scenes is usually that nothing worth achieving can be had without pain. But Jones resists this kind of unsubtlety. The real messages here are about the manipulation of knowledge. Unthinking action always goes unrewarded. The denouement of the novel and the children's success comes not from the spontaneous grabbing of the tooth, which traps them in Biddy's hut, but from the ways in which they then face off with Biddy. The circle they form might not be magical—Biddy mocks its vulnerability—but a ring is powerful in creating connections and allowing communication, and it enables Vernon to knock the tooth to one of the other children, knowing that it will land near one of them. The necessity of dual use and interpretation operates even on this mundane level.

Wilkins' Tooth is a fairy tale, so the solution to the problem has to come from the mechanisms of fairy tale: the witch must have an Achilles' heel. Biddy's Achilles' heel is the treatment of her cat, punished with starvation for not bringing the children back. "The cat was sitting on the table staring at her spitefully. It looked as if it hated Biddy quite as much as Frank did."[20] But before they can get the cat's cooperation, the children have to apologize for throwing spoons. Friendship to the animal–familiar world is crucial in fairy tales, and the children must treat the cat as an equal, talk to it, and assume it understands the hint about Puss in Boots; knowingness allows them to trick Biddy. Similarly, although Suzanne Rahn is correct to argue that the ending is weak, that Biddy is "hardly the type to be taken in so readily,"[21] Biddy's ego demands that she work within the rules of fantasy. As John Clute describes a similar scenario in a novel by Patricia McKillip, it is "the moment of joy, because it is a moment when the tale is obeyed both by the characters within the book, and (if I am correct about the reading protocols necessary for the proper comprehension of fantasy) by the reader as well."[22] Biddy's insistence on truth telling, even if it is riddled truth, and on her assurance that there is a way to break the curse, even if it is impossible to find, provides Jess with the means to manipulate Biddy, if she can only work through the fairy tale. This she achieves by pandering to Biddy's ego, persuading her to prove that real magic exists by transforming herself into first the traditional elephant and then the traditional mouse. On a more mundane level, knowingness reminds Jess to get the mouse to run across the circle to tempt the cat. However, although the scene performs its function, the magic feels grafted on. Not only is it the first time we have seen unambiguous magic but it also is almost too ostentatious a use of fairy tale. Deborah Stevenson has argued that "academic recovery of a book cannot reinvent the initial response,"[23] and here, where both Jones and Jess act as "academics" critiquing the fairy-tale text, one can see the difficulty. The original exuberance of the tale is muted by too great an awareness of its significance. Jones does not repeat this mistake in her later books.

More interesting is the structural role that this tale has played throughout. *Puss in Boots* is one of the few fairy tales told from the point of view of the companion. The cat pretty much tells his "prince" what to do. Puss is also the go-between who negotiates with the principal actors. Frank and

Jess, assuming themselves to be protagonists in their own narrative, rapidly become instead messengers, but like Puss, they retain control of the moral outcome, reinterpreting the demands of Martin, Frankie and Jenny, and Buster according to their own understanding of fairness. *Puss in Boots* is woven into the narrative structure from the beginning.

The conclusion of the novel is more straightforward. Having proved her worth by holding and hiding the tooth, Jenny has, in a sense, rescued herself. Her heirloom is as much her own bravery as the emerald necklace that Vernon finds out of the corner of his eye. Biddy, it turns out, hid the treasure in the rubbish dump that surrounds her hut; it cannot be seen straight on, only in glimpses, transformed into bicycle chains and tin cans, a metaphor perhaps of the transfiguration she had performed on Buster and his gang and quite possibly a reference to the jewels found in the witch's hut in *Hansel and Gretel.* It is a reflection also of Biddy, who hides herself in the knowledge that the absolute truth will not be believed.

Reading the novel, and particularly on rereading, one is struck by the shifting roles of the characters. On a mundane level, good and evil are no longer as easy to identify; friends and enemies have become the same people, and it is no longer clear, by the end, that this is Frank and Jess's adventure. The character shifts that Jones has depicted are the most telling aspect of the parallel structure I have outlined, and the area in which she is most subversive.

When we first met Buster, Frank, and Jess, the structure of the novel and their presentation appeared firmly social realist. Frank and Jess are the primary protagonists, the principal viewpoint characters. But in terms of the social hierarchies of the text, they are positioned neatly in the middle. Martin is the most upper class, with Frances and Jenny positioned along-side him as (apparently) fallen gentry. On the other side, there is Vernon Wilkins, who represents an ethnic minority and the respectable face of the British working class, while Buster is of the lowest class, white and unrespectable. Jenny, Frances, and Jess are positioned to show three perspectives on femaleness at a time when the portrayal of young girls in children's books was being contested. These choices weigh the book down. Jones's later novels, which are often less apparently balanced in their casts, handle the integration of class and gender and the challenging of stereotypes, with far greater felicity (race is much less considered).

From the point of view of the fantastical, however, each of these children also operates within classic fairytale archetypes: the hero or heroine of a fairy tale needs assistance to perform great deeds.[24] Buster functions as the giant or wild animal who can be tamed through gratitude; Martin initially plays the prince, determined to secure his inheritance; Frankie and Jenny are the missing heirs—abandoned princesses; and Vernon is the sidekick. Frank and Jess begin as the wronged children, but as they emerge into their full role they increasingly come to play the role of mage or wizard, dispensing advice and completing tasks that are not, in actuality, their own.

The ensemble structure, whether social realist or fantastical, is an ideological stance in itself, and one not unfamiliar in children's fiction of this period—the idea of the hero has here been subsumed into the concept of the community effort. This is the period in which people produced books of noncompetitive games for children. But although Jones emulates the archetypes of the fairy tale, in part to endow her ensemble with depth, her purposes are different. As I discussed in the introduction, Jones revisions heroism.

For Jones, heroism is the very stuff of children's literature: "In every playground there are actual giants to be overcome and the moral issues are usually clearer than they are, say, in politics."[25] The way in which she explores this subverts the realist and fantastical alignments. Crucial to the ethical and narrative structures of Jones's work is the belief that knowledge, and specifically knowledge of each other, is the key to perceiving each other as human and to understanding what bravery is. And Jones, in rethinking heroism, subverts our understandings of who the villains are and who the heroes are, beginning with the idea that girls cannot be heroes.[26]

The desire to produce the female hero (not heroine), or at least not a predictable one, is one of the distortions that affect this book. As I have already pointed out, the cast is evenly balanced; three boys, three girls, carefully composed according to class, with Frank and Jess as the fulcrum. By the end of the book, however, Jess and Jenny are the principal heroes, with Vernon and Buster as their most significant supports. Frank and Martin, the two who seem to have been placed to lead, have taken a back seat; Frank rather resentfully.

The established archetypes are broken down early, first when it becomes clear that Frances and Jenny are both persecutors and persecuted; their harassment of Martin calls into question the ease with which Frank and Jess label Buster's gang as "evil." Second, the attribution of roles rapidly becomes problematic in both the mimetic and the fantastical interpretations. Very quickly we realize that Martin is not the child of rich parents but is living in a large house that has been converted to a residential home. It also emerges that it is Vernon who is the leader in the relationship—far from being the sidekick: "It was Vernon who seemed to be the bossy one. At least, somehow, they all kept doing what Vernon said."[27] This causes Frank some difficulties. Frank has controlled the structure of his and Jess's summer, even assuming that any money he and Jess earn will be directed first to the payment of his debts. Frank has three lessons to learn: that he is not a natural leader, although he might be in charge at times; that he has a tendency to value people according to the extent to which they will defer to him—as Jess points out, he prefers Martin to Vernon because Martin will acquiesce to his leadership; and, as the novel develops, that it is Jess who is the more creative and imaginative of the two. It cannot be insignificant that we are never told which of the two children is the elder. Jess is allowed to emerge as a leader because she has the talent. It is Jess who figures out the way in which to use the eyes and how to manipulate the fairy tales within which Biddy operates. The exercise of knowledge and thought that Jones indicates in *Wilkins' Tooth* is essential for heroism, is as radical a notion as allowing the girl-child to emerge as the hero.[28] The same qualities lift Vernon's status and undercut any opportunity for the reader to see Vernon as a marginal character because of his color. When we learn that it is his younger brother Silas who protects the young white child Kevin from bullying in the playground, our stereotypes about bullying are further depressed. Vernon, far from being the sidekick, emerges as the unrecognized prince. Although Jenny is less significant to the narrative, we see at the end that it is her bravery, rather than that of her older sister or any of the boys, that facilitates Jess's victory.

Frank and Frankie see themselves as leaders, perhaps because of gender, or in Frankie's case because she is the elder. Both act on impulse and judge character by instinct. Both are dethroned by the leadership characteristics of others, specifically their sisters. Jess and Jenny emerge as braver and more thoughtful, and, alongside Vernon, continually emphasize that bravery without thoughtfulness leads to unethical decisions and danger. Although this appears obvious, by paralleling these roles, Jones neatly elides the fact that she has shifted the focus of the novel from the boys to the girls. Although the title indicates that this book is about a boy, Vernon Wilkins, and the presence of Frank and Jess allows for identification by both sexes (that unquestioned desire of the unimaginative critic). Rather than using the ensemble effect to create these different routes of identification, Jones subverts the structure. By the end of the book, Jess, on her own, is the primary viewpoint character. Male readers will have been led into sublimating their identity within a female hero.

Elsewhere, Vernon and Buster oppose rather than parallel each other. Both face the world with force, but whereas Vernon is oriented to community, to family, and to collective well-being, Buster operates on the assumption that his interests are in the interests of his gang. However, Buster is not a nice child; before the story starts he has beaten Vernon while Vernon undertook his paper round. In the story itself, however, Buster is not threatening Frank for money; Frank freely admits that he owes Buster, although owing Buster is not a pleasant position to be in. Similarly, although Vernon is resentful that Buster wants a tooth, he appears to see the scratch on his arm as within the boundaries of normal behavior. He does not accuse Buster of bullying. That Jones subverts our expectations of Vernon's status is obvious, but it is easy to miss that we are denied our expectations of Buster; he behaves in ways very similar to Vernon. Both characters are highly protective of their people; for Vernon his family and friends, for Buster his gang. Both will take risks, and Buster, although thoughtless and selfish when he sells his gang to Biddy for petty revenge, is much more willing to accept responsibility and rectify his mistakes than is either Frank or Frankie, both of whom tend to look for other people to blame.

For a novel of only 170 pages, *Wilkins' Tooth* is astonishingly complex. If this book leaves the reader with a sense of failure, it is because it attempts far too much and is not really comfortable with the mimetic structures and ideas that shape its earlier chapters; but the ways in which it does not work are fascinating and herald the emergence of a profoundly self-conscious and critical author. It presents the reader with at least three strands: the mimetic, the fantastical, and Jones's own critique of these elements. It achieves the notable affect of creating two female heroes in the midst of an ensemble novel without marginalizing the male characters, and questions the nature of leadership and of apparent bullies without either lecturing the readership on psychology or producing a miraculous transformation in anyone's character. Buster, for example, is essentially unchanged. It is just that he now regards Frank, Jess, and the rest as his people. The strongest message might be to keep an open mind and to refuse the conventions of the mimetic world—that there are things that are real and things that are not—and also those of the fairy tale, which would have every unprepossessing character be a fairy in disguise.

Finally, if at first we are presented with an essentially mimetic view of the world in *Wilkins' Tooth*, the parallel structures of event and interpretation that emerge in this book can be understood as a series of portals. Each event-interpretation archway through which we pass deflects us further into the fantastical until we no longer have a choice of direction and our understanding of the world has been profoundly changed. In later books, such as *Witch Week, Hexwood,* and *Deep Secret,* Jones refines this technique so that the segues are seamless and the moral structures of the novels less intrusive, but in *Wilkins' Tooth* we can already see the outline.

CHAPTER 2
AGENCY AND JONES'S UNDERSTANDING OF ADOLESCENCE

Much of children's literature is concerned with the need of children to gain autonomy and pass into adulthood. In part because children's literature is frequently seen as a tool for socializing the child and because the process of growing into adulthood is of ferocious interest to children, the "most pervasive theme in children's fiction is the change within the individual from infantile solipsism to maturing social awareness,"[1] although as Melvin Burgess proved with *Junk,* and *Lady, My Life as a Bitch,* the result is not always regarded by adults as a desirable outcome.

In children's fantastic fiction, the acquisition of magical power—or magical gifts—frequently marks emergent adulthood. Magical events and intrusions (ghosts and poltergeists) are a common metaphor for the state of uncertainty that exists on the threshold of adulthood and for the disruptions of the every day: divorce, death, and poverty. Quests—searches for swords and identity—map onto the search for the accoutrements of adulthood (cars and credit cards) and the sense of self.[2] The patterns occur in books for children of all ages: magic is an effective metaphor for growth and the process of constant change, and negotiation with the change that is adolescence.

However, in children's and adult's fantastic fiction, all too frequently adulthood is reduced to a mere matter of power, disengaged from emotional maturity or complexity. The element of the fantastic suffers because it becomes an adventure playground in which the depiction of the fantastic becomes a description of what happens if you press a particular button. This is particularly central to one subgenre of fantasy, the quest fantasy, in which something must be found in order to resolve the chaos. In this narrative, the magical and the doing of magical deeds—however important in the search for what Nick Lowe has termed *plot coupons*[3]—is only a portal. The transition from the mundane to the magical becomes more significant than the exploration of the magical. Similarly, the moment of transition from adolescence to adulthood is given more significance than is the potential it unleashes, in part because adulthood becomes a plot coupon, something labeled and clearly defined, rather than a process.

J.K. Rowling's Harry Potter sequence suffers from this problem: Harry Potter's future and therefore his adult self is iterated in the very first novel. C.S. Lewis is even more reductive: in *The Lion, the Witch and the Wardrobe*, Peter is given a sword and shield to symbolize his role as a warrior, Susan is given a horn so that she can always call for help, and Lucy is given the small vial of healing water. In *The Dark Is Rising* sequence, Susan Cooper embedded an arcane knowledge of one's adult self into her very definition of adulthood and magic. The Old Ones have inborn knowledge, but conscious awareness emerges only with the onset of puberty, and the first magical event is the moment of realization. Wisdom and magic are gifts of birth, and this is true even of the nonmagical children in the sequence. Jane is told in *Greenwitch* and in *Silver on the Tree* that she has an instinctive wisdom. Gillian Spraggs and Fred Inglis both argue that too much dependence on instinct or destiny creates protagonists "who need to strive neither to *do* anything nor to *become* anything, because they are defined as adequate to whatever may happen."[4] Of *The Dark is Rising* sequence, Spraggs argues that Will discovers an "endless series of miraculous powers" rather than any sense of who he is as a person.[5] His sense of realization takes place in the moment.

One result in all of these novels is that the adventure becomes determined rather than exploratory. The end is predicted by the quest, and the novel describes how that end is reached, rather than challenging us to consider what that end might be or the process by which the journey is traversed. To maintain tension when the outcome is predetermined, the author must become endlessly inventive about the content of his or her world—to produce thrill after mystery—which concentrates the author's gifts on the descriptive, in an irony of mimesis that tries to convince through detail. Similarly, because realization in these novels is momentary, it does not connect to growth. Adventure becomes the substitute (an irony of maturation if you will), distracting from the relative lack of agency that the protagonists, steered through the map of their adventure, never acknowledge or correct because they are absorbed by the power that the accoutrements of adulthood—swords and car keys—seem to provide. What these tokens do not provide is choice, although choice can become the point of the novel (as in Bran's choice to stay with his foster father in *The Grey King* and again in *Silver on the Tree*). The structured, deterministic choices that we can see in Lewis's, Cooper's, and Rowling's work elide the distinction between the risks of adulthood and its challenges. They conflate magical power with maturity. Occasionally this is deliberate; Lewis, a Christian, associates adulthood not with freedom and choice but with the acceptance of a yet more powerful father figure.

Jones, along with authors such as Margaret Mahy, Lloyd Alexander, Anne Fine, William Mayne, Alan Garner, and David Almond, is distinctive because she reverses the route map to adulthood. Jones posits that power is a direct consequence of the acquisition of agency. Because agency is about the ability to make conscious choices—the realization that one obeys because it is the wise thing to do, rather than because an order has been given by an authority figure—agency cannot be acquired solely with the conferring of power. Power without agency creates either a more powerful servant or an individual unable to harness his or her own power effectively. One can envision Harry Potter in this relationship with Dumbledore, and the more sinister figure of Mordion in Jones's *Hexwood* in relation to Reigner One. Abdullah, in Jones's *Castle in the Air*, is a good example of power without agency. His early use of the genie's wishes mimics the children's mistakes in Nesbit's *Five Children and It* and betrays his lack of control over the situation. On occasions magic comes with that acquired agency, but it can also be the catalyst for its development. For example, Margaret Rumbold made a powerful argument that in *Power of Three*, the middle child (Gair) is marked out from the start as special because of his looks, his family line, and his oppositional relationship to his cousin Orban—portrayed as large, brash, and aggressive. Gair's acquisition of "sight unasked" merely confirms his rightful inheritance of his father's mantle as chief of the tribe.[6] But even here, in this example of destinarianism, Gair's real worth is less in his gift than in his character. When his father boasts of him, the gift comes third, as a trump card, after his father has recognized his wisdom and courage. Gair's gift is only of use insofar as it is linked with the qualities of adulthood. The same issue plays out in *Charmed Life*, in which the consanguinity of Cat's parents determines his destiny.

The point here is not that Jones is unique in using magic as a metaphor for adolescence but that as her work develops, she increasingly deploys magic as the tool rather than the problematic. This has implications for her plots and for the stylistic development of her work. Where other writers provide a pathway through the adventure to adulthood, bounded by spiky and obvious wrong choices,[7] Jones requires of her protagonists a constant negotiation with possible right choices and attractive wrong ones. Furthermore, it is the making of choices not the choices themselves that are the route to adulthood. Vigen Guroian describes the changes Jones writes within her child protagonists as the development of a moral imagination, "not a *thing*, not even so much a faculty, as the very process by which the self makes metaphors out of images given by experience, and then employs these metaphors to find and suppose moral correspondences in experience."[8] This all sounds very worthy, but as we shall see, in Jones's work is the starting point for the Rabelaisian. What it means for the development of the narrative is that instead of a moment of realization, realization as an ongoing process becomes the message. One consequence is an open-endedness to Jones's plots.

Frequently we reach the conclusion of a Jones novel only to discover that consequences continue beyond the borders of the text (compare this to *Silver on the Tree* in which we have to be told this by the resonant and prophetic Merriman Lyon, or by Dalben at the end of Lloyd Alexander's *The High King*, a book that otherwise agrees with Jones that adulthood is mostly process). There are consequences of this for Jones's style: we do not have the need for the continual obvious choices—between pathways, gifts, or leaders—that punctuate many other texts of children's fantasy. The fantastic might retreat, becoming the background against which the protagonist is tested or the context in which they become competent. Magic becomes a metaphor not for the moment of adulthood but for the adult world, complex and with its own rules. The conclusions to Jones's novels show protagonists who have acquired the ability to negotiate precisely this extended world.

When Jones's characters develop magic it is as a vital aspect of who they are, but it does not usually serve as a shorthand description of their personalities (the exceptions are Zillah in *A Sudden Wild Magic* and some of the students in *Year of the Griffin*); like other talents magic must be developed and understood, assimilated into the character rather than pinned on like a magical cloak. Learning to deal with one's talent is the route to agency and to power. Magic itself does not confer agency. In this Jones makes a radical break with her own first novel, *Wilkins' Tooth*. Inevitably, this repositioning of magic does not appear immediately. In this chapter I want to explore its appearance and development as perhaps the overriding theme of her work. Although I do not consider every novel in this chapter, I intend that this chapter will function as a comprehensive introduction to the nature of Jones's work. It is, therefore, the only chapter that functions roughly chronologically, although the reader should check the bibliographies for a clarification of the order in which the novels were written.

Eight Days of Luke, The Ogre Downstairs, and *Dogsbody*, all early novels, stand apart from the rest of Jones's work because they are not immersive fantasies—fantasies set within fantastic worlds in which the characters are fully competent in their setting. Instead, they are intrusion fantasies— fantasies in which the fantastic intrudes on the fictive normal world, creates chaos, and is negotiated (or managed) by the protagonists who return the world to an altered normality (although that may prove an illusion). In these three books, Jones uses the narrative structure of the intrusion fantasy as a metaphor for the issues she is discussing, paralleling the intrusion of the fantastic with the intrusion of a more mundane element. Jones then wields the Rabelaisian properties of the fantastic to allow her child characters to override the interpretation of the unknowing adults in the eyes of the reader.[9]

In *The Ogre Downstairs* two sets of children are forced to share the same house when their parents marry. Neither set is happy. Caspar, Johnny, and Gwinny resent their stepfather, an Ogre who shouts and lays down the law. Malcolm and Douglas have been taken out of their school because there is no longer enough money for fees. They did not like their school, but it was still a disruption. To keep them quiet, the Ogre gives to each set of children a chemistry kit, the second layer of which proves to have interesting properties. The intrusion is both the chemistry kit and the stepfather; the two act distinctly until relatively late in the book. As the children learn to cope with magic they also learn to see adults as human beings rather than as archetypes. The magic, like power generally, proves unpredictable. Efforts to rely on magic as a quick fix, without the ameliorating element of planning, prove disastrous. In *The Ogre Downstairs*—and in each of these three early novels—one protagonist lacks the ability to change anything, is bullied, and reacts with spite or retreats; another has too much power but no control. The pattern does not repeat in later books, so we need to consider what Jones achieves with this pattern and its limitations.

Each experiment the children perform in *The Ogre Downstairs,* with its little disasters and major consequences, shifts their perception of where they fit into the world and addresses the egocentricity and solipsism of youth. Magic shifts the protagonists' and reader's perception and dislocates understanding in both metaphorical and literal ways: flying above the city, Caspar, Johnny, and Gwinny note, "Another surprising thing was the way the bent streets looked straight, and streets they had thought straight had unexpected little twiddles and curves to them";[10] a metaphor perhaps for an adult (or at least alternative) perspective on other's lives.

Dogsbody similarly relies on perceptual dislocation, although here it is reversed. *Dogsbody* has two plot elements: it describes the life of Katherine, an Irish child living in an English family that does not want her, and the life on earth of Sirius the Dog Star, condemned to live out his life on Earth unless he can find the Zoi he is accused of using as a weapon. *Dogsbody* anthropomorphizes the universe, giving each star and planet a sentient resident. C.S. Lewis did something similar in *The Voyage of the Dawn Treader,* which was the favorite of the Narnia series for Jones's children, but her inspiration might rather have been the Milky Way Circus in *Mary Poppins Comes Back.*[11] Sirius must come to terms with mere earthly understandings, rather than the distanced gaze of the luminary. Where Caspar, Johnny, and Gwinny gain by distance, Sirius reinterprets by proximity. When Sirius first begins to search for the Zoi, his dog nature perceives the town as smells, his luminary nature wants to bend it into a sphere, and the learned human perception wants a nice, flat diagram. Sirius is quite physically shown the need for a consideration of other people's perspectives, but the lesson goes deeper than that. Only when he allows the three natures (plus a fourth, the "yell-hound" inheritance from his supernatural parentage) to interact can he find the Zoi; only when he consciously thinks about that interaction can he begin to relate to and judge the world around him and read his incarnated Companion for the rather cold individual she is.

In *The Ogre Downstairs* magic forces the children into a more realistic assessment of themselves. Central to this shift is the acknowledgment that intent is as important as external behavior. All the children have been incapable of perceiving their elders (brothers or adults) as confused, afraid, and inexperienced. Adults are supposed to know. When Caspar and Malcolm exchange bodies, this fairly conventional trope provides Caspar with an opportunity to rewrite his internal narrative of grievance and to reassess the behavior of the eldest child, Douglas, in terms of Douglas's behavior not to himself but to Malcolm, and by doing so to accept that he, Caspar, is not at the center of the world's narrative. Caspar realizes that although the Ogre might be a bully, neither he nor Douglas is wholly innocent:

> "You sounded just like the Ogre when you said that," said Caspar.
>
> "Are you trying to be funny?" growled Douglas.
>
> "No," said Caspar, who was in no mood to be bullied. "Sometimes I'm surprised Malcolm even survives the way you sit on him."[12]

The realization that they revert to bullying when they feel most powerless provides the epiphany that both boys need to reevaluate their relationship with the Ogre. Jones closes the circle when Douglas, finally angry enough to stand up to his father, argues that it is not that he and Malcolm are better behaved but that they have learned not to be caught. Bullying teaches irresponsibility and more bullying, not responsibility and collaboration. The denouement of the story is therefore the Ogre's one-to-one discussions with Gwinny in chapter 7 and Johnny in chapter 9 and the joint shopping trip, rather than the discovery of the philosopher's stone in the chemistry kit that turns things to gold and solves their financial problems. However even this momentary magic is significant: although it superficially parallels the discovery of the jewels in Biddy's waste heap in *Wilkins' Tooth,* Jones is much more in command of her material here. Gwinny's discovery of the philosopher's stone becomes relevant only because the Ogre and the boys have now widened their worldview to take notice of Gwinny's contribution. And even then the lesson is not complete: having excluded Sally (the [step-] mother and a rather shadowy figure) from much of the strife, the family discovers that her inclusion might have led to a greater reward. *Dogsbody* has similar lessons to teach: Basil (Katherine's eldest cousin) bullies because he has no other role model and is himself bullied. Robin, still young, is already learning the same behavior. Alice Mills points out that the story deals with one of Cinderella's stepsisters, but "in this optimistic reworking ... all the child characters achieve some degree of individuation."[13] The lesson is both for us and for Sirius: although Sirius's innocence is proved, Jones forces him to compare his own bluster as a luminary to that of Basil. Sirius's crux moment is when he abandons a potential feud, and instead of leaving Tibbles to the brutal bullying of Duffy, rescues the cat who has gotten him into trouble. He could have accepted the role of bully-by-proxy that Basil has taken on. Sirius's refusal to play this game—he also rescues Robin from bullies—and his acceptance of responsibility for Katherine undermines the solipsism of his quest narrative.

In *Eight Days of Luke*, Luke (Loki) erupts into the life of David, a young boy living in a distinctly unhappy extended family. David and Astrid (cousin Ronald's wife) learn from the intrusion of chaos that their unhappiness is in part due to their own complicity. Astrid's own behavior demonstrates that adults can be disempowered and made childlike. Astrid's lack of title (she is never referred to as "Mrs." anything, or "cousin") reinforces her subordinate status. The adults in *Eight Days of Luke* are solipsistic: each member of the family struggles to force his or her narrative upon others; failure to do so results in a loss of self-esteem, but the narratives are themselves damaging to the ego. Astrid breaks free only by disrupting that narrative. Luke breaks free in a similar fashion, rein- forcing the pattern of doubled characters that pervades these three books. For David epiphany occurs early when he watches Luke and the fire: he realizes that falling in love with one's own narrative is fundamentally sociopathic but that he is in danger of acquiring the same characteristics. There is just enough input (from the children next door, from his school) that he is not utterly crushed and that his value structure allows him to despise his family, but this in itself is a dangerous distortion. Although he can seem completely depressed and without self-esteem, David has come to see himself as superior by reason of his difference—what cognitive therapists call the entitlement schema.

> The trouble was that David, particularly in the holidays, was so used to feeling guilty that he had come to ignore it whenever he could. He found himself pretending the fire was nothing to do with him.[14]

David is a sociopath in the making.

The rest of the novel is structured around the process by which David, Astrid, and Luke reconnect to the world and to an awareness of others. Jones handles this delicately: we are even provided with a spokesperson (Mr. Wednesday) whose role is to relieve David of guilt for his own (ungrateful) behavior and for his failure to achieve agency prior to the appearance of Luke, but the message is clear: adulthood is about standing up to oppression and acknowledging the other.

Dogsbody is perhaps the most interesting of these novels. Its protagonist is the child of an Irish terrorist (the book was written at the height of the troubles and while anti-Irish prejudice was still strong in the United Kingdom). There is never any doubt that Katherine's father has done something awful, and we are never led to expect that his imprisonment might turn out to be a mistake, which in itself holds us apart from the usual consolation of fantasy.

Katherine's problem is that she has no ego and little sense of self, and she has come to regard herself as marginal to the world. She accepts the bullying of Duffie as somehow fair: like David she assumes that she should be grateful for receiving even resentful care. The bullying of Katherine is repeated over and over again in all the relationships in the book (even the objectionable Duffie is bullied by her husband on the rare occasions he takes an interest).

Katherine is in a terrible position: bullied at school for being Irish and a convict's child and in her uncle's home because she is unwanted, Katherine gains agency not from her own magic or that of Sirius (the Dog Star turned dog) but through her own slow acquisition of skills: through her rescuing the puppy, learning to clean house, defending her dog, and defending herself, Katherine gains confidence. It is confidence that grants her the ability to make decisions and eventually to improve her situation. It would have been perfectly plausible to write this element of the story without introducing the fantastic, which is not true of many other children's fantasies, or of most of Jones's work; however, running alongside Katherine's tale is that of Sirius, the Dog Star. Sirius is an old and powerful star. Unlike Katherine, he has authority, status, and magic, and he is utterly without agency. He is gullible, reckless, and wild: his power is a liability. As her dog, Sirius the Dog Star—himself a character who needs to learn that he is not the center of the universe (a nice bit of metaphor on Jones's part)—pulls Katherine back into the action; he gives her responsibility and relationships and allows her eventually to impose her own interpretation of the world on others. Most of all, however, he teaches her that only loving care is worthy of gratitude and that she is special. Jones structured the novel not merely to demonstrate that Sirius must learn control but to ensure that he learns from someone ostensibly much weaker than he is.

At the end of *Dogsbody*, Sirius's dog body dies, and he and Katherine are parted. Katherine has already had to deal with the death of her father—it is this which leads her to smash Duffy's pots. It is clear that Katherine does not even fully comprehend the link between the luminary and her beloved Leo. Both Sirius and Katherine have succeeded in changing their lives, but agency in these terms is about managing frustration and enduring loss. Growth means leaving the loved one behind. This is a common trope in fantastic fiction (e.g., J.M. Barrie's *Peter Pan*, Lloyd Alexander's *The High King*, and P.L. Travers's *Mary Poppins*), but it is actually made relatively little of in most of Jones's work. Later Jones will be more ambiguous: in *Fire and Hemlock*, for example, it is implied that magic is a gift that cannot be taken away, and the ambiguity of the ending makes it unclear whether the romance at the heart of the novel has, or has not, been ruptured.

In these early novels children learn to cope with upset, distress, and chaos in the real world and in the fantastic world without the use of dream metaphors or artificial quest themes (see chapter 4). In *Eight Days of Luke* and *Dogsbody*, the quests that emerge at the end of the novels are brief—David must find Thor's hammer, Katherine finds herself seeking a Zoi for Sirius—and serve to ratify the protagonist's newfound confidence, not to create it. This is bound up with the fact that in each case the quest is for something that belongs to someone else: the object cannot materially benefit them, and in Katherine's case, the securing of the Zoi will deprive her of the one individual she loves. Importantly, the children are marked at the end of these quests. Unlike the classic intrusion fantasy (of which horror is the best exemplar), while chaos abates or is held at bay, normality is not fully resumed. Jones demands that the encounter and negotiation must change the individual's understanding of normalcy in the first place. This is hinted at with the implausible conversion of Buster's gang in *Wilkins' Tooth* and, more subtly, with the emergence of Frances and Jess as the real heroes of that novel, but in *The Ogre Downstairs*, *Dogsbody*, and *Eight Days of Luke*, we see a transition from an insistence that "everyone is nice really" to an understanding that individuals are complex and that adulthood and agency must be built on an understanding of this and an awareness of how one must continually negotiate the intrusion of others into one's own internal narrative or private fantasyland.

The emotional drive of *The Ogre Downstairs* and *Dogsbody* could be represented entirely without the element of fantasy, but the intrusion allows Jones to disassociate her protagonists in ways that give them freedom to reassociate with the world. In both books the protagonists are already disassociated by trauma—the acquisition of stepparents on the one hand, and the complete dislocation of Katherine through the imprisonment of her father on the other. The further disassociation provided by the fantasy serves to underline the connection of the protagonists to the real world, so that Katherine's loss of her dog is crucial to her reentry into human relationships, specifically with the retired schoolteacher Miss Smith. At the end of the book, Katherine and Sirius lose their hearts' desires (each other), even as they achieve their goals: for Katherine a home, for Sirius the Zoi. In this book, for the first time, we see the full equation that creates much of the tension in Jones's work: adulthood is a combination of agency, power, and the ability to withstand loss.

Nowhere is this clearer than in *Fire and Hemlock*, a much later novel aimed at a rather older audience. A simplistic description of the book is that it is a retelling of the ballads of "Tam Lin" crossed with "Thomas the Rhymer." This description will do for the moment: a more sophisticated analysis is offered later, particularly in chapters 6 and 7.

At the age of eight, Polly is drawn into the life of Thomas Lynn, who is held in thrall by a manifestation of the faerie queen…and other mythic avatars, Laurel.[15] Much of the novel is about Polly's decision to train to be a hero and how she models her actions on the heroes she reads about. Ironically (or not) this means she plays out her heroism in public, which is, of course, also what heroes do. They might not ask for acclaim, but performance is, as Jones points out, part of the heroic ideal. Polly first experiences this when she attacks the school bully. Jones based this on a real-life incident and included in the portrayal the reality of punishment, because that is how the story of the school rules must go, alongside rather embarrassing adulation that is the story of the hero.[16] The crucial lesson in the incident, that Polly actually fails to remember at the critical moment, is that the hero must never be embarrassed to step forward or to make a fuss.

The rest of the novel leads up to the point where Polly is old enough and wise enough to free Tom. The novel begins with the intrusion of magic, but Jones racks up the tension by holding the boundaries of magic permanently in doubt (see the discussion in chapter 6). At the conclusion of *Fire and Hemlock,* Polly rescues her prince (Tom), but the suggestion is that having held on to him throughout the novel, she must now let him go to meet the terms set by faerie. John Stephens' assertions to the contrary, we are denied the determinate closure that he associates with Jones's work, and this denial is duplicated in the Dalemark books, *The Time of the Ghost* and *The Homeward Bounders*.[17]

However, as Elizabeth Kedge pointed out, we might be examining the wrong character. By narrating the story from Polly's point of view, Jones set up the assumption that this is Polly's story. When she has written about the tale, Jones has said that Polly is both Penelope and Telemachus, the one who stays at home and narrates the tale of waiting.[18] This directed gaze can explain the ambivalence of the ending: has Polly won or lost Tom? If, as Kedge suggested, we reverse this and focus on the Thomas the Rhymer poems that structure the text (they provide epigraphs for each chapter), then the book has a much clearer message: it is the development of Tom's agency that we are watching.[19] Throughout the book Tom has manipulated Polly. Laurel's gift to him, that what he says will come true, offers the possibility of liberation if he has the wit to use it, but instead Tom uses Polly's wit and imagination. Tom breaks free of Laurel only at the point at which he is forced to rely wholly on the abilities and strengths that he has developed in his years as an independent musician and writer. It is Tom who wins, and Polly is a spectator (a quite different interpretation is offered in chapters 6 and 7).

From here on, magic becomes a central element in the development of agency in Jones's work, as protagonists discover that their choices can have larger, perhaps even world-shaking, consequences.[20] In Jones's work, magical abilities become part of the package of change and trauma that adolescents experience, in contexts that render the whole experience of adolescence, but magic especially, problematic. It is this emphasis on context that makes these texts stand out. *Witch Week* is perhaps the clearest example of Jones's corollary that it is the context of talent that shapes character.

Witch Week is set in a rather miserable boarding school, in a classroom divided by internal conflict and externally imposed fear. Although the world we see is apparently just like ours, in this world magic exists, but rather than being a source of entertainment, it is a threat. Witches are despised, feared, and burned. Of the four major characters—Nan, Charles, Brian, and Nirupam—only Nirupam wields his talents (both magical and intellectual) with any control or concern for others, but this is not because he is inherently superior to anyone else—Jones's comments on destinarianism, expressed in Nan's riff on real boys and girls, are a stinging critique of the fantasy tradition—but because of the four protagonists he is the only one who has experienced a warm and nurturing family. Brian's behavior is reckless and selfish in part because that is how he has perceived the behavior of his father, who refuses to explain the realities of their situation. Nan is quiet and secretive because her entire life has been structured around a major secret, whereas Charles has great power and great intellect, which have been channeled, through misunderstanding, into resentment. The result of all of this is that only Nirupam achieves more or less what he aims to achieve when he applies magic. Brian and Charles exercise the most spectacular overkill, while Nan's magic supplies her deepest wishes rather than her immediate needs. To become adult the children must learn to accept their own selves so that they are able to negotiate with their magic. However, the way in which each of the four comes to terms with this paradigm is very different.

Nirupam has already learned self-control but has also learned that safety lies in hiding his talents and diverting attention to others. He is the first to reveal publicly that Nan's real name is Dulcinea (after the legend-ary arch-witch), encouraging the others to tease her. His decision to stand with Nan and with Charles, although partially about self-protection (he is the only one of the four who has met an inquisitor), is an acceptance of communal responsibility, as he acknowledges that although the four of them together are generating danger through their interaction, they are stronger together.

Brian accepts the existence of his witchcraft, but whereas Nirupam resents the consequence of exposure, Brian resents the secrecy. Brian's frustration over the use of magic has become bound up with his status as class victim. Overreliant on his belief in his magical powers were he allowed to employ them, Brian has trapped himself into passivity. As Nan points out, "SS [Simon] is so certain that he is the real boy that he has managed to convince Brian too."[21] Brian's growth begins when he realizes that magic does not work either: the appearance of the birds in the music room (rescuing him from the exposure of a solo) serves only as a tempo-rary distraction and does not give him the leadership he craves. Similarly, his attempts to blame the witch for his illness and to create a witch kidnapping only increase his isolation and misery while also leaving chaos behind to focus attention on his activities. But all of these actions fail to change Brian's perception of himself, and so fail to propel him toward agency. Brian learns to be (in Nan's terms) a real boy only at the very end of the novel when he no longer has magic, but this manifestation has nothing to do with niceness. Nan's "real boys" are not nice.

Nan and Charles are rather different from either Nirupam or Brian: both come to learn of their own gifts by accident, Nan when she is accused of witchcraft and decides to live up to it, and Charles when he inadvertently renders himself invisible to the seniors. Both of them experience moments of realization that are quite specifically beyond their control. This is characteristic of these two individuals. Nan has been living down to low expectations all her life, but suddenly failure seems attractive. Charles, a classic outsider, has effectively deflected others' gaze from his real self: a troubled and disturbed child, the glare he uses to try to see into others' intentions has been misinterpreted as hostility. The more Charles has resented the world, the more he has withdrawn from it, until his diary is written in a code intended for others to see and misinterpret. Charles's intelligence and powers of analysis have contributed to his withdrawal. Although it is not presented in quite this way, the most traumatic moment of his life centers around his mother's refusal to explain the witch burning he has witnessed.[22] Unlike Nan, who accepts others' dismissal of her value, Charles sees their lack of perception as a judgment on them. Although Charles is treated with sympathy, Jones seems to be arguing that his estrangement from others has placed him well on the way to becoming the classic evil enchanter-sociopath for whom only his own feelings are real, reversing Nan's understanding of the real and the not real. The result is to leave him free to perform whatever witchcraft attracts him, but each such performance is distorted by his solipsism. Wrapped in his own world, and, as Deborah Kaplan points out, trapped within the limited vocabulary he has created with which to communicate with the world,[23] it does not occur to him to specify to his magic that it is his own shoes he wants to find, so all the school shoes are brought to the hall. He wants Simon to look foolish, but he succeeds in giving Simon the power to change the world. Charles is able to use his power effectively only when he accepts that he is not an island, not the only real person. But Charles is the longest holdout; he owns the most powerful magic and so has the most to lose and the most to gain by a change in the world. It is easy to posit Nan as the most imaginative of the four, but it is Charles who constantly reinvents what he experiences and who can change the world of his mind. Consider Nan, listening in horror to herself describing the food at High Table:

> Why doesn't he stop me she thought. Why do they let me go on? …
> And all the time she could hear herself talking. "These did in fact start
> life as peas. But they have since undergone a long and deadly process.

They lie for six months in a sewer, absorbing fluids and rich tastes, which is why they are called processed peas."[24]

Nan is actually quite clear about the separation of fantasy and reality. In contrast Charles's attempt to burn memory and fear into himself with a candle results in a bewildering mixture of regret and terror—this mixture of emotions is typical of Jones's portrayals. But Jones refuses to allow this as a moment of epiphany for Charles. Later, thinking about the blister he got from the candle flame, he "found he rather enjoyed being frightened, once he got used to it. It made life more interesting."[25] It is not fear that forces Charles to cooperate in the end but his growing belief that he can make a difference.

Charles cannot write a line that is not censored, and he has placed an entire wall between him and the world, a wall that, when it breaks, results in a flood of uncontrolled magic. In contrast Nan is incapable of self-censorship, writing compulsively in a diary she knows will be read by teachers. Where Charles has been overscrutinized, Nan has been ignored and is desperate for recognition that, as with Brian, manifests in her magic. Nan needs come to terms with her gifts, working out what they are and what they are not. Looking up her ancestor Dulcinea, she makes the classic mistake of assuming that talent has only one form. As Chrestomanci points out, however, it has many manifestations and heredity guarantees nothing. She cannot count on Dulcinea to give her a "witchy inner confidence."[26] Although Nan talks in terms of her right to be a witch, in part because she has come to see the world in terms of those who are or are not entitled, Jones seeks to break that connection endemic to children's fiction. This might explain why at the end it is clear that it is Charles (together with Brian, the least responsible of the five children) who might just get to keep his magic. There is no justice in the world, even if it is magical. But for Nan, learning to control her compulsive behavior allows her to become the vital element in someone else's magic (an idea that Jones has exploited elsewhere, in *The Magicians of Caprona*), but more important her own reassessment of bad behavior as valuable leads her to reevaluate herself.

Although she is a minor character, Estelle Green, a friend of Nan, is worth considering. Estelle transforms in the reader's eye from the empty-headed acolyte of *real girl* Theresa Mullet to a smart and resourceful young woman; however, she has always been smart and resourceful. The emulation of Theresa is a combination of insecurity and a very real desire to hide. Estelle is the least powerful witch of the five children, yet of them all she is the one who best copes with the responsibilities of adulthood. While Jones gives a clear context to what Estelle has learned (her mother ran a witches' safe house), it remains important that this distinction is made clear: far from providing a route to maturity, the message in this book seems to be that talent is all too often used to excuse the individual from responsibility.

The Time of the Ghost is one of Jones's most structurally complex novels and offers a challenge to reader position that is repeated in Jones's later works. Its sinister tone is shared only with *The Homeward Bounders* but, in its theme of lonely, neglected children, it seems to belong with the more straightforward *Eight Days of Luke* and *Dogsbody*. It begins with a ghost. The ghost knows something is wrong and knows that she is one of four sisters, but she is unclear which one. In the first half of the novel, the ghost's central concern is finding out who she is, but the method by which she does this is part of the message of the novel. The ghost uses two tactics: she tests herself against the external image of the four girls as she perceives them, and she tests herself against others' external perceptions of the four. Lesson number one, as it turns out, is that no one can be judged entirely by the image he or she presents to the world and, number two, is that one cannot define one's own character by how others want or expect one to behave. Looking inward is the only solution, but this ghost cannot, at first, look inward. When she does, she finds only a hollow, dug through her own compliance with others' demands.

The related and equally important aspect of the novel is the extent to which the characters are shaped by parental expectation and parental misunderstanding of the world. The four girls are lonely and neglected, but one thing they understand is that this is not how their parents comprehend the situation. Their mother, Phyllis, sees them as competent and responsible rather than neglected and wild. Like the parents of England's Bohemia, she seems to feel that the less attention they receive, the "freer" their souls will be.[27] Phyllis regards settling their career as a form of caring, not as a form of entrapment, but she has mistaken image for substance: Imogen, for example, is to be a concert pianist because of her angelic profile, not her talent. As it turns out, of the four girls it is our ghost who has most accepted her parental assessment: she is trapped by acceptance first of what her parents, in their casual neglectful way, desire, and then almost out of habit, by what the dangerous Julian Addiman wants of her. This becomes entangled in her dealings with the goddess.

Brian Attebery argues, "In Jones's terms, the ghost has no way to hide from the goddess until she learns to draw the magic circle of identity around her Self."[28] The ghost fails to achieve agency when obsessed with destiny and expectation, and she finally finds her place only when she accepts the freedom wrested by the simple decision to make choices and to insist on self-definition, which might involve rejecting the inevitability associated with talent, in particular the odd but common assumption that one enjoys what one is talented at. The conclusion of the book is a challenge to the idea that talent and destiny might be synonymous.

The Homeward Bounders focuses throughout on the theme of agency: the original premise, that the world is run by all-powerful beings, that there are rules, and that these rules control even those expelled from the game, generates an expectation that protagonists and readers will have to play by the rules to win. The book begins when Jamie spies on these secret masters and is set to "walk the bounds," expelled until such a time as he finds his home again. In *Homeward Bounders* Jones manipulates the structures and tropes of the portal fantasy that take us from the reality within which we are competent to that which we must explore, negotiate, and accept—and then changes the game. Our characters move from acquiescence with the rules, to proficiency, to manipulation, and eventually to the stage where they discover that the rules themselves are merely rules; the creation of consensus space. They break with the consensus, and glorious anarchy ensues. The portal and our understanding of it is a social construct that we can choose to reject.

Jones seems to argue that one grows into one's magic only as one learns to accept both the humiliation of one's limitations and the scariness of one's abilities. Recognizing and acknowledging this might be humiliating as well as rewarding, and both *Charmed Life* and *The Homeward Bounders* explore this idea. Cat in *Charmed Life* and Helen and Joris each have powers that they are not wholly willing to acknowledge. In *Charmed Life* the orphaned Cat is desperate to be protected, and so ignores the evidence of his own talent and the indications that his sister Gwendolyn cares not a jot for him. His self-esteem is so low that he does not at first realize that he has magic: this is identified first by Janet and the readers, and then, only when it is unavoidable, by Cat. There is an indication here that Cat does not recognize his power because to do so would be to accept agency and he is just not ready to do this (a theme that is extended in "Stealer of Souls," where he resents the presence of a boy younger than him). The link between emotional maturity and real power is absolute.

Helen of *The Homeward Bounders* plays a different part. Born in a hell world where the frail do not survive, she has been saved from infanticide first by a determined mother, then by her magic, and finally by the priest. Her father has rejected her for the deformity that is her arm; the priests have feted her for it. Her personality has been destabilized by the obsessive focus on one element of her body. Here Jones plays a neat trick on us, because we are fully led to expect that it will be as a consequence of her magic that Helen achieves agency. We are even presented with the scene in which her arm becomes the living blade that frees the world, but Helen has achieved agency before this—in Jones's understanding she must do so. Her agency is achieved less through her confidence, which it turns out is based on certain misunderstandings, but through her growing cooperativeness with the principal protagonist Jamie, a boy displaced from nineteenth-century England. Only that cooperation facilitates the fulfillment of her destiny (one of the very few occasions Jones resorts to destiny). Of the three protagonists, each of whom has his or her own story of maturation, it is Helen who emerges as the most changed by her understanding that she is not enslaved by her gift.

Jones is at her most interesting in this regard in *The Lives of Christopher Chant*. Christopher Chant is taken from his family home to learn to be an enchanter, while being vaguely aware of a seediness about his family situation and taking refuge in oddly substantial dreams. Christopher becomes aware of his status as a powerful enchanter in the first third of the novel: he blows the roof off his tutor's house and must learn to control his magic in order to put it all back together again. Much of the rest of the book is devoted to positioning Christopher so that he can use his power and gain authority thereby. There is also a fascinating thread in which Christopher begins to reinterpret the characters who surround him. But if we are to pursue this issue of agency, then the emerging agent is not Christopher but the minor character of Tacroy–Mordecai Roberts. A superficial reading of this book has Tacroy liberated from the powers of his home world (ruled by the Dright) by Christopher's decision to rescue him. Although his challenge for Tacroy's soul rests on Tacroy's willingness to lie for Christopher "for a whole day," that set of lies is not the fulcrum on which Tacroy's liberation turns. Lying to save Christopher, although an act of generosity, does not fundamentally sever him from the network of obligations to the Dright and to the enchanter, Christopher's uncle Ralph Argent. The critical decision is made much earlier in the book when Tacroy takes Christopher to the House of Asheth to steal a temple cat. Christopher, lying at home in bed after an accident caused by the cat, liberates it. We learn later that Mordecai Roberts has found it in London and sent it to Chrestomanci Castle. Although we do not realize it at the time, Roberts and Tacroy are one and the same, and this decision is the first fully independent act that Tacroy undertakes. Everything else follows on from this break with Ralph Argent.

In the novels I have discussed so far, characters' self-comprehension is negotiated in part by their interaction with the outside world, and almost always in dialogue with an adult companion. In *Cart and Cwidder* Moril, the youngest child in a family of singers (and revolutionaries), discovers his own abilities and his ability to take action predominantly in dialogue with himself or occasionally with Kialan, a rather mysterious passenger in the family cart who turns out to be the heir to an earldom in the free North. Breaking with adult interpretations of behavior and character is crucial to Moril's self-development, but Jones does not present this in an antagonistic fashion; instead, adults are shown to misdirect.

Repeatedly, Moril is told to bring together his two worlds, the two aspects of his character. Because Moril's parents are admirable, we too listen. Only in the power vacuum left by their absence is Moril left free to act (a traditional trope in children's adventure fiction), but what he does first is to observe and evaluate: first his sister Brid "not as clever as she thought she was" but with her mother's efficiency and sharpness, and then his brother Dagner, who lacks the personality to carry off their father Clennan's in-your-face secret identity. Moril then turns to his own character, considering its divides and ripples. It is a small but significant point that Jones allows Moril to accept that he is part of his family, taking both good and bad from them: much children's fiction is keener to assert separation and difference than it is to accept commonalities. But Moril's crucial insight is that accepting this reality is the key to using the power of the cwidder he carries, the instrument of the legendary Osfameron. To use it one has to accept the truth of what is and also the power of metaphor that one can still be anything. In this way only can Moril bring his two sides together while remaining in both.[29] They do not need to be united, only linked. This is a much more radical notion than it at first appears. The convention in fantasy is that the individual must choose between magic and the mundane (Eilonwy at the end of *The High King* gives up her magic; the children leave the world for permanent residence in Narnia at the end of *The Last Battle;* and in the first three books, Harry Potter must leave his magic behind at the end of term), but for Moril it is precisely the understanding that one is a metaphor for the other that is the revelation: "The important thing was that Moril *was* in two halves."

But Jones refuses to allow such epiphanies to form passages into adulthood. Adulthood is not wondrous, and it cannot be magical. The most moving and important part of the novel is not when Moril rescues Kialan but when he admits that he brought down the mountains on an army (which he knew to be conscripted and unwilling) because of the death of the family's beloved horse and not for any of the reasons he had claimed to the cwidder. At that moment Moril is not a hero but a child again, clinging to the coat of Keril (Kialan's father). His true moment of maturity is somewhat later, when he works out,

> What he had done was to cheat the cwidder. That was the worst thing. If you stood up and told the truth in the wrong way, it was not true any longer, though it might be as powerful as ever. Moril saw that he was neither old enough nor wise enough to have charge of such a potent things as that cwidder.[30]

At the end of the novel, Moril realizes that even the death of the vicious Earl Tholian has diminished him, and that his own freedom has been bought at the price of others' deaths. There are two things buried in there. First, that truth can be used to lie, which is manipulated to different effects in *Fire and Hemlock* and in *The Homeward Bounders*.[31] Second, another of Jones's radical turns: usually in fantasy the refusal of authority is rewarded with a crown (or material equivalent), which is seen as an indication of suitability. Jones refuses that easy elision. Moril is not rewarded in any way for his realization. The nature of the interaction between Moril and self is repeated in *The Spellcoats* in ways that bring up another issue: for Jones, the act of creativity is the act of self-comprehension. As Moril discovers his sense of self by composing on the cwidder, Tanaqui acquires self-understanding through the process of weaving, and similarly brings together the multiple aspects of her nature, as villager, outcast, heathen, mage, and finally perhaps goddess.[32] The cliché that Jones extends in this work, that the pen is mightier than the sword, forms a significant strand of her critique of fantasy, as we shall see in the final chapter.

Although self-comprehension and agency are the resolution of *Cart and Cwidder,* they form the structural lattice on which *Archer's Goon* is constructed. *Archer's Goon* is much the most complicated of these mid-age novels. The father's story (Quentin) replicates that of many of the earlier protagonists: a sense of helplessness and distance from decision making is replaced by self-knowledge and engagement. But his son Howard's story is structured around other ideas. As the novel opens, Howard is already taking on the responsibilities of adulthood in his interactions with his sister, Awful, and in his attempt to protect both of his parents. This is simply what the eldest in a family does, but it is a hint of what is to come. Each of the siblings who rule the town displays behavior that emerges in part from his or her place within a large family. Archer offers the protection of an elder brother in return for sibling submission; Dillian and Shine rail against the unfairness of not being born first; Erskine demonstrates the annoyance of the penultimate child, usurped by a small person he must then cherish. Only those who are capable of overcoming sibling resentment can liberate themselves, can step over the threshold of maturity. The recognition of entrapment, however, does not necessarily change one's condition. In his moment of recognition, Howard chooses not to abandon the role but to embrace it more enthusiastically than before.

In *Archer's Goon* Jones seems to argue that agency emerges from an acceptance of the world as it is behaving, whether this fits one's expectations or not. Self-delusion, whether about the external world or internal world, one's own narrative, is dangerous. Howard's father, for example, has deluded himself into believing that it is normal to pay one's tax in words:

> Dad's being a passenger again! Howard thought angrily. ... Fancy running up a twenty-three-thousand-pound bill for taxes! Fancy writing all those words for years without bothering to find out why![33]

And it is never clear that Quentin ever really stops being a passenger. In his final scene, writing the exit for Venturus's siblings, he argues strongly that he is merely a passenger for his ideas. His creativity becomes both his means to control the world and to abandon responsibility for himself, even at the last.

The spine of this novel is the role of portals and thresholds in Howard's growing understanding of himself and of the limitations that one places on oneself. Each of the siblings forces Howard over a threshold to meet them, but almost every portal is not into somewhere more vital (in the usual tradition of portal fantasy) but into somewhere that is only a fragment of the whole, and that by enlarging a single characteristic of Archer, or Shine, or Dillian, or Torquil makes them somehow hollow and unreal. All four of these characters attempt to use their sliver of self to dominate Howard, and they fail because they cannot influence those who accept themselves fully: we see this momentarily when Shine loses control over Ginger Hind (in a scene reminiscent of *Wilkins' Tooth*). The only sibling whose portal is into somewhere of greater interest than the real world is Hathaway, but as we quickly learn, this is precisely because he has allowed himself to grow into a real person within the space he has chosen to occupy, with all the emotional accoutrements that this involves. Hathaway is trapped but as with Erskine and Howard, the entrapment is a consequence of adult rather than childish, choices. His place in the past is secured as much by family and friends as it is by the aging process should he travel into the present.

Toward the end of *Archer's Goon*, Howard discovers a portal into a hangar where he is building a rocket ship. The portal ages him as he enters, and Howard must confront himself and the equations of agency. First there is the shock he feels at his own unfolding power, and the moment he understands the ease of selfishness. Second, Howard realizes that traversing the portal is not ordained, and he rejects this quick route to maturity, a nod perhaps to the lessons learned in Nesbit's *Five Children and It*. This time around (having grown up as the eldest, not the youngest, child) the arrogance of the unsocialized and individualistic Venturus horrifies Howard; this arrogance has influenced even the design of his spaceship, resulting in unmanageable controls.[34] The portal trope—the falsity of which is tested repeatedly in this novel—loses the element of inevitability and progress inherited in fantasy from the Campbellian monomyth. Instead it comes to stand for the tension of adolescence and of choice that is the real hallmark of adulthood. This idea is repeated in *Howl's Moving Castle*, which provides perhaps the clearest statement of Jones's understanding of adulthood and the role of agency.

The text of *Howl's Moving Castle* opens with a direct statement of denial: "In the land of Ingary, … it is quite a misfortune to be born the eldest of three. Everyone knows you are the one who will fail first, and worst, if the three of you set out to seek your fortunes."[35] The rest of the book is structured around the attempts of various people (her sisters, Mrs. Pendragon, Howl) to deny this aphorism and convince Sophie Hatter that her position in life is determined only by her talent and effort, opposed by the energy that Sophie puts into convincing herself that she can only fail. The structure of *Howl's Moving Castle* reverses the usual tropes of quest fantasy: Sophie sets out to seek her fortune only when artificially aged; she struggles, not against other people's expectations but against her own.[36]

This reversal is reflected in Jones's structuring of the fantastic. *Howl's Moving Castle* turns, unexpectedly, into a portal fantasy when we discover that the castle door opens into four different locations. Sophie repeatedly tests the alignment of the portal, curious to see the world at the other end of the black daub of paint. In the end Howl takes her through into Wales, resulting in a superb manipulation of the style of portal fantasy to provide a (mis)interpretation of the fantastic world found within (to be discussed further in chapter 4). But for Howl, the portal is a false route to adulthood: Howl loses confidence in Wales, and his agency is diminished by his own avoidance of confrontation. Only in what has become his home world is he able to self-consciously manipulate his own cowardice into recognizably adult self-control and authority. However, it is in Wales that Sophie discovers authority and dignity, although the magic that she faces down is the emotional blackmail wielded by Howl's sister; a magic that we all know can reduce the sternest souls to mere jellies. Like all returning questors, Sophie is able to apply the lessons she learns to both her handling of Howl and her understanding of her sisters and stepmother. Jones reminds us that movement has direction, and some portals and choices take us the wrong way.

Most recently, Diana Wynne Jones has turned her attention to that most nebulous of fields: the young adult and adult market. *Hexwood, Fire and Hemlock, A Sudden Wild Magic* (the first written and marketed for adults) and *Deep Secret* share two extended emphases: responsibility for others and for one's own actions becomes the hallmark of adulthood, and the ability to cope with the unexpected and to accept the chaotic willingly into one's life—to retain an element of the childlike—become the markers of enjoyable maturity. Whereas the children in the earliest novels seek agency that is focused on control and stability, the characters in these four novels all attempt to destabilize a situation or realize at the end that this was what they sought. The result is that the books have a roaring rambunctiousness expressed most vividly in the greenwood scene toward the end of *Hexwood*, in the conga at the end of *A Sudden Wild Magic*, and in the continual chaos of the science fiction convention in *Deep Secret*. In all three of these books, agency is what one can negotiate out of a bad situation: whether in *Hexwood* the slave continues to talk with the Girl in his head and to smile at Veirran when there is no other way left to rebel; Zillah in *A Sudden Wild Magic*, runs from her lover in fear of the absence she sees in his character; Nick and Maree Mallory in *Deep Secret,* create entire fantasylands to avoid absorption into someone else's power fantasy. For these characters, the agency they develop—however confined it might appear—provides them with the strength and personal autonomy to grasp liberty with both hands when it appears.

In *Hexwood* what appears to be a self-contained fantasy is opened up by the questioning of its game players: the immersive qualities are undermined by the unwillingness of Vierran and her colleagues to accept the consolation demanded by the initial game player (a maintenance technician at the site who requested of the computer a fantasy game with hobbits and elves). The test that faces the unwitting protagonists is for them to be able to create space for themselves (agency) within the Bannus field: of those selected to play, some are used to having agency and others are utterly deprived. Most deprived is Mordion, Servant of the Reigners and—unbeknownst to Vierran—the Slave whose voice she has known most of her life. Within the Bannus field Mordion has the chance to rediscover himself, to bring up a child without fear, and to shed his guilt for the children he failed. But the Bannus cannot do everything, and Mordion, conditioned to never feel good enough, punishes himself repeatedly. He has no self-respect because he knows he is not worthy of respect: he cannot understand [Vier]Ann's assertion, "One person ought to treat another person properly, even if the person's himself."[37] But although Ann is a catalyst, Mordion must heal himself: the Bannus makes this clear with the lessons it offers to other characters. Hume, reexperiencing childhood, learns to kill his own dragons; Vierran learns that revolution is not a game; and Reigner One learns that victims are not without resource. It is in *Hexwood* that many of Jones's ideas about agency come to their completion. And we see this in the way that in her later books she moves away from the question of how to develop agency, to examine instead the manifold forms that it can take.

The heroine of *A Sudden Wild Magic* is Zillah, a single parent, undirected and considered rather a failure in worldly terms: her unwillingness to train her power has reinforced this perception. But what others see as aimlessness is for Zillah a quiet negotiation. Her evasiveness around her sister Amanda is much more effective than standing up to her would be. She has the affair with the man she wants, removes herself when it seems untenable, and takes herself elsewhere when that seems the right thing to do. Everything in this novel revolves around Zillah the unassuming. Zillah has a knack of making friends and allies. People want to help her.

Everything that looks like weakness is in fact strength; her apparent pliability disguises her pursuit of her chosen path unheeding of opposition. Within this novel it is overcontrol that denies one self-knowledge: the ability to be adult enough to behave like a child is vital, and it is specifically the childishness that is valued—misuse of adult qualities (Roz's manipulation of sexual attraction) does not wreak the same kind of chaos (the right kind of chaos)—as does the simple joy of the conga (Flan) or the delight taken in good food (Helen). Both of these are communal and require responsibility for one's own actions, a celebration of oneself, and a willingness to surrender one's dignity. Flan and Helen represent the definition of agency and adulthood that Jones offers. What is most liberating perhaps is that at the conclusion of the novel, Zillah is not tamed. In contrast to the conventional trajectory in which the wild girl passes through puberty to gain control and hence power,[38] Zillah never does gain control of her magic. Its wildness is her strength.

Maree in *Deep Secret* offers a different perspective: her apparent humility masks a fierce pride and determination that as yet lacks direction. Maree deals with being ignored and resented, but at all times she maintains choice. In *Deep Secret* almost all the workings of magic we see are minor. The really important elements on which the plot hangs are choice and self-control; but the idea of which is the central plot continually shifts, with each new element the tone of the book changes, keeping the reader and the principal protagonist, Rupert Venables, continually off guard. Like most adults he expects his perceptions of the worlds he explores to be reliable and cumulative; instead he is continually forced to accept new paradigms. His determination to keep his different missions distinct breaks down when the inhabitants of his portal world cross into his own, reversing the role of colonized and colonizer and so forcing him to reevaluate his role as adult in this adventure. In the end, his destiny is appropriated by his much more relaxed older brother.

What is very clear from this overview is either that Jones's understanding of what agency has shifted or that Jones is quite clear that the process manifests itself in a variety of ways shaped in part by age and context. This is not a revolutionary notion, and it does not in itself distinguish Jones's work. Instead what remains distinct is that magic is not a metaphor for the process, nor is it simply analogous to the turmoil of adolescence (although Jones does link emotional trauma to magical jinxes in *Year of the Griffin*).[39] This is perhaps clarified in the roles played by those children who either do not have access to magic or are not themselves magical.

Jamie of *The Homeward Bounders* manipulates the magical terrain without having magic. So too does Janet (the alternate of Cat's sister Gwendolyn) in *Charmed Life,* and she is easily more adult than Cat. Jamie and Janet between them make it clear that it is the intelligent negotiation with magic, rather than magical power, that leads to agency. This connects to one of the principal contentions, made first in chapter 1, that will be continually emphasized in the later chapters of this book: that in Jones's fiction what matters is knowledge, and the ability to use that knowledge to shape one's own world whether literally, through magic, or metaphorically, through description and action. The most powerful people in Jones's fantasies are those who can use words, not those who use magic.

A corollary of Jones's insistence that the route to maturity is through agency is a thread of rage that runs through her work, directed at those who seek to restrict the moral or creative agency of others. This manifests as a fascination with conventions, rules, and structures. Jones's concern is the borderland between rules and conventions and the way in which adults (and evil villains) frequently blur the dividing line for children. The point at which convention becomes rule lurks at the heart of *Black Maria, Dogsbody,* and *Deep Secret.* Each of the protagonists in these novels is held in place by an oppressor who has turned convention into law. In each book it is the recognition that what is being asked is convention and not rule—that men and women wield different kinds of power; that children are subservient; and that someone who is dependent on another for support should be grateful—which is the liberating factor. Although parodying the conventions of genre, Jones reserves her real ire to attack the assumption that adulthood is synonymous with submission to convention. Jones cements her argument between the building blocks of her worlds. The magical structures that conspire to deny agency such as the skeletons of expectation and dependency that go into prophecy-based fantasies are all excoriated. Particularly in Jones's sights has been the prevalence of gods, secret rulers, and god-games in fantasy and the way in which protagonists are expected to abandon their agency and become as little children. One of her neatest critiques of this scenario is to be found in the novella "The Sage of Theare."

The gods of "The Sage of Theare" seem very Chinese. They are people, they have characters, some are brighter than others, they have relationships with mortals, and they are very, very concerned that the rules they have established are kept. The gods of Theare are the most rigid gods of the known multiverse: "Everything was so precisely worked out that every god knew his or her exact duties, correct prayers, right times for business, utterly exact character and unmistakable place above or below other gods."[40] There is even a god of prophecy to ensure that all prophecies are known and effected. In their desire for rules, the gods of Theare restrict the agency not simply of mortals but also of themselves.

When the god of prophecy reveals that the Sage of Dissolution has been born, the gods panic. When they identify the child—who turns out to be the the son of the god of prophecy—they decide to deal with him by displacing him to another world. There, Thasper is found by Chrestomanci—the Enchanter from *Charmed Life* and its sequels—and returned seven years later to his home world of Theare.

Thasper grows up, hears about the Sage of Dissolution, who has begun preaching, and follows him. What is interesting in "The Sage of Theare" is the way in which Thasper's danger to the gods is made manifest. Thasper is not dangerous because he is the son of a god or because the attempts to get rid of him almost collapse the world into a crisis of temporal inconsistency. Thasper is dangerous because he asks questions. Thasper, unlike the other rule-bound people of his world, is growing into an adult in Jones's understanding of the term. In a rather neat emulation of the cognitive stages of the child, Thasper has moved from the three-year-old's constant demands to know why something is so, through the child's obsession with collating lists and making up rules, to at age fifteen the realization "Why should one's mind not climb right out of the rules?"[41]

As Thasper comes face to face with the Sage, who is of course himself, he calls on Chrestomanci, who arrives and takes him to challenge the gods. In what might be termed a *homo ex machina* (man saves god), Chrestomanci forces the gods to accept the existence of the Sage and their possible dissolution and to accept that they are adults who must deal with the chaos of the every day, not children making playground rules. Jones argues that it is the proper role of mortals to question the rules, conventions, and paradigms with which they are gifted.[42] It is those around Thasper who are infantilized by their relationship with the gods, and in Jones's portrayal of the gods as rather hail-fellow-well-met types, she suggests that the gods have not been well served by the current order either.

The insistence that characters question the environments and the tales in which they find themselves if they are to be fully in control of their own lives is a tenet of those of Jones's books that make most use of the reader's cultural capital, what we might call the "deep secret" books. Each of these books is underpinned by a known plan of action, a story, a poem, a nursery rhyme, or a set of theses advanced by Jones. In other hands, they might become destinarian. For Jones, however, the point of this kind of hidden knowledge is that it gives one a lever to move the world. This is why the knowledge of the deep secret of these books does not necessarily structure the plot (as opposed to the story). *Eight Days of Luke,* for example, is underpinned by Norse myth, but although knowledge of the legacy texts of the novel can indicate a possible trajectory, it does not dictate the conclusion. These are tales of modern people whose reactions are fundamentally different from those of their ancestors. A protagonist's success in these books hinges in part not only on learning the rules but also in the willingness to climb right out of the framework to challenge destiny.

In each of these books, someone is trying to manipulate someone else. Conventions are conflated with rules, and the status of rules is used to coerce. Texts underlie this manipulation, and the more they are kept secret, the more powerful they are. In each book, recognition of story—a moment identified by John Clute as a crucial part of full fantasy[43]—grants power to resist the directed narrative of someone else.

The most frequently discussed of Jones's novels, *Fire and Hemlock,* is the classic story of this type. *Fire and Hemlock* makes use of the "Tam Lin" and "Thomas the Rhymer" ballads, but is also structured around a series of paintings the child, Polly, helps the musician Thomas Lynn choose, and is planted with information from fairy tales, from *The Golden Bough,* and from myths and legends and classic novels. For many readers, the process of decoding this book is itself a god-game in which Jones is the god in charge of whether we find meaning (and what meaning we find) at the end of the game.

Neither Polly nor Thomas Lynn is a free agent. Thomas Lynn has been enthralled by Laurel Leroy Perry, mistress of the Big House of the area. Already the first hint of a secret is waved beneath our noses—Perry (Peri). But Thomas Lynn is neither Tam Lin nor Thomas the Rhymer. Unlike his predecessors, Thomas Lynn understands what is happening; he knows the story and its trajectory. Although severely circumscribed, aware that Laurel and her companions keep close watch, and like Thomas the Rhymer sent away with a double-edged parting gift—that everything he says should be true and dangerous—Thomas Lynn's knowledge of the story confers power to resist the game that is being played. To resist the game however, he must draw someone else into it. He must do to another what has been done to him.

Thomas Lynn must educate Polly in such a way that she can have her own recognition of story. He makes sure Polly reads the two most pertinent ballads, but he is even more concerned that she read fairy tales and legends, which form the substructure of Laurel's game. Tom comments, "Only thin, weak thinkers despise fairy stories. Each one has a true, strange fact hidden in it, you know."[44] This idea of hidden knowledge pervades the book. But we need to be cautious in the way we read Tom. We like Tom; it is all too easy to take at face value his assertion that fairy tales are there to teach people to think, without considering that they may teach people to think in a particular way; they are not ideologically neutral. Terry Pratchett's Tiffany Aching (*The Wee Free Men*) regards fairy tales with suspicion: "It seemed to her that it [the book] tried to tell her what to do and think. Don't stray from the path, don't open the door, but hate the wicked witch because she is *wicked*. Oh, and believe that shoe size is a good way of choosing a wife."[45]

We can, of course, combine the two interpretations, Tom's and Tiffany's sensibilities. The tales do teach Polly to think, but they also trap her into a way of thinking. In the end Polly recognizes this. When Polly ignores some of the lessons she has learned, from tales such as *East of the Sun and West of the Moon*, it is in part because she has become resentful of her place as a counter in the game. Only when Polly shapes the tales, rather than let them shape her, and only when she becomes an active reader and therefore a writer of a new ballad of Thomas (Tom) can she move within the tale that Laurel has written and take control. *Fire and Hemlock* is an intense battle between those who wish to deny agency and those who refuse to acquiesce. Both Pratchett (in *Witches Abroad*) and Jones are arguing with the insistence that the world is shaped by the monomyth: just because the monomyth is all pervading does not mean one has to acquiesce to it any more than to any other coercive narrative.

The commonest form of coercive narrative in genre fantasy is prophecy: conventionally, prophecy brings destiny, and destiny is generally a good thing. Jones's revulsion with this idea is easiest to see in *Power of Three*, one of her earlier novels and one that is closer to the raw material of traditional story than some.

Power of Three is set on a moorland shared by three peoples: Dorigs, who live in dry caverns under still water and who are shape changers, Lymen—the people whose point of view dominates—who live in mounds sealed by words of power, and Giants (us), who have the power of electricity and mechanical ingenuity.

The three peoples become bound by a curse attached to a gold torc that has been stolen from a young Dorig by a murderous Lyman. The children of all three peoples come together, first out of mutual curiosity and later to prevent a new reservoir from destroying the Lymen and the home of the Giant children (although it would actually rather benefit the Dorigs). Gair, the middle of the three Lymen children—and in his mind the least gifted—is the first to realize that there is a curse on the gold torc in the Giant's house and that its influence is affecting all the people on or under the moor. In an attempt to negotiate with the Dorigs, he inadvertently places himself and Gerald (the male Giant) in the power of the King of the Dorigs, who decides to sacrifice them to the Powers who fuel the curse.

The Old Power is appeased when the stone is lifted from the Haunted Mound and when Hafny, the Dorig child, deliberately puts himself in the hands of the Lymen in penance for having inadvertently handed Gair over to his father, the Dorig King. The Middle Power, which "asks for blood, as all living things need to feed" is appeased by Gair's free offer of his own life, in place of his and Gerald's lives coerced. But it is the Dorig King's exasperated refusal of this sacrifice, his decision not to sacrifice either child, that appeases the New Power, "the most mysterious ... the Power of birth, growth and Future time."[46] The King too has been trapped in a game, this time one shaped by secrets and meanings to which he never has full access. At the moment the King—who has reigned in the knowledge that he was the younger son, never meant to be King—refuses the sacrifice he achieves his own agency. Because this is not one of the strongest pieces of Jones's writing (the scene is, frankly, weak), its radical turn can be missed. The King rejects the prophecy. His resistance, not destiny, is what brings him to agency.

In *Power of Three* destiny and the Powers rule humans. In *Fire and Hemlock* it is faerie and the power of story. Elsewhere, Jones turns her sights on secret rulers and guardians of the universe. Secret rulers (or guardians, or masters) protect or manipulate a society, either for "its own good" or for hidden purposes to the advantage of the rulers.[47] When they are particularly vicious, they play god-games in which humans are merely players in their pageants. They are, as Nicki Humble pointed out, "the terrible willful beings of King Lear's rage-filled visions."[48]

In *Deep Secret* Rupert Venables' insistence to Maree Mallory that he is not some kind of secret ruler is part defensiveness, part an acknowledgment that there are secret rulers (the Upper Room), and part a rejection of the whole idea that this would be a proper thing to be. However benevolent, Secret Rulers deny agency to others: Rupert is consumed with a feeling that he is being treated as a child, never quite trusted to do the right thing or to know enough—another way of considering the division of the Babylon verses. Although powerful in his own sphere, Rupert cannot escape the sense that he is a counter in a god-game.

A god-game is not a simple relationship between gods and mortals but rather "a tale in which an actual game (which may incorporate broader implications) is being played without the participants' informed consent, and which (in some sense) is being scored by its maker."[49] Jones's critique of god-gaming ties together all she has to say on the matter of agency: when humans accept the rules of the god-game, they infantilize themselves. Most of Jones's protagonists refuse the god-game, attempt to subvert it, or, even when they acquiesce continue to rage against its injustice. Sometimes they tear up the book.

Within the god-game, the moment of recognition and story is linked to the moment at which the actor turns an action upon the owner of the game. The true god-game, of which we have seen only hints so far, requires that there must be a victim, there must be a plot in which each action of the victim is in fact a reaction, and there must be an owner of the game "who is in some sense present while the game is being played, *and who stands in judgment.*"[50] This is why *Archer's Goon* is not truly a god-game, although it uses our expectation of the form to shape how the reader understands the book. *Archer's Goon* is the perfect inversion of the god-game. The wizards are not forcing Howard to react; they are similarly caught in a god-game in which they react to the game set up by the youngest brother Howard (Venturus).

Hexwood fits the rules far better, at the same time displaying Jones's arguments about the roles of players. There are several god-games here. The most obvious is played by the Bannus, a god-game designed to select the rulers of the galaxy. Because *Hexwood* reads in most ways as science fiction (even the appearance of Arthur Pendragon is described in science fictional terms, as his having been in stasis for fifteen hundred years), the parallel between the Bannus's aims and those of the standard genre fantasy are most visible in the trappings that accompany the game—the medieval castle, the dragon, and the grail. But the convention that those who play the gods' games are rewarded is subverted. At the end of *Hexwood,* the new hand of Reigners is selected by the degree to which they disrupt the game; to win they must stand up and declare, "I will no longer play."

The most ruthless of the god-games in *Hexwood*, however, is one that would not conventionally be seen as a god-game but that makes the point more vividly than anywhere else of the essential abusiveness of the god-game structure; and this is the upbringing of the Servant. Mordion has been brought up in isolation, with only five other children, each of whom died as they failed the tests. His education and testing almost exactly parallel the conventional Bildungsroman of the genre fantasy: he is of unknown parentage, he is to be trained to greatness by a great man who will oversee his future, and he is to be in the service of a prophecy or an empire. But all of this is in the service of someone who is evil. This is not simply an issue of who is served: in *Hexwood*, Jones demonstrates how essentially wicked are the taken-for-granted narratives of the conventional heroic fantasy of the predestined king. Part of Mordion's process of recovery is his attempt to impose a more benign version of the same trajectory on the boy Hume, who he thinks was created from earth and magic. The Bannus, as both god-gamer and participant in the god-game, forces Mordion into a position where Mordion and Hume—who has tried this with other children in his own real past—can recognize this parallel and can see that it is the principle, not the method or intention, that is at fault.

The one unequivocal god-game Jones has written is *The Homeward Bounders*. Along with *The Time of the Ghost*, it is also one of Jones's most frightening books, and its threat lies in the degree to which Jamie, our point-of-view character, is helpless within the structures of a god-game in which there might be no purpose. Far from being the direct victim, as a Homewardbounder Jamie exists outside the rules. He can see the games as they are being played—and they are literally games, played on boards and with dice—and as the book proceeds he becomes increasingly angry at what They (the players) are doing to other worlds. At the same time, his own movements appear to be constrained by the rules of what we might call a supragame, a game in that They are also only counters.

Although the games played by They appear in many forms—as versions of Dungeons and Dragons complete with dice and character attributes; as war games based on strategy; as games of diplomacy; and as card games—the supragame bears some resemblance to chess, with the worlds as the squares perhaps, and some resemblance to Go, in which pieces are positioned to control the boundaries. This is particularly relevant to the overall explanation of the quiet place where a Prometheus-like character is bound. It is the square to capture, but it is also the central node from which the fault lines of the world split and multiply. Each of the worlds that They play with is held in place by their control of boundaries or the lines on the board.

Jamie, although angry, is trapped by his own acceptance of the situation and the necessity of working out the rules as he goes along. Jamie is like a chess player who knows the pieces and their moves but, having learned them at board-eye level, cannot lift himself above the game to strategize. In contrast Helen has had the chance to study the handbook; she understands the theory of the game and can distinguish between the binding physical laws to which they have been subjected and those rules they have been taught that socialize them to helplessness. Helen can stand above the game and set herself up as a rival dungeon master. With the aid of Konstam the demon hunter, Joris his slave, Jamie, and Jamie's descendants Adam and Vanessa, Helen can change the paradigm of the game. As with the other deep secret books, in *The Homeward Bounders* Jones argues that individuated information is not enough; one must read widely and one must synthesize.

Yet *The Homeward Bounders* is not without its supra-supragame. *They* are not completely free agents. To preserve their game space, they have had to create the conditions in which it could be destroyed: their anchor is a man who must retain hope; the homeward bounders must believe they can get home; and there must be a prophecy that makes it possible to break into their place. Although Helen is able to rise above the game book, she is also one of the most powerful pieces in this supra-supragame and in the end, Helen cannot escape. Neither can Jamie, who takes Prometheus's place as the anchor for the worlds, returning us to the *homo ex machina*, or man saves god, that is such a feature of later books.[51]

In her construction of the fantastic, Jones suggests that within all rule systems is the potential of their own destruction, that no system can be completely closed, and that it is a human responsibility to find the loopholes. Jones maintains that magic is about understanding, it is about the ability to both comprehend and challenge apparently rigid structures. On one level these are societal and cultural; on the second level, and the one with which this book is most concerned, is a description of Jones's arguments with the ossified nature of much fantastic fiction. In the succeeding chapters we will see how Jones applies this idea to her own writing and seeks to find some of the loopholes in the rules that bind the fantastical universe.

CHAPTER 3
TIME GAMES

In most works of fantasy, time travel just happens. Characters step back in time, walk through portals, light candles, or dream themselves elsewhere. In most time travel stories for children (Alan Garner's *Red Shift* is a notable exception), either moments in time travel at the same pace in all time spaces or protagonists are returned to their own time as if nothing ever happened. Time travel in fantasy is frequently very convenient. Elsewhere in this book I have insisted on Diana Wynne Jones's position as a fantasy writer, but her approach to time travel has been distinctively that of the writer of science fiction. Her time travel narratives exist in the world of the rational, not of wish fulfillment: they deploy recognized theories of time travel.

One of the distinguishing features of science fiction is that time travel must affect one's experience of the world. *The Homeward Bounders*, although it reads as fantasy, is driven by Einstein's theories of relativity and the belief that the universe is curved. Anyone traveling out along the curve of the universe (in a rocket, for example) would, on return, overleap the years in a parabola, just as a stone thrown in the air comes down at a slight distance from the point at which it was thrown. Similarly, the further out Jamie travels from his own world, the further he deviates from the straight line of world time.

The result is that Jamie's family extends three generations into the future, while Jamie lives rather less. although he loses count after the first

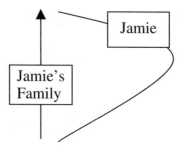

Figure 3.1 Einstein's Twin Paradox

few worlds. Elsewhere, "The Sage of Theare" applies a relentless logic to its time fantasy. When the infant sage is placed in suspended animation for three years, his over-ordered world tries desperately to reunite the sage's personal time line with the time line of events that prophecy has dictated.

The general assumption is that writers turn to mathematicians and metaphysicists in search of their rationalization, but, as Paul Nahin pointed out, it has been the work of science fiction writers that has frequently inspired the mathematicians in the first place,[1] so although in this chapter I will be ascribing theories of time travel to the philosophers, physicists, and metaphysicists whose names are associated with them, it is worth bearing in mind that in many cases these are ideas that first appeared in the pulp science fiction magazines of the 1930s and later. "The Sage of Theare" demonstrates vividly Jones's very distinct awareness of this fictional tradition and of the two major divisions in the conceptualization of time: McTaggart's A-series and B-series (or relative and absolute time). These two divisions are held by philosophers, and physicists and mathematicians, respectively.

A-series time (which this chapter will actually consider second) is relative time. It locates events in the past, present, and future, and events move away from one, backward into each. B-series time is absolute time. Rather than locate events in time, it orders them, fixes them within a series of coordinates: an event happens earlier than another, later than a second, and simultaneously with a third. The publication of Jones's first children's novel, *Wilkins' Tooth/ Witch's Business* (which in A-series–relative time terms happened in the present of 1973, but our past) occurred twenty-three years after the publication of *The Lion, the Witch and the Wardrobe* in 1950 and twenty years before the publication of *The Merlin Conspiracy* in 2003. The B-series–absolute time is a stable order of events; the A-series–relative time is concerned with the flow of time, what Heather Dyke has described as "temporal becoming."[2]

One consequence of this configuration of time, McTaggart argues, is that if time consisted only of B-series–absolute time, change would not be possible, because B-series–absolute facts never change: "Facts about the B-series relations between events are fixed; they do not change. If there is only a B-series so that all events are equally real, no matter when they occur and no event ever changes its B-series location, then nothing really changes. Reality is a fixed and unchanging entity."[3]

The Time of the Ghost might have been written to demonstrate this hypothesis. It is a novel whose premise is that the past cannot be changed but which apparently depends on changing the past in order to achieve resolution. Sally wakes in a hospital bed not knowing who she is, aware only that something terrible has happened. Visiting the past as a ghost, she becomes convinced that something that was done or not done has left her life at the mercy of a goddess, the wrathful Monigan.

The problem Jones is faced with is how to create a time travel narrative while asserting one cannot change the past. The narrative mode Jones deploys is that of the thriller: all thrillers are essentially countdowns, ineluctably time bound; the voice she adopts is that which Dorrit Cohn terms *psychonarration,* which "combines an omniscience ('the narrator knows more than the character'), external focalization ('the narrator knows less than the character') and fixed internal focalization ('the narrator knows as much as the character') in a mixture in which the techniques are inseparable but highly ambiguous."[4]

Sally's sojourn in the past takes place in real time: the dual bands of time—the then and the now—run side by side, hour for hour, and Monigan ensures that every minute Sally experiences in the past is a minute used in the present. The tension of the book increases as we realize Sally might be running out of time. Time in this book is absolute; it cannot be cheated by traveling outside of time.

The past in *The Time of the Ghost* is narrated by the watching ghost. It is a peculiar narration, one held together by a unity of time but not of place. The ghost dances from place to place, observing events that she could not have witnessed at the time they occurred, but she initially observes them in a linear progression. This linear progression is part of the deception that Jones enacts. Charlotte (or Cart), Sally's eldest sister, has already told us, "The only thing you can alter is the future. People write stories pretending you can alter the past, but it can't be done. All you can do to the past is remember it wrong or interpret it differently,"[5] a statement strongly reminiscent of the Russian religious philosopher Nikolai

Berdayaev's assertion, "The past which we so much admire has never really existed … it is merely a composite part of our present; there was another present in the past as it actually was, a present with all its own evils and shadows."[6]

The linearity of the ghost's visitations, their fixedness within the B-series–absolute coordinates, invites us into an ironic deception that because events are processing in order relative to each other, they can therefore be stopped; it is the apparent rigidity of the B-series–absolute time that makes it possible to move around in it. So it is not a coincidence that only once Sally has accepted *both* that the past is not perfect and that she can change only her memory of it that she is able—as the ghost—to travel to moments she chooses. B-series, because it is a set of coordinates, might not be changeable (although we will see a different set of arguments in *A Tale of Time City*), but it is within reach. The nonunity of space that the ghost experiences is the clue. If she can move from place to place without passing through the connecting land, then she can do the same in space-time.

This movement is possible because one way to conceptualize B-series/absolute time is as something with geographical density in which one can move around. Block space is probably the easiest of the images for the nonmathematician to hold in his or her mind. It is simply a cube of space-time, which one can leave and then choose to reenter at another coordinate on the map. Michael Friedman describes it so:

> Our theories all agree that space-time is a four dimensional differentiable manifold. … Space-time has a *topology:* given any point p in space-time, we have the notion of a *neighborhood* of p—a set of points all of which are "close" to p.[7]

Once time is realized in this way, not only is the past accessible but so too is the future. It might not have happened yet (A-series–relative time), but it exists as a B-series–absolute coordinate.]

Understanding this is what helps Sally to realize that changing time is not the point. Its very stability is what allows movement. Sally can move away from the first half of Cart's statement—that the past cannot be altered—and focus on the second half: "All you can do to the past is remember it wrong or interpret it differently."[8] It helps Sally to understand that although for Monigan all times run side by side, some are in focus and some are not. Knowing this, she can return to a moment when Monigan's eyes are away from a younger sister, Imogen, and persuade

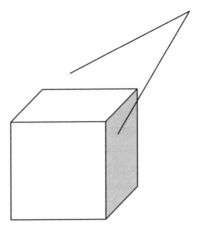

Figure 3.2 Negotiating block time.

Imogen to return and make her sacrifice, a sacrifice she has already made—because in block time all events coexist—and that a thunderstorm has thrown from her mind. Monigan is not trying to prevent Sally from changing the past but is making sure that Sally cannot remind Imogen that a bargain was struck, that the past is not what they think it was. Imogen is the only one to realize this and its relevance to Cart's earlier statement, and can respond, "It's the future I'm trying to change."[9]

Block time is the context for *The Time of the Ghost*, but in *A Tale of Time City*, block time and the argument about whether time is changeable are the rationale for the plot.

A Tale of Time City is perhaps the only indisputably science fiction novel in Jones's portfolio: Maria Nikolajeva suggested in 1988, "Time fantasy ... never, unlike science fiction, ... depict(s) apocalyptic visions of distorted time." There are other reasons why this book is science fiction, but certainly Nikolajeva's comment reinforces the point. *Hexwood* and *The Homeward Bounders* are much more conscious of the blending of science fiction and fantasy.[10] *A Tale of Time City* is the novel in which Jones, understandably, most directly considers the nature of time as described by philosophers and understood in modern physics; however, it is not what is commonly understood as a time-slip novel.[11] Vivian Smith, the child from Earth, is not strictly from the past. Time City to which she travels is outside time; its apparently futuristic elements are representations not signifiers. Time in this novel has cyclical, linear, and static (or block) expressions, but Jones requires the reader to hold all three of these concepts rather than choosing from them.

The premise of the novel is that a city can exist outside of time. To do this time is constructed as a cycle in which that which is "within time" moves in one direction on the wheel while the city moves in the other direction. Antonia Barber used a very similar image for time travel in *The Ghosts* (filmed as *The Amazing Mister Blunden*) but envisaged time travelers moving through the spokes of the wheel, an idea for which I can find no parallel in the physics texts or from the philosophers. Jones's construction is, however, consciously Platonic (one of the characters, Professor Wilander, tells us so).

However, Jones does not leave Plato's conception of time untouched but marries it with the idea of block space-time; something that one can exit from and return to, so that rather than seeing the whole of time as one circle on which we are traveling in different directions one could envisage Time City's relationship to the universe as two wheels facing each other.

From wheel X, it is theoretically possible to reach any point on wheel Y. Of course the reverse is also true, but this is hidden from the citizens of Time City because, as Professor Wilander points out, they refuse to accept that Time City is also bound by the same equations that affect the world, or the place that they insist on calling "in time," a label that might make this section rather confusing.

Access to "in time" is possible because although the citizens of Time City see time as circular and repetitive, they also see it as a block to be entered at any point. The best visual image might be if the block of space-time became a ribbon and was twisted into a moebius strip. There is no

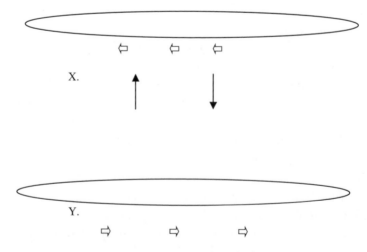

Figure 3.3 Time as conceived in *A Tale of Time City.*

beginning or end, and it can all be accessed anywhere. The real pecu-
liarity appears, however, in the way in which Jones has blended the
concept of block time with possibility theory.

If we return to McTaggart for a moment, block time is theoretically
feasible if we accept that all events are fixed by the events that occurred
before and after them. They have coordinates. Usually, changing these
events in science fiction novels would change the present substantially
or launch the protagonists into a future that is not their own: the time
line would split into a range of possible futures. This is what has happened in Jones's worlds of Chrestomanci: the series of worlds is created
by possibilities that have split endlessly. But in *A Tale of Time City,*
Jones departs from the assumptions usually made about block time
while not actually deviating from the fixity of the B-series–absolute
coordinates as McTaggart outlines them. In *A Tale of Time City,* as
time in the outside world unravels, a careful observer can see that the
events of B-series–absolute time—the world war, the invention of
nuclear weapons, the application of nuclear technology—remain intact
but have been compressed.

The structural premise of *A Tale of Time City* is that the circular time
we have already noted is constructed of four large fixed, or stable, eras;
several shorter ones, "put in to confuse";[12] and four unstable eras.
Within the unstable eras history is a little unpredictable and can be
shaken. From the point of view of Time City, all moments happen at
all moments (i.e., there is never a time when Kennedy is not being
shot). When someone begins to play with time, and to remove the
time-weights that keep it balanced, time begins to roll. In the twentieth
century the Second World War starts eight months early at Christmas
1938, but it still starts.

The implication is that time has a momentum, a fabric of its own. It
can be folded, pleated, or shrunk. Individuals can move about the landscape of time. In one of the most vivid descriptions of time in the novel,
the Guardian of the Iron Casket tells the children,

> "I did what I could. When I saw the theft begin, I ran back to the
> Age of Iron and from there I ran back to the late days, pulling the
> threads of history as I came … the allotted span of the city is ending
> and it made my power to summon weak. Only you two answered the
> summons. … So then," the Guardian's thin voice muttered on, "I

surrounded the thief in the threads of history and wrapped them round any who would help in the Age of Iron, to drag them together."[13]

The degree to which Jones seeks to manifest time in the visual fabric of Time City is very noticeable. As Time City moves backward through the cyclical time it observes, the cyclical manifests in the physical structures of the city. These confuse the 1930s child, Vivian Smith. Lee House "was built mostly of metal in a most modern-looking style, and yet she could see that it was very old from the gigantic flowering tree trained up the front of it." In contrast, the newer houses are built of brick and wood.[14]

Time City is marked with monuments: habit ghosts leave their marks like cattle trails; once ghosts distort the landscape with their emotional force. Some of these monuments have been made in the future. In Time City, as much as "in time" the existence of everything at any given moment undermines the A-series—relative of time (that notion of events moving past us, from future, to present, to past). Yet despite the denial of the citizenry, each of these is an indicator that Time City is just as much subject to the concept of block space-time as is the external world. Time City does have its own internal time, because people are born, age, and die. Wilander explains to Jonathan that of course Time City has a history but nobody keeps a record because part of the conceit of Time City inhabitants is that existing out of time makes them immune to history, but the refusal of history is indicative. Wilander says,

> You can only tell from outside, here in Time City. And it isn't only that nobody *in* an Unstable Era knows what's going to happen in their future—nobody knows. It can differ from day to day.[15]

> What do you think is the real reason we have records of every single year of history and none of the City itself? Because those records wouldn't stay accurate, of course. And do *you* know what's going to happen in the City tomorrow?[16]

Time City's Calvinistic sense of predestination, reinforced by the time-ghosts, is seriously awry. Vivian realizes this when Jonathan is badly hurt during their trip to the age of Gold: "The two time-ghosts meant that we came *back*! Then she thought, this is an Unstable Era. Anything can happen."[17] There has been a hint in this direction. When the children go on a picnic by the river, they hear that there are more habit ghosts at the time-locks than there have been previously. The idea that the ghosts are predictive is destabilized, and therefore the assumption of Time City's inhabitants that they are free in time is also destablized.

Jones's idea that some places in time are more accessible than others is a science fictional conceit: it constructs time as a spiral in which one can reach only the points at which the thread crosses. Having tested it as a narrative device in *A Tale of Time City* and produced an adventure that continually crosses and recrosses the same moment of time—the train station where Vivian is first met—Jones exploits the idea to the fullest in *The Merlin Conspiracy* more than twenty years later. In *The Merlin Conspiracy*, an indirect sequel to *Deep Secret*, Nick Mallory (Maree's brother) cannot reach or change his own past, but because he can move between universes, and time travel in the process, he can drastically affect his own future by affecting the childhood experiences of those who are already adult during his childhood.

Frank Sadler, in his 1984 study *The Unified Ring: Narrative Art and the Science Fiction Novel*,[18] threw out a challenge to science fiction writers to develop a way of writing about the world in general, and time specifically, that would reflect twentieth-century physics and ways of understanding time; in particular Werner Heisenberg's argument that "for the smallest building blocks of matter every process of observation causes a major disturbance."[19] If we keep Heisenberg's theories in mind, then the plot of *The Merlin Conspiracy* makes sense both as a narrative and as an argument.

The temporal narrative of *The Merlin Conspiracy* is complex and combines the notion of fixed-coordinate B-series–absolute time with a new one of backward causation, "a causal signal traveling between two events in space time such that the time direction of travel is from 'later' to 'earlier,' i.e., the relation of causal precedence is opposite to that of temporal precedence,"[20] so that one can have a causal sequence of ABCD and a temporal sequence of BCAD, an idea that summarizes rather well the narrative structure of *The Merlin Conspiracy*.[21] *The Merlin Conspiracy* is a farrago of a novel in which the main plot revolves around a kidnapped Merlin (the title of the chief magician of Blest), an England—not UK—analogue and Nick Mallory's desire to be a Magid.

A rather more complicated time line can be constructed of Roddy's and Nick's experiences of each other. Within the author's and reader's construction of the narrative, Nick meets Roddy in the astral plane quite some time before Roddy goes into the trance that calls him. In *The Merlin Conspiracy* moving between universes does not mimic the equations of relativity. Nick does not automatically travel forward in time when he

TABLE 3.1 Temporal Narrative of Nick's Journey in *The Merlin Conspiracy* (references from UK 1st edition, references rendered as section/chapter/page)

MINUS TEN YEARS	STARTING POINT
	Nick leaves Earth—spell possibly laid on him to attack Romanov
	Plantagenet Earth
	Meeting with Romanov
6/1/169 Nick meets the Prayermaster and his boys in Loggia.	
6/2/185 Nick meets the embroiderers—describes meeting with Romanov as "this morning" (?).	
6/3/198 Nick gets to Romanov's place with Mini for his third sunset in a row. Mini is young here.	
6/3/202–224 Nick finds Romanov sick; Nick answers the phone and alienates Sybil from Romanov; Nick turns Sybil's voice around so she cannot talk to Romanov for the next ten years; Prayermaster and boys arrive on island; Nick asks if they paid Romanov to eliminate him. They did not in this time but did put a spell on him to lead them to Romanov; Nick laughs at Japheth, and Japheth declares that now he really hates Nick.	
7/2/228–29 Maxwell Hyde arrives, having got very drunk: "Hadn't bargained for Romanov's island being in the past. … Ten years or more behind the times, this place is … though I believe parts of the island must be in the future too. (7/2/229)	
7/3/248 Nick suggests the spell was on him before Romanov turned up with the contract on Nick.	
7/3/249 Nick thinks he went back ten years when he took the fork to Loggia (there had been a trace of Romanov in both forks).	
	11/2/397–99 Nick gets all the children back to Romanov's place, by following the goat, to find himself ten years in the future from when he first met Mini. Three weeks have passed for him—he has traversed time; Romanov comments that he dreamed ten years before that Nick returned with a crowd of children. Nick dismisses it as a fever dream.

(continued)

TABLE 3.1 Temporal Narrative of Nick's Journey in *The Merlin Conspiracy* (references from UK 1st edition, references rendered as section/chapter/page) (continued)

MINUS TEN YEARS	STARTING POINT
	11/2/405 Nick realizes that it was Sybil he "tuned out" of Romanov's life ten years before—possibly provoking her.
	11/4/411–12 Arriving in Loggia City Nick realizes the devastation his comments on the craftwork have wreaked on Joel and Japheth's city.
	11/6/424 Meets and recognizes Joel
	11/6/425 Joel reveals that it was he—as an adult—who sent Romanov, in this time, and was the one who sent Nick off from London, just before kidnapping the Merlin. His own actions as an adult set Nick on the path that offended him in the first place.
	12/2/447 Nick meets up with Japheth again, who is still nursing hate caused by Nick's laughing at him when he trod on an egg. "I'll show you what of it! I've dreamed of you dead for ten years now!" (12/2/448)

traverses. Instead space-time becomes a map that one can, if talented enough, navigate in a variety of directions.

The consequence is that B-series–absolute time structures the plot—the coordinates of events that must be worked out by the characters in order to establish what it is the villains are up to—but the tale is told in A-series–relative time, in which Nick has a quite different understanding of what is past, present, and future than do the other characters. His time line is "kinked." See figure 3.4 for a visual image of what the time line might look like.[22]

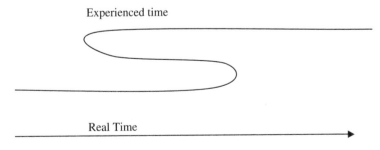

Figure 3.4 Kinked time line.

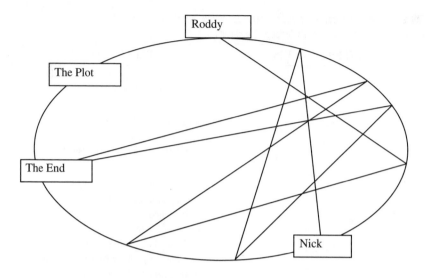

Figure 3.5 Nick and Roddy on intersecting time-lines.

But figure 3.4 is Nick's time line, not Roddy's, and if we were to add Roddy's experience, the diagram would look much like a game of cat's cradle. The only way to conceive of plotting it is to place the linear plot—what happens—on a circle and allow Roddy and Nick to criss-cross it.[23]

Nick meets Roddy in his narrative before we know why she is there, and it takes Roddy another three chapters to explain her presence in the interstices of the universe. Her presence there is not simple, and it reveals that Nick and we have missed at least three steps in time, not merely one.

The plot in *The Merlin Conspiracy* is linear, but the protagonists' experience of the plot, and the structure of time in *The Merlin Conspiracy*, is hologramatic (try adding Roddy's grandfather, Maxwell Hyde, to that circle). Jones has taken the idea of time as a dimension and realized the way one would actually move through it if it were possible to construct this in the mind. The entire plot relies on the assumption that time is folded and that it is possible to move through the folds. This is a much more philosophical understanding of time than we have hitherto considered. With the exception of the wormhole theory—the idea that space is curved and that one can drill holes through it like a wormhole in an apple—the idea that time might be folded is not one that physicists seem to have dabbled with, although it has turned up in science fiction. Space-time as it is depicted in *The Merlin Conspiracy* bears a strong resemblance to philosopher Donald Williams's "doctrine of the manifold":

> The conception that nature, all there is, was, or will be, "is" (tenselessly) spread out in a four-dimensional scheme of location relations which intrinsically are exactly the same, and hence in principle commensurate, in all directions, but which happen to be differentiated, in our neighbourhood at least, by the *de facto* pattern of the things and events in them—by the lie of the land, so to speak.

Later he writes,

> It is conceivable, then, though perhaps physically impossible, that one four-dimensional part of the manifold of events be slued around at right angles to the rest, so that the time order of that area, as composed of its interior lines of strain and structure, runs parallel with a spatial order in its environment. It is conceivable, indeed, that a whole human life should lie athwartwise of the manifold, with its belly plump in time, its birth in the east and its death in the west, and its conscious stream perhaps running alongside somebody's garden path.[24]

This, of course, takes us right back to A-series–relative time. Some of the players in *The Merlin Conspiracy* literalize Williams's conception: they lie athwart the B-series–absolute structure of time and can make moves in this hologramatic understanding of the world in which past, present, and future are all equally accessible. Romanov, the wizard who lives in an island made of times and places, can choose his actions carefully because he knows what is not worth doing; why threaten a prince when you know that he will lose much of his empire shortly after his ascension anyway?

All the magic users in *The Merlin Conspiracy* have some relationship to time. Mrs. Candace does know to expect Judith and the children: "*Space is as a folding screen to the little people,*" said the witch's knowledge inside Roddy's head, and this is a pretty good image for the magics that are worked throughout the book—whether Mrs. Candace's folding of space and time for Judith to shorten her journey,[25] or the range of images we receive when Nick travels through the universes. The most startling image is in chapter 11, when it is the goat that takes them through: Nick's dark paths, seen the way a goat might see them, become "a line of bright islands. They were just hanging there, like unstrung beads, or huge stepping-stones. ... Each island was a slightly different shape from the others,

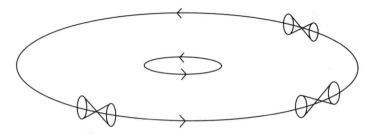

Figure 3.6 Gödel 1949: Space-time with closed time like curves. Gödel, "An Example of a New Type of Cosmological Solution to Einstein's Field Equations of Gravitation," *Review of Modern Physics* 21 (July 1949): 447–50; http://www.utas.edu.au/docs/humsoc/philosophy/Time_Travel/lectures/10a.html[7]

but each shone out in various greens and golds."[26] This movement through and over universes bears a very strong resemblance to the pictorial depictions of Kurt Gödel's understanding of time travel.

Gödel argues that it is possible to travel in time by moving from universe to universe (each is depicted by the butterfly cones). Einstein's corollary to this is that it is possible if the universe is infinite and stable. Unfortunately ours is finite and expanding.[27]

The formation of magic in modern Blest shares the imagery of time enfolded and interwoven with space. The little person explains the way the land's magic is formed as "magic all laid together close, over and under, like weaving."[28] Where, elsewhere in Jones's writing magic has often linked most directly to words, here it is linked to the land and to the passage of time—it feels much more physical. Mrs. Candace explains, "...the magic of Blest is most intricately interlaced with itself—the hugely old, the old, and the newer *and* the most recent—so that each part supports the others."[29] Romanov, the character who has most facility with traversing time, lives on an island that connects to at least ten other places, each of which is in another time.

> You could see the lines dividing the different kinds of water if you half closed your eyes. ... Even the sun, setting in the midst of red and purple clouds, was divided into an orange part and a smaller slice that was much redder. It looked really odd.[30]

We are told so frequently that Romanov lives in both the past and the future that it is incumbent on us to take notice, but it is very easy to miss the point that it is in the interweaving of past and present that the motive for the senior conspirators is hidden. Counterpointing this tale of the traversing of time are the figures of Sybil, Joel, and Japheth, who cannot traverse time but instead bring time—in the form of grudges—with them. This is even drawn on Joel's physiognomy.

> It's strange how some people hardly change at all as they grow up. When I first met Joel, as the older of the Prayermaster's two boys, he had had this thick pile of dark hair, cheekbones that stuck out, and eyebrows that seemed to express disgust with the whole world. Those eyebrows were just the same now.[31]

The moebius strip of time turns out to structure the conspiracy and the novel. Nick's actions in his own past have triggered responses that create the present. Maxwell Hyde (Roddy's grandfather) dismisses Nick's sense of responsibility, but in this book determinism is reversed and, in contrast to *The Time of the Ghost*, the future does change the past. This takes place in both the metanarrative and in the small details of the plot: admiring a tapestry destroys an economy; a phone call and laughter create enemies.[32] Again, time is less traversed than it is interwoven.

This image of the weaving of time infects even the relationship of time to the landscape. Nick mistakes the dragon for a fossil in ways that emphasize the connection between time and land—a trope usually associated with Alan Garner—and remind us that most travel through time is by the slow route. Roddy's maternal grandfather, Gwyn ap Nud, is one of the great powers of Blest (and Earth). Space folds around him, time spent with him does not quite match up with time in the real world. To Gwyn ap Nud, space and time can be indistinguishable; he sends Roddy in search of magic to a ruined village, but a place so much of the past that it has become somewhere of now, and this nowness is communicated in part in the way Roddy sees it:

> It was like an accidental garden strewn with heaps of regularly piled stones. Small rowans and hawthorns had grown up among the stones, along with heather and gorse, big bushes of broom and small shrubs of bilberry. In between, there was every kind of wild flower, from foxgloves and poppies and yarrow, through buttercups, down to speedwell and tiny heartsease. I was particularly enchanted with some flowers like dark blue trumpets nestling in sunny spaces and by the drifts of frail, wiry harebells.[33]

One can consider this as a sort of eternity-gram. An eternity-gram is what beings outside of time, in "hypertime," would see, because they can see the past and future all at once.[34] Terry Pratchett offers us the following very clear example. Death bends down to stroke a cat; because Death sees all times simultaneously, he can see the cat as kitten, mature cat, and old cat simultaneously so that the cat looks a little like a fluffy carrot.[35] Gwyn ap Nud's understanding or vision of this village is not of ruins and the past but of growth and the future. It is nature that allows the witch, another character for whom time is but a another landscape, to reach down to Roddy through the centuries.

The Merlin Conspiracy is related as two diaries, and two time lines, one told by Nick Mallory, the other by Roddy, who lives in Blest. The reader, however, is on yet a third time line, which is at the intersection of theirs. In this time line Jones withholds and plants crucial information as she sees fit: in the third part of the novel, Roddy has seen the Merlin go off in his car and is "interested to see that the Merlin was back."[36] Much later we might realize that his speedy return is an indication that it is not the same person, but as long as we remain wedded to the straight line of consequences, this is not obvious. Jones combines the different understandings of the physics of real time and of time travel with the manipulation of experiential time. It is to the techniques she employs to create a time narrative within the mode of telling, and the manipulation of A-series–relative time we now turn.

A-series–relative time is about the relationship of experience to time and is simultaneously metaphysical and metaphorical. Although, as I have demonstrated, Jones uses B-series–absolute concepts of time and the theoretical models of time travel with great facility, it is in her manipulation of A-series–relative time that her work achieves its fullest complexity. This is first hinted at in *The Magicians of Caprona,* a novel that is not about time travel at all.

Jones uses A-series–relative understandings of time as a narrative technique. In *The Magicians of Caprona,* Jones does not set out to manipulate our perception of time, but it is here that we first see Jones experiment with tense and rhetorical structure to create, in effect, a mode of time travel that is facilitated by language rather than by visible machinery or the description of time travel. In this it foreshadows *Hexwood.*

Chapters 1 and 2 of *The Magicians of Caprona* take us from the distant past to the present by using a rhetorical structure more usually associated with nonfiction writing. Each section of these chapters (sometimes by paragraph, sometimes not) goes from the general thesis, to a summary of the evidence, to a specific example, to a quotation, and then to analysis;

TABLE 3.2

The great houses of Petrocchi and Montana go back to the first founding of the State of Caprona—seven hundred years or more ago. And they are bitter rivals. They are not even on speaking terms. If a Petrocchi and a Montana meet in one of Caprona's narrow golden-stone streets, they turn their eyes aside and edge past as if they were both walking past a pigsty. Their children are sent to different schools and warned never, ever to exchange a word with a child from the other house	Distant past	General thesis
Sometimes, however, parties of young men and women of the Montanas and the Petrocchis happen to meet when they are strolling on the wide street called the Corso in the evenings. When that happens, other citizens take shelter at once. If they fight with fists and stones, that is bad enough, but if they fight with spells, it can be appalling.	Recent past	Summary of the evidence
An example of this is when the dashing Rinaldo Montana caused the sky to rain cowpats on the Corso for three days. It caused great distress to visitors.	Immediate past	Example
"A Petrocchi insulted me," Rinaldo explained, with his most flashing smile. "And I happened to have a new spell in my pocket."		Quotation
The Petrocchis unkindly claimed that Rinaldo had misquoted his spell in the heat of battle. Everyone knew that all Rinaldo's spells were love charms.		Analysis

they simultaneously mix three positions of the A-series–relative past (the distant past, the recent past, and the immediate past) and do this consecutively. One of the shortest examples can be found on page 10 and is perhaps best set out as a diagram.[35] The pattern recurs throughout the chapter but is not extended into the rest of the book.

One of the difficulties that fantasy often faces is that the narrative direction of the plot is to resolve a problem whose origins are in the past, not unlike the crime novel. In Jones's work the clearest manifestation is in *The Lives of Christopher Chant,* a straight-forward crime novel in which Christopher catches a smuggling ring, but we can see the pattern in *Fire and Hemlock, Archer's Goon, Power of Three,* and *The Magicians of Caprona.* In each book there is an event or story in the past that must be related in order to establish the story of the present.

The consequence of this need to divulge the past is that the point at which the relevant information is made available can seem contrived; the legend can be delivered in portentous tones by the resident mage or through personal reverie, or it found in a book of legends. The technique Jones uses here evades all of this: a great deal of necessary history is covered, and the shuttling between past and present reinforces the plot theme of vendetta constantly renewed and reinvigorated over time. If there is time travel as plot in this book, it is the vendetta that has traveled, and it has traveled in words: through the tales told of the past, the embroidery attached to small incidents, and the toleration of bad behavior, all of which are rehearsed in the rhetorical structure. The very relativity of A-series–relative time, the degree to which the present is allowed to become the past, is at stake.

Alongside the time travel of the vendetta, the reader too has been transported: the internal rhythm that shuttles us through different periods of the past allows Jones to deliver us apparently effortlessly to her present.[37] In the final scene of the first chapter, Tonino's great uncle, Old Niccolo, asks the Casa cat Benvenuto to befriend Tonino. At the beginning of chapter 2 we are with Tonino, firmly in his present, waiting for Benvenuto to join him. And then Jones plays a neat trick: chapter 2, we discover, was not the present of the story but its immediate past. It ends, "What worried them far more was their gradual discovery that things were not altogether well in the Casa Montana, nor in Caprona either."[38] We have traveled in time once more.

There are traces of the thesis structure throughout the book, but elsewhere the order is frequently reversed. An exclamation from Aunt Francesca about the harvests is followed by a report that "all these years Paolo and Tonino had been at school, they had grown used to hearing that there had been this concession to Florence; that Pisa had demanded that agreement over fishing rights."[39] The new rhetorical rule, if there is one, seems to be that no elaboration is written in the same tense or mode as that which it is elaborating. If one is direct speech, the other is delivered in another manner, so that we are continually kept off guard. One irony is that it is frequently the adults who speak in the immediate present, reacting unthinkingly to crises, while it is the children who consider the past.

Once we have reached the present, most of the book moves firmly through the present with the occasional pause for "meanwhile," but instability of time is not a major theme in the novel. However, chapters 13 and 14 contain scenes that are narrated in directly the reverse order to that in which they occur. In chapter 13 Paulo and Renata are overwhelmed by the noise of flying metal griffins:

> Renata began to laugh. "Now that *is* Angelica!" she said. "I'd know her spells anywhere."[40]

"What is it? A call for help?" Panted Paolo.

"Must be," gasped Renata. "Angelica's spells—always—mad kind of reasonableness."[41]

But it is in chapter 14 that we see this spell cast. The Duke wants to get
the two families to the palace but without the Duchess' knowledge, and
Angelica suggests that she cast a spell, on the grounds that the family
would know it to be hers. She suggests a charm to call all the rats and mice
in Caprona to the palace. To Tonino: "If you did the calling, we'd fetch
something."[42] On page 194 they see the griffins flying toward the palace.

This reverse ellipse infuses urgency into the scenes with Paolo and
Renata, whereas Tonino and Angelica's scene is more relaxed: they have
sent their cry for help and have done all they can. It also allows the two
threads to join at the same point in the characters' time lines. If the spell
had come first, and we had to wait for Paulo and Renata to see it, it would
have required an extra scene to get Paolo and Renata to the top of the
cathedral. Instead, Jones is able to let their activity take place while
Tonino and Angelica get on with things after the spell. The scenes are
structured to parallel each other, rather than for one to follow the other.
B-series, or coordinate time, is something we are left to construct for ourselves. Experiential time is at this point most central to the creation of
drama. This technique, as we have already seen, is vital to the narrative
structure of *The Merlin Conspiracy*. It reaches its fullest complexity in
Hexwood with the construction of a series of temporal heterotopias.[43]

It is in *Hexwood* that Jones most successfully combines A-series–relative
and B-series–absolute understandings of time, both with the Heisenberg
principle and the manipulation of the narrative techniques developed in
those first two chapters of *The Magicians of Caprona*, and it draws attention to a truth: one cannot separate philosophical thought about time
from metaphor. Metaphors are repeatedly used to prove that our ability to
think about time, and the ways in which we think about it, are a priori,
evidence that metaphors are themselves truths.

In *Hexwood* Jones used the combination of A-series–relative and B-
series–absolute time to narrate a particular story and to play with our
understanding of the nature of time. In *The Time of the Ghost*, Jones was
concerned primarily with the nature of the past and retrieving a true past.
In *Hexwood* the ways we move through time, our narrative expectations of
time and time travel, are applied to build the fantastic, to create Todorov's

moment of hesitation, which is why this novel, until very late in the narrative, is understood by the reader as fantasy, not science fiction.

Jones's choices of metaphors in *Hexwood* enrich the sense in which time is the subject of the narrative and the focus of the fantastic: Ann's illness is time bound and has erased her own sense of time as a passage; pain is endured in centuries; Vierran amuses herself by dressing the Reigners in out-of-date clothing; and Reigner Five tries to attack Vierran and falls into the river. His death and dying are a function of subjective rather than objective time.

> His back was broken. The water was forcing his body between the boulders, rolling him onwards, pressing him over to drown too. It took him a while to give in and admit that he had been dead all along.[44]

Alan Garner said, "…the whole process of writing is in coming to terms with language … the nature of language."[45] In *The Magicians of Caprona* and *Hexwood*, Jones reminds us that language constructs our understanding of time.

Hexwood plays both on our understanding of how time and the past are linked, and on the expectations of fantasy time that most experienced readers of children's fantasy will have acquired. Jones writes knowing that almost all of her audience will have read *The Lion, the Witch and the Wardrobe* and that we will have absorbed into our subconscious the idea that time ellipses, juxtaposed against instant time, authenticate the fantasy. The result is that it takes some while for the reader to question the time narratives that pass in this book.

The book starts straightforwardly with the decision of Controller Borasus to go to Earth to investigate reports that machinery might be out of control. Chapter 1 is told mimetically—this later proves to be a clue. Events are pinned down firmly into their B–series–absolute pattern of "this happens, then this happens, then something else happens." The construction of B–series–absolute time is authoritative. The second chapter is told as if in a dream and quite firmly within A–series–relative time in which experience of time will take precedence over the events of time: a boy finds himself in a wood, meets a dragon, and is found by a silver creature. The mood takes us out of time, away from internal referents. The boy has no past and little sense of self. But he does have a future, and a future that has already happened. In very deliberate echoes of T.H. White's *Once and Future King*, the silver creature responds to the news of the dragon: "It was killed. But maybe we have yet to kill it, since I see you are quite small right now."[46]

The future is something that has already happened. "If the reptile is alive, we have come to the wrong time and we must try again."[47] Because time is a product of experience, it can be accessed at any point, and the past can slide through beyond the future. The chapter concludes at a fork in the wood.

> "This wood," Yam told him, "is like human memory. It does not need to take events in their correct order. Do you wish to go to an earlier time and start from there?"
>
> "Would I understand more if I did?" Hume asked.
>
> "You might," said Yam. "Both of us might."
>
> "Then it's worth a try," Hume agreed.
>
> They went together down the left-hand fork.[48]

Jones embeds in this section coziness, clues, and disorientation. She uses the simplicity of a small child and the way adults spin metaphor to answer a child's impossible questions, to fold us into the story. Yet in *Hexwood*, narrative linearity is deceptive, and the principal effect of this deception leads us to trust—quite incorrectly—the disruption of time we witness and to assume that the A-series–relative of past, present, and future remains intact. The reader needs to keep an eye on what is said: the boy pesters the creature with questions including whether they have met before; the creature replies "many times." Later we may come to believe that these times are in the future. But the creature has already told us that it is experiencing life in an order different from the boy's. Narrative time is always an unreliable guide in this book. The real key to what is real and what is not will be mood.

To attempt a summary of the time narratives is essential to further consideration of *Hexwood*. *Hexwood* is constructed of concentric circles of time. As with *The Magicians of Caprona*, if you track the narrative voices carefully it is possible to see a link between the depiction of the fantastic and the understanding of time. The outermost circle is the linear time experienced by the Reigners and their servant and by Vierran and her family before they arrive on earth. In this narrative the events form the coordinates that we understand as B-series–absolute time. This part of the story is always written in the third person, and its demotic voice encourages the reader to understand it as nonfantastical and hence somehow more true. There are few internal narratives, and we, the readers, clearly sit outside of the events, watching them unfold.

The second narrative is that of Ann Stavely, who is recovering from a severe viral illness when she decides to explore the local wood, into which she has seen several men disappear.[49] Ann discovers that her adventures in the wood are not linear. Ann's tale takes place within more than two time narratives. After going home for lunch, she returns to the wood, where she meets up again with Hume:

> She had a moment when she was not sure who he was. But his brown shaggy hair, his thin face, and the way his cheekbones stuck out, were all quite familiar. Of course he was Hume. It was one of those times when he was about ten years old.[50]

There are two slippages here. One we are clearly expected to notice is that Hume is older; we are in a fantasy world in which time passes differently. The other is more unnerving. Ann should not yet have worked out that Hume will be a different age each time. She has, theoretically, only been there once before, yet already she has memories of future visits. Her own internal clock is out of synch. Already, she needs to question the meanings of past and present. This moment of time travel extends the narrative ellipsis we first witnessed in *The Magicians of Caprona* and makes of it fantasy.

> Hume had this way of knowing things before she told him, Ann thought, gathering a small bunch of the violets. ... Sometimes it turned out that Hume had asked Yam, but sometimes, confusingly, Hume said she had told him before.[51]

Ann's own entry into the wood can take place at any point in the apparent lives of Mordion (the man she seems to have released from a stasis tomb) and Hume (the boy Mordion has created from his and her blood). Mordion's and Hume's event coordinates are experienced in a different order by Ann, and the A-series–relative of past, present, and future are experienced differently by each. The significance of this last matter is easily missed: because we mostly view the behavior of Mordion and Hume from Ann's perspective, we accept that Mordion's and Hume's A-series–relative ordering of events is the same. Our belief that Hume is not real further encourages this. But Hume is real, and when Mordion and he are separated, they quickly move to experience events in different orders. There is, then, no reason to accept that if each of them were questioned, their own experience of their time together would contain the same pattern of experienced time. That they are seen together does not mean they experience together. It is Ann's ability to reorganize the events she witnesses into a chronology of her own that signals she has gained control of the Bannus, the computer that is in charge of the narrative.

Then there is the issue of the voice of these sections. Unlike the very direct external narratives of those sections concerning the Reigners, "Ann in the Woods" is narrated with a much stronger internal voice, and a rather more elegiac quality. These scenes are not fully dreamlike, as was the first scene with Yam and Hume, but they are constructed as if on an emotional island. In their abstraction and disassociation from outside concerns, the scenes acquire the intensity of the conscious dream, in much the same way that our understanding of time as flowing past us is held internally, a quietly ticking clock. This enables Jones to create yet another layer of the time narrative.

Ann's time in the local housing estate is poised between the elegiac memories in the woods and the very direct tone of the sections about the Reigners. If we work out this rhetorical hierarchy, we can take a guess as to the levels of reality we are dealing with quite early, but there is no encouragement to do so. Instead, the mimetic style persuades us to understand Ann's place in the housing estate as a marker of reality. When Ann leaves the wood after her second visit, the voices she has in her head tell her she has been there only once. This is the first time she has exited the wood.

Time is not simply unstable in the wood; it is also complex. As the narrative unfolds, it emerges that it is not objective time but subjective time, the metronome in our heads, that is being manipulated. Although the distinction is not as clear as in the first chapter of *The Magicians of Caprona*, once the plot resolves we can see the way that time as manifested in the external plot of the Reigners, in the theta field of the wood and in the plans of the Bannus, is narrated slightly differently in each case in ways that match the original A-series–relative and B-series–absolute concepts with which we started this chapter:

1. *Reigner time:* Reigner time is linear time, narrated in the direct third person, a clear mimetic style that assumes full immersion into the story as normal. Reigner time is B-series–absolute, with clear coordinates in which one event

proceeds after another and the coordinates do not change, even when the length of time in which they have taken place becomes obscured.

2. *Bannus time:* Bannus time is linear and repetitive and is narrated in a midway point, allowing Ann self-consciousness of her actions. This is essentially A-series–relative time, an attempt to make all events "before," "now," or "after" while allowing the position of those events to change with regard to other coordinate events.

3. *Wood time:* Wood time is spiral, intersecting with itself at various points, and is narrated in the third person but from Ann's point of view, it has an elegiac quality, like a waking dream, told in the immediate past but interrupted with moments of awareness of the continuous present in which Ann has moments of conscious awareness but otherwise accepts the given reality at any moment, even accepting knowledge of her future. "*What* year forty-two? she wondered. It *can't* be *this* century, and I refuse to believe we're a hundred years in the future. And Hume *knows* the robot! How?"[52]

Ann's awareness of the wood comes from her ability to spot the dissonance between the A-series and B-series time lines. Her position in the narration of time is crucial to the maintenance of the intersecting and illusory time narrative. The assumption of authority traditionally ascribed to the authorial voice is here used to convince us of the reality of the illusion and eventually to control its deliberate dissolution. The more self-conscious and analytical Ann is, the closer she is to her own reality as Vierran, child of the House of Guaranty, and part of an intergalactic empire. Sitting in the hotel feeling sorry for herself, Vierann plays the tape her father made. Immediately after his message she finds one from herself: "Vierran. This is Vierran speaking. Vierran to myself. This is at least the second time I've sat in the bedroom despairing and I'm beginning to not quite believe in it."[53] What Vierran realizes is that the Bannus had "rendered her journey from the House of Balance correctly enough, but it had cut out all the disembodied conversations."[54] Although those conversations were with her voices, they are also the analytical aspect of Vierran's persona. And when the Bannus wants that aspect of Vierran, it allows the voices to be heard in the repeating scenarios. Vierran's realization heralds the merger of the different modes of storytelling. Scenes within the Bannus-field told by a Vierran aware that notions of past, present, and future (the A-series) are unstable and have a very different feel. Compare Sir Fors's internal thoughts, under the complete influence of the Bannus, "Another was the king's bride, but the least said about *her* the better,"[55] with

"How long has today been?" Vierran asked Mordion as she slid back on her bench beside him.

"Too long," he said, wondering what was the matter. "The Bannus sometimes likes to fast-forward things. We seem to have caught it at it for once."

"Or it's let us see it at it," Vierran said distrustfully. She wished she had her voices to check how long it had been, but there was only silence from them, making a miserable gap in her mind.[56]

Jones plants clues throughout the novel about the nature of time: the most obvious is the cut on Mordion's wrist that does not heal because no real time has passed—the cut is a B-series–absolute clue to the falsity of the illusory A-series–relative time played out in the field. The more subtle indication is Ann's voices, that she can hear only when outside the wood. Given that Mordion turns out to be one of her voices, it later becomes clear that she is communicating with her voices in their past. But Jones also uses our awareness of the time ellipses to play with the reader's sense of subjective time, of "reader-time" if you will. *Hexwood* becomes a comment on the construction of story: a different point of entry results in a different narrative; all the characters need to be gathered together before the story can start. Yet experiential time helps to construct a narrative and temporal unity that underpins the apparent fragmentation. In *Hexwood* B-series–absolute time is initially depicted as rational and intellectual, whereas A-series–relative time is experiential and hence less reliable. In the conclusion, however, it is those depicted as most firmly convinced of their understanding of the B-series chronology of events—the Reigners—who prove most susceptible to the Bannus's manipulation of experienced time; like the citizens of Time City, the Reigners have mistakenly assumed that their sense of past, present, and future is more real than that of others. Time is the complexity and the reward in this novel, expressed in the gift to the wood of its own time, and hence its own story, and in the reunion of the new Hand of Reigners who formed Veirran's voices, the only characters who have traveled in time by the oldest and most traditional means—sleeping through it.

CHAPTER 4
DIANA WYNNE JONES AND THE PORTAL–QUEST FANTASY

Chapter 3 considered the relationships between Diana Wynne Jones's protagonists and time. This chapter, and the two immediately succeeding it, will consider the relationships between Jones's protagonists and their worlds and the ways in which Jones critiques and reconfigures the expectations of fantasy's built worlds.

In the portal fantasy a character moves from the mundane world into the fantastic otherworld and proceeds to describe what is witnessed, much like a character in a utopian novel or a travelogue, and although his or her impact is ostensibly large, the fantasy world is often left relatively untouched. Most often, what change takes place returns the world to a semimythical perfection of the past. Although many quest fantasies start in a full otherworld, the rupture when they move into the wider world is as large as if they had stepped through the portal. The wider world is always unfamiliar to the protagonists, with the result that quest fantasies function in the same way as portal fantasies.

Jones uses the portal–quest fantasy genre very little, and in fact has only one true portal fantasy, *The Crown of Dalemark* (a time travel fantasy set in another world), and this functions as the only clear-cut quest fantasy as well (although one or two novels, such as *The Magicians of Caprona* and

Castle in the Air, are what Geoffrey Trease called "the treasure hunt"[1]). But in a number of her works—the Chrestomanci series, *Howl's Moving Castle, The Homeward Bounders,* and her most recent book, *Conrad's Fate*—Jones shuttles back and forth across portals, crosshatching her worlds in ways that intensify their connection.[2]

Jones uses the portal to shift perspective within the book, to introduce outsiders into a sealed world, or to question the nature of portal fantasy. This last point unifies the rest. Portal fantasy has always operated on the assumption that what is seen by the protagonist and narrated to the reader is *true.* It is not that there cannot be treachery or mistakes, but we are usually convinced that the interpretation by the protagonists of the world around them is correct, at least according to the evidence available at the time.[3] In a number of her novels, Jones challenges this, and in doing so she destabilizes the foundations of the subgenre. In Jones's hands the descriptive realism of the portal–quest fantasy becomes something much more ironic.

Portals mark the transition between this world and another, from our time to another time, from youth to adulthood. The most familiar, and archetypal, portal fantasy in the United Kingdom is *The Lion, the Witch and the Wardrobe* (1950), whereas in the United States the *Oz* tales are perhaps better known.[4] Within this type of fantasy, the two key elements of the narrative strategy are transition and exploration; the overall theme, one also common to children's books, is moral growth or admission into the kingdom, or both, or redemption. Although Jones accepts the theme of moral growth, her writing of the elements of transition and exploration frequently expresses a cohesive critique of the form's narrative assumptions.

Although modern quest fantasies often spend entire books turning travel into a place for and a metaphor of the transition to adulthood and into the magical world, most modern portal fantasies spend relatively little time on the transition; the time spent in Lewis's wardrobe, despite its impact, is only a few paragraphs. A recent portal fantasy, K.C. Dyer's *Seeds of Time,*[5] although presenting the exploration of the portal (a time travel tunnel) as a specific activity, is not terribly interested in its nature and moves on quickly. In K.A. Applegate's *Everworld* sequence, the children simply fall through a lake into another universe. Generally speaking, Jones spends far more time considering the actual transition through the portal, both its mechanism and the experience.

Even in Jones's most explicitly fantastic novels, the portals must make sense, so that Christopher Chant's travels to other worlds in *The Lives of*

Christopher Chant are structured as a walk around a corner[6] to a location that is at the center of things, a place between the worlds reminiscent of *The Magician's Nephew,* Jones's favorite of the Narnia books.[7] Sophie and Howl simply open a door, but one that can be set to different coordinates. In *The Homeward Bounders* Helen and Jamie work out a mental map and a theory of the boundaries that reduce the randomness of their travels and reassert control. In *Deep Secret* and in *The Merlin Conspiracy,* the journey elsewhere becomes a journey through a landscape.

Although the description of traversing the islands of the universe in *The Merlin Conspiracy* is detailed and exotic, it is perhaps the exception. For much of the time, Jones prefers to keep her transitions mundane in their deceptive simplicity: Christopher's corners (*The Lives of Christopher Chant*), for example, or Nick's travels in *The Merlin Conspiracy* that begin quite suddenly with a voice, "Off you go then."[8] With the exception of the transition in *A Sudden Wild Magic,* in which inhabitants of the bus become caught in a cosmic storm, Jones's transitions lack the trauma or surprise that usually accompanies portals: there are no whirlwinds, no tunnels to fall down. Even in *The Homeward Bounders,* Jamie understands and accepts what happens to him; the moment of surprise and shock is very limited. This might connect to how Jones understands children specifically and people generally, as animals who unless given cause to react otherwise tend to take their surroundings for granted and to react with inquisitiveness rather than amazement. This affects the subsequent development of Jones's adventures, because what is frequently missing in her interpretation of the portal fantasy is the passive acceptance of what is seen and explained.

Jones's protagonists are aware of the process of journeying, and their reaction to the transition is one means by which Jones establishes character. Christopher "thought everyone had the kind of dreams he had. ... He did not think they were worth mentioning."[9] Christopher's besetting sin will be the degree to which he does not consider issues worth mentioning and takes for granted the ways in which people behave without ever applying any analysis. Jamie's preference for experimentation with the boundaries will reveal him as the person best equipped to maintain them—he is adaptable. Jones's portals are active in the story, unique to the individual and shaped by that person's way of seeing the world. Tacroy, Christopher's friend, understands the Place Between only as mist, whereas Christopher sees it as woods and valleys. Unlike the wood between the worlds in *The Magician's Nephew,* the interstices of the world are vulnerable to personality. Funniest is the view Jones offers us of portals as seen by a goat: "a line of night islands ... just hanging there, like unstrung beads, or huge stepping stones, for as far as we could see."[10] One of the most elegiac is Roddy's journey into the past to inherit knowledge from the witch in *The Merlin Conspiracy*. It is one of the simplest transitions Jones writes. First there is "a perfect cloud of butterflies," and then "We stepped inside onto the green, moist grass. And there the thing happened that my grandfather must have sent me for."[11] Roddy is taken back into the history of the land and Blest, like its analogue England, is a land of depth, with "many legends milling about" layered in time and space.[12] This texturing of the fantastic with the landscape, and the landscape with the fantastic is, Peter Hunt suggests, a very English construction of the fantastic.[13] Jones makes less extensive use of it than a writer such as Alan Garner (for whom "legends milling about" was coined), but the thread is there in the appearance of Herne the Hunter in *Dogsbody* and in the construction of the town in *Archer's Goon* and in the mythic threads that run through *Fire and Hemlock*. But in *The Merlin Conspiracy*, the entire novel is structured around the sense that the *Land* is a living, breathing thing. At the end of the novel, when the land rises, the dragon of Blest takes hold of it and it too moves through a portal to become a subtly different land in a slightly different position in the figure of infinity. Jones's portals, and hence her worlds, are essentially the creations of humans and act as signifiers, rather than facilitators, in the text.

Someone who has decided to traverse a portal is much less passive and vulnerable to external pressures than is someone forced through a portal.[14] Jones clearly wishes us to understand this. In *The Time of the Ghost*, a novel that is not strictly a portal fantasy but that makes heavy use of references to *Alice* in its opening sequences,[15] the disorientation of the ghost is precisely because she is not in control of her movements. Only when Sally chooses to go back in time to be a ghost again can she control her movements. *A Tale of Time City* takes an entire novel to move Vivian Smith from the passive mode to the active: each time she chooses to return to Time City she is more in command. One of the very few passive figures (relatively speaking) is Janet in *Charmed Life*, who is precisely not in command of her fate. This is an interesting novel in the terms of this chapter anyway because, unusually, the reader sees what it is like for the portal world to receive a traveler who is not the locus of the disturbance. And Jones twists this again by turning Janet's competent confusion in a strange world into dependence on Cat (Eric), forcing a shift in his perspective and behavior. This moves us to the second pillar of the portal–quest fantasy, the degree to which the explorative mode shapes the rhetoric of the fantasy.

To restate the point, the portal–quest fantasy is essentially a tale of exploration in a strange new land. Its mimetic form is the travelogue, and just as with a travelogue it is a form that relies intensely on the assumption that what the reader is told about the configuration of the world is true. In the fictional form, the protagonist—usually the one who has traveled through the portal—acts as proxy for the reader. He is dependent on the protagonist's viewpoint for the narrating, explaining, and decoding of the plot, the motives of the characters around him or her, and the world in which the adventure is taking place. This is so much the normative position of most storytelling that its consequences in the fantastic world are easy to overlook.

One of the defining features of the portal–quest fantasy is the degree to which landscape becomes a substitution for knowledge of the world. In the proxy relationship between the reader and protagonist, the world is unrolled to us in front of his or her eyes and through his or her analysis of the scene. One result is that the world is flattened thereby into a series of descriptions made possible by the protagonists' unfamiliarity. This is not to say the technique is necessarily bad; it can be deployed to great effect, as in this extract from Charles Butler's *The Fetch of Mardy Watt*:

> Usually she could see no more than twenty metres ahead before the next street corner. Tenements, warehouses, boarded shops she passed, sometimes a municipal park or a messy, granite statue. Now and then, aimlessly exploring, she came across one of the broad, straight avenues that sliced the city, cutting into the twisty streets as cleanly as a blade.[16]

In this mode of fantasy, the fantastic is constructed not by rendering the unfamiliar as strange but through the reactions of the protagonist to the landscape (in the previous example we are told of Mardy's fear) and through the layering of detail. What is distinct about this detail is the distortion of perspective by the insistence of the complete visibility of the surroundings. Within the example, although Mardy can see only twenty meters ahead, everything within compass is taken notice of. A visual comparison might be with the landscapes of the pre-Raphaelites, which, although retaining the mathematics of perspective, eschewed representations of focus. In a Millais landscape every detail is depicted; focus comes from where the viewer chooses to look rather than channeled by the interpretive eye of the artist. In John Brett's *The British Channel Seen from the Dorsetshire*

Cliffs, the absolute mathematical perfection of the perspective is distorted by the impossible perfection of the detail of the distant cliffs. True vision does not work this way, but the description of the landscape in the portal–quest fantasy (whose historical antecedents lie contemporaneous with, and in some of the same names as, pre-Raphaelite art) frequently applies this intensity of eye. To continually revive the sense of wonder in this manner, such fantasies often continually embroider the landscape: invention substitutes for imagination; diegetic overkill, in which the representation of ostensibly insignificant details—jumping frog chocolates, lembas bread, or clothes that change color—acts a substitute for realism.

The result is to heighten the sense of the fantastic at the same time as rendering it mundane through equalization across the land. This kind of description, like this approach to painting, assumes that the eye must be constantly engaged with the new. Jones rejects this formulation by concentrating her descriptions of landscape on what her character might be interested in: we understand one of Christopher Chant's worlds only through what a small child might want to do when away from home: "He went to the Anywhere with the silly ladies several times. It had blue and white sand, perfect for digging and building in,"[17] but there is no real surprise, because to the small child everything is new and wondrous. In contrast, Nick Mallory, old enough to be confused, is confused and understands the new world in a series of similarities, of "things I thought were helicopters"[18] and "the Thames winding underneath among crowds of houses, so I knew we were in London, but in a dreamlike way there was no London Eye ... and where I thought St. Paul's ought to be there was a huge white church with three square towers and a steeple."[19] Crucially, no one explains this to Nick, and he does not explain it to us (although science fiction readers may realise it is a London where there was no Great Fire). The same holds true even when Nick is a more experienced traveler: his depiction of Loggia is that of a person caught in a crowd, and it is the crowd he notices. Much later, the magician Romanov will explain it to him, as Christopher Chant will learn about the mermaids from his guardians at the castle, but the explanation comes as a clarification of confusion, not as a downloaded guide to a new place.

In most portal–quest fantasies, the emphasis on description of place and people creates a need for the new; this in turn encourages movement through the fantastical space—hence the ubiquity of the quest in the portal fantasy. If the protagonist stays still too long, there might be nothing left to describe.[20] The irony is that this movement through the action and the world's stage can impose an assumption of unchangingness on the indigenes. "New" is what is new to the traveler, not to the people left behind. This kind of fantasy is essentially imperialist: only the hero is capable of change; fantasyland is orientalized into the unchanging past.

The guidebook form of the portal–quest fantasy has other consequences. Too often in fantasy we are told what evil is, what it is called, and (it is often implied) that it has always existed: a glossary becomes a substitute for cultural understanding. In addition, portal–quest fantasy often has very imperialist expectations: the outsider from our world shows people in the otherworld how to put things right, and functions as a catalyst for change in an unchanging society. Jones ironizes this in Janet Chant's solution to Chrestomanci's allergy to silver cutlery—stainless steel—and more extensively in Vivian Smith's wonder at the structures of Time City in which the more primitive is often the newer, and in Vivian's position as a protagonist in an ostensibly more advanced society that regards itself as fluid and changing, and that prefers to consider itself as the culture from which observers are *sent* rather than received. Vivian is the equivalent of the African missionary bringing Christianity to heathen London: it jars with the British sense of themselves as the civilizers. In this way Vivian's presence draws attention to the stasis and complacency of Time City, which can stand for the stasis of many societies that portal protagonists enter.

The unrolling of the landscape in many fantasy novels can create the feeling that nothing else outside the path taken really exists. As Jones pointed out in *Tough Guide,* even the maps that accompany such tales reinforce this point: any place that will be on the journey will be on the map, any place which is not, will be omitted.[21] The result is a world with blanks such as a medieval projection. If the protagonist does not go there, it cannot be real, which creates a fantasy reworking of the philosophical problem "if a tree falls in a forest..." In effect, the world is allowed to exist only in reality because of the presence of the protagonist. This is clearest in the Narnia sequences in which all the really important events of history occur only when children from another world are present.

The Dark Lord of Derkholm, the novel written to satirize mainstream fantasy, subverts the trope in a number of ways. First the story is told from the point of view of the guide (of which more later in the chapter) and of the inhabitants of the land; very little is described. Instead, the layout of the land and the possibility of the magical creatures, are simply accepted. The main characters know their world: it is the "frame-world" of the story. The narrowness of the Pilgrims' or portal protagonists' knowledge becomes an element in the plot, and the degree to which the world's natives refuse to play the game reinforces and mocks the conventions of knowledge acquisition rife in quest fantasies. In *The Dark Lord of Derkholm*, we know the prophecies that drive the portal–questors are a fiction. To make matters more complicated, so do the Pilgrims. The Pilgrims, those on the quest, and Mr. Chesney, the businessman, are intruding on the world so that instead of the rhetoric of exploration, understanding, and correction, we have a structure of intrusion, understanding, defeat and negotiation, and the return of the intrusion to its own world. And because this fantasy world we are in is actually the originating frame-world, Jones relates it as if it is the only world, in an irony of mimesis— an immersion fantasy in other words, as we shall see in the next chapter. The hollowness of the full fantasy quest novels is exposed.

Archer's Goon contains a number of portal sequences, in which Jones exploits the rules of the classic portal fantasy to create specific emotional affects. Each time Howard goes through a portal, the book becomes intensely descriptive; the entry to Archer's kingdom, for example, beginning with another homage to Alice's rabbit hole:

> Its walls were lined with pigeonholes, so that there was only a narrow passage down the middle. He looked into some as the young man led them through. He saw black cashboxes, brown leather jewel cases, and bundles and bundles of important-looking envelopes. Some of the lower pigeonholes had doors across, perhaps to hide money. But there was not much chance to look because Archer led them straight through to another, much smaller door at the back. This door was just as thick, and they all had to bend to go through it except Awful. Beyond that they came out into a huge place.[22]

Jones is able here to manipulate the expectations of her implied readers —it is a fair assumption that most British children will have read *Alice*—and use the disorientation of rapid travel and the discomfort of size to leave both readers and the protagonists unsettled. The impact of the moment of arrival is hence deeper and more disorienting, it forces the protagonists to depend on the cataloging of detail, distracting them from a focus on what is important.

They all stopped, in a huddle, and stared around. There were installations, machines, cabinets, read outs, winking lights, screens, dials, illuminated plans, displays flashing, in all directions, almost as far as they could see. There were machines in the distance quietly at work running on rails, pushing more displays into place. Other machines were humming along the girders overhead.[23]

Howard and his companions are overwhelmed: they can see everything—that intense detail again—but can comprehend nothing because everything is portrayed as of equal value. In contrast, when by the end of the book Howard goes through his last portal into the future, into Venturus's home, he has learned how to filter out the extraneous information, and we get a description that focuses not on the detail but on the important:

Here there was a round antechamber with two vast arched doorways leading off it. On the floor of this round space was a heap of typewritten paper, some of it old and yellow, some of it white and new.[24]

Just as Jones depicts character by the way in which individuals understand portals, so in *Archer's Goon* can the understanding of portals indicate character development and whether the character belongs in the space. Howard does not need to describe Venturus's home, because he is Venturus, and the lack of description is in part an indication of this if we know how to read the rhetorical cues.

Furthermore, *Archer's Goon* reifies the protagonist-in-the-forest construction of the portal fantasy. In the portal–quest fantasy, the land we see and the possibility of land is confined by what the protagonist experiences. In *Archer's Goon,* as I will discuss in much greater detail in chapter 7, it is quite possible to see the entire adventure as literally confined by what Howard (the protagonist) is experiencing within the pocket universe of the town, and Venturus's home does not exist in this time until Howard arrives.

The descriptive structure of the portal–quest fantasy is intensely political: its apparent neutrality discourages questions and encourages belief in a monosemic understanding of the world and often of the nature of good and evil. It does this primarily by allowing the reader to assume that what is described in the understanding of protagonist is described correctly. The portal–quest fantasy by its very nature needs to deny the possibility of a polysemic discourse to validate the quest. There are some exceptions—the original grail stories offer polysemic narratives and question the reality, desirability, and possibility of goal, as do some modern quest fantasies

(China Miéville's *The Scar* and K.J. Parker's *The Fencer* trilogy)—but more generally this issue extends into the world building of fantasyland, reducing history, religion, and politics to mere attributes. There is no theology in portal–quest fantasy, only catechism. However, once we accept that the protagonist is essentially a tourist in the world and therefore able to construct only the most superficial understanding, this monosemy becomes vulnerable. One of the most interesting techniques Jones uses to make this point is to reverse the direction of the portal.

Howl's Moving Castle is a fully immersed fantasy in which the world is thoroughly known to the protagonists as we experience them. That caveat is necessary because Howl is in fact a foreigner, but for most of the time this is not relevant to the case. The world is described in mimesis, as if real, although the introduction to the book is itself a portal into a fairy tale: "In the land of Ingary..." But partway through the tale, *Howl's Moving Castle* contains within it a portal fantasy that underlines the differences in language for immersive and portal texts. Howl, Sophie, and Howl's assistant Michael travel through the entrance of the Moving Castle into Wales: "Beyond that was a flat, hard looking road lined with houses on both sides. ... Like all the other houses, it was square and new, with a front door of wobbly glass."[25] Immediately we are into the conventions of portal fantasy. The characters obey a guide (Howl), ask questions, and describe to us what they see. No longer must we just exist and interpret a foreign language; instead, the protagonists (mis-)interpret the world on our behalf: "Michael's jacket had become a waist-length padded thing. He lifted his foot, with a canvas shoe on it, and stared at the tight blue things encasing his legs."[26]

Jones reveals the intensely descriptive and falsely mimetic nature of the portal–quest. Our usual understanding of the portal fantasy leads us to expect that the descriptions of the travelers will be true and accurate. Sophie—assuming that Howl's computer-game-playing nephew is really at risk of his life—reveals their unreliability. Despite the book's diversion into our primary world, it remains High fantasy because this glimpse of our primary world is rendered in the extravagant detail of the portal fantasy.

Sophie's inability to either prioritize or interpret forces her to the descriptive: "a large window filled with a white curtain and a notice that said: TEAS CLOSED"[27]—note the way the lack of punctuation on the sign renders it meaningless to Sophie. The mundanity of the tea shop is rendered fantastic.

This use of perspective to undercut the false consciousness of the portal fantasy is also deployed by Jones in two short stories: "Little Dot" and "What the Cat Told Me." The use of the cats' point of view functions to shape the tales as reversed portal fantasies because the cats are not fundamentally a part of the human world and do not truly understand what is going on. Their understanding is at variance with that of the human protagonists. In "What the Cat Told Me," the cat's misunderstandings counterpoint the naïveté of the young boy she companions. Her descriptions of the world they inhabit are, although detailed, partial and skewed; the spirits called up by a magician resolve as "delicious beauties ... the light burnt sort of dingily,"[28] and the cat continually deviates to what really interests her—the well-being of her kittens, not understanding why her gift of the kittens does not cheer the boy up. Brindle, the cat, understands the danger that the Old Man represents, but her comprehension is only partial. In the end, however, she is able to help the boy and his princess to the necessary magic through her own attributes—the classic role of the assistant–companion in the quest fantasy.

In "Little Dot" we see a farmyard through the eyes of a cat: the territorial spaces and the places that are important. The result is a remapping of a mundane area as a fantastic space in which are played out the battles and rivalries of different factions. When the safety of the farmyard is breached by the arrival of the Sphinx, the configuration of the cat's response mimics the grand alliances of *The Lord of the Rings* and its successors. In the background has been the human story, of magic and spells and the hunting of the Sphinx, but we see almost none of that, because we are tied to the cat's point of view.

In most portal–quest fantasies the comprehension of the protagonist goes unquestioned and is reinforced by the figure of the guide, who stories the world for us by dispensing knowledge and moral judgment as and when it is needed. In the classic portal–quest fantasy, this is commonly done in extremely obvious ways, through related history, a found past (old books are common), and fragments of prophecy leaked throughout the adventure. There is almost always a guide in the portal–quest fantasy: the Evangelist in *Pilgrim's Progress* (arguably one of the earliest quest fantasies), the raven in George MacDonald's *Lilith,* the beaver and Aslan in *The Lion, the Witch and the Wardrobe,* and Gandalf in *The Lord of the Rings.* The journeyman succeeds or fails to the extent he listens to those wiser or more knowledgeable than him, whether these are spiritual, fantastical, or human guides. Philip Pullman's *His Dark Materials* sequence provides Lyra with a multiplicity of guides, and although this could have broken down the monolithic view provided by the single guide, there is so little disagreement among these individuals that this never occurs. Despite the significant intellectual content of many portal–quest fantasies, it is hard to escape the feeling that this situation is infantilizing, requiring the readers to abandon their own moral understanding at the portal. It is probably not coincidental that the classic portal fantasy (in which a recognizable portal is crossed) is more typically found in children's fiction, whereas the adult genre focuses on the quest fantasy in which the transition from the "familiar" to "unknown lands" is rather less flagged and the dependency on the guide less visible.

The Tough Guide to Fantasyland strikes at this point ruthlessly: the tour book takes the place of the guide. But there are few ostentatious guides in Jones's work, in part because she has never written a classic portal–quest fantasy (*The Dark Lord of Derkholm* is too obviously an attack on the form to count). This is because her work continually asks us to consider the reliability of whoever is offering to guide us through the dark woods.

Many of Jones's novels play on the degree to which we as children and as readers trust the guide figure in our lives and in our narratives. In *The Lives of Christopher Chant*, the conspiracy at the heart of the novel and the behavior of Christopher Chant on the other side of the portal, are dependent on his default trust of his guide, his uncle Ralph Argent. Ralph Argent's friendliness, his bonhomie and his apparent willingness to explain things, allow Uncle Ralph to interpret the world for the naive Christopher. What Ralph says is truer than Christopher's own observations: for example, Christopher has observed the ladies with tails who live out in the harbor, but he never questions for a minute the fishy-smelling parcels that his uncle brings in from that world—and initially neither do we: Ralph Argent is the guide, and he decides on our behalf what is right and wrong. The realization that we have been duped is a shock because it breaks the rules of the portal fantasy, not simply because an apparent nice guy is not but because we are reminded that our own analysis would have served us better than relying on the mediation first of the guide and second of the young child Christopher. We have abandoned moral responsibility because in a portal fantasy we are used to thinking we cannot question the protagonist unless (as in the depiction of Edmund and the White Witch) we are directly told to. The entire game played out in *Hexwood* depends on this understanding; Ann (and the other members of the Hand) achieve adulthood when they challenge the Bannus in its role as Dungeonmaster. The same is true for Howard in *Archer's Goon*. Each time Howard traverses a portal, he falls victim to the assertions of the guide–the sibling to whom he is talking, and is further misled by the Goon who poses as a stupid guide, burying his manipulation in apparent foolishness. In *The Crown of Dalemark*, the guide figure (the magician Wend [Mallard]) turns out to know less than Maewen the time tourist.

This untrustworthy guide is repeated in *Castle in the Air* when Abdullah takes up with the soldier. In this case, though, we know the soldier is a stranger in Ingary and is simply that bit more familiar with it than Abdullah. He succeeds to his place as a guide largely through bluff, and he keeps both us and Abdullah unbalanced, wanting to believe his knowledge even while we are repeatedly reminded that his knowledge is flawed and his judgment is terrible. It is ironic, therefore, when the unreliable guide turns out to be intensely knowledgeable about the kingdom because he is its prince. There is one easily missed trick that Jones pulled in this book. Throughout, the soldier—as in the traditional dancing princess tales on which the novel draws—is never called anything else but "the soldier," and Abdullah never asks his name.

Elsewhere, building on the know-all soldier, Jones draws guides from her protagonists. They are not people who know more but people who believe that they can judge the story for others. In *A Sudden Wild Magic*, all the principal protagonists are thrown into a strange world of which they know little, but one woman, Roz, is immediately (and wrongly) convinced that the secret power of the brotherhood they have been sent to undo lies in its celibacy, and she coerces almost every other member of the group into a pattern of sexual procuration in much the same way that in many quest fantasies tasks are assigned to individuals. In much genre fantasy the estrangement from the home context renders the protagonists vulnerable to this interpretational coercion, not unlike the situation of Kate in *Taming of the Shrew*. In *A Sudden Wild Magic*, the situation has been rendered traumatic by the unexplained death of some of the young people in the bus. The first to generate a coherent response to the trauma can control the responses of others. But its sustainability is also due to the narrative convention of the club story that has been adopted wholesale into the portal–quest fantasy.

The club story is simple enough to describe: it is a tale or tales recounted orally to a group of listeners foregathered in a venue safe from interruption. Its structure is normally twofold: there is the tale told, and encompassing that is a frame that introduces the teller of the tale—who might well claim to have lived the story he is telling—along with its auditors and the venue. "At all levels of sophistication, the club story form enforces our understanding that a tale has been told."[29]

The completeness of story is perhaps the crucial contribution that the club story offers to the portal–quest fantasy. The teller of the tale, the one sitting in the narrator's chair, is uninterruptible and incontestable. In the portal–quest fantasy, much of the narrative is delivered in this club story mode among a group of friends isolated from the wider world in a context in which they will not be interrupted. The guide delivers in portentous tones both the history of the conflict in which they are involved (complete with an established interpretation) and the orders for the quest.

There are touches of this in the narrated form of *The Homeward Bounders:* its delivery as a diary or autonomous monologue is hard to contest.[30] In *The Merlin Conspiracy* the presence of two diarists should undercut this, but the agreement between the two narratives means that they serve to reinforce the impermeability of the tale while constructing an internal argument about which story is the story. However, argument is the primary method by which Jones undercuts the club narrative of the guide. In Jones's works attempts to enforce monochrome analyses of good and evil are greeted with questions and arguments. Roz quickly loses control of the women she assumes she is leading. Abdullah spends much of his journey into Ingary arguing with the soldier about the dissonance between what the soldier says and the facts on the ground. Even in *Deep Secret,* in which edicts and prophecies come down from the upper room, the magid (or mage) Rupert continually argues with explanations and prophecies, while Nick's narrative in the sequel, *The Merlin Conspiracy,* begins with his disgust at his dependence on guides.

The closest Jones comes to the closed club story is in *Cart and Cwidder* and through the character of Clennan the Singer. Clennan educates his children through tale and interrogation. The past is laid down in neat little stories that he coerces his children into repeating back as epigrams. Only once their quest (for sanctuary) begins do they begin to unpick the stories and to rework the past into a much more complex history, and to realize that Clennan has made story of politics, in doing so erasing many of the details they actually need to know. In *Drowned Ammet* and *The Crown of Dalemark,* Jones pushes the point home even further. When we accompanied Dagner, Brid, and Moril to the North, we accepted them as our guides: what they discovered must be correct, and their judgments of the people they meet are naturally reliable. In *The Crown of Dalemark*, we are separated from their interpretations and, through the eyes of Mitt, we get to see another side of the "good guys."

The club story is supported by the notions of the closed past that we have already discussed, and also by the idea, implicit in many quest fantasies, that those who went before knew more. The portal-quest fantasies' links to *The Pilgrim's Progress* are revealing because the assumption of knowledge lost can be a consequence of the importance of the Fall in the Christian tradition. As we fall further away from God, we are naturally less well informed of his desires than were our ancestors. One consequence for many portal-quest fantasies is that the adventurers can go forward only by knowing what it was the past wanted them to do: prophecies are a distinctly positivist way of shaping the future. The usual ending is to complete the prophecy and present the world with free will again, but the effect is to render the future a blank for which no tools have been developed.

Clearly, Jones does not reject this entirely: the magic in *Deep Secret* is buried in nursery rhymes, in *Wilkins' Tooth/Witch's Business* in fairy tales, and in *Eight Days of Luke* in the legends of the Norse Gods. In addition *Fire and Hemlock* and *Hexwood* require an extensive knowledge of the myths and legends of the past, but generally Jones defies modern fantasy traditions by insisting that knowledge is best secured by building on what is already known and applying the scientific method. Take, for example, *Fire and Hemlock*—which does not really fit into this chapter—in which Polly takes her knowledge of several versions of the Tam Lin–Thomas the Rhymer cycle, and her own grandmother's experiences, and constructs a solution for herself. There are no fixed answers to the problems she will face, because those problems have changed with time, just as all similar historical events are actually quite different. *The Ogre Downstairs* (also not a portal-quest fantasy) is precisely about magic as experiment: it arrives in a chemistry set, and scientific discovery and the rejection of held social prejudices go hand in hand. In *The Dark Lord of Derkholm*, Derk is appointed as the year's evil magician precisely because he is an experimental geneticist and will look to the future, to new ways of doing things, rather than to perpetuating the old approaches that have kept the world in thrall to Mr. Chesney (a businessman from another world who uses this world to organize tourist quests). The sequel, *Year of the Griffin*, is even more hostile to the idea of the discovered past. The Wizard Howl, in *Howl's Moving Castle*, teaches his apprentice magic through experiment. *The Magicians of Caprona* begins with a narrative of the past very similar to the setting-up prologues of many quest fantasies, but the narrative structure of the section serves to emphasize the unreliability of communal memory, and the subsequent story goes on to undermine the perceived past.

Only in *A Sudden Wild Magic* is the knowledge of older peoples regarded as somehow more powerful. When the King of the Orthe[31] decides to disrupt the Brotherhood of Arth, he looks for wild, untamed magic: a throwback centaur (spindly and apparently underdeveloped), a throwback gualdian (clumsy and highly strung), and his own nephew, whose birthright is outside the usual structures of magic. These are joined by Zillah, from our own world (assuming the Earth is our own world, which is a big assumption to make), whose magic is also undisciplined. But even here Jones does not look for old ways of doing things. These are people who cannot use the current modes of magic, but their actions return to original principles and reexperiment. They are not dug out of a book and, consequently, they do not invoke stasis on the process of history. One of the neatest bits of magic in the book is Herrel's attempt to create some kind of safety for his son by building a magical playpen. This is contrasted with the strongly ritual magic of the Ladies of Leathe. The experimental goes up against the traditional and ossified.

"The True State of Affairs"

The ultimate subversion of the portal in Jones's portfolio is an early story, "The True State of Affairs," which was written in the 1960s. This novella, the first Dalemark story (although not wholly of it, as Maureen Kincaid Speller pointed out),[32] began as a self-conscious critique: Jones has written (in the introduction to *Minor Arcana*) that this was a reflection on *The Kingis Quair*, a true story by James I of Scotland. Imprisoned and bored, he fell in (courtly) love with a girl seen in the distance and courted her with notes. "Of course it all stopped when he was released. It occurred to me to wonder what the girl felt about it."[33] In Jones's version the tale is told from the point of view of the girl courted, and she too is a prisoner. Furthermore, she seems to have come from another world, perhaps ours, although not our period. The story contains, in one place, many of the issues outlined in this chapter. It is brilliantly uneasy because it is laced with genre expectation, both of romance and fantasy, and because it destabilizes the reader's sense of the present and the past.

In "The True State of Affairs," Emily finds herself on the banks of an unknown river. She is persuaded to swap clothes with one of the women there and then is surprised to see the party break up before it moves off. Later she is captured and imprisoned, at first because she is thought to be the woman with whom she exchanged clothes, later because no one knows what do with her. The story is then about Emily's imprisonment, the relationships she builds with her jailors, the picture of the world and its civil war that she constructs, and her growing friendship with the prisoner in the other tower.

"The True State of Affairs" is told in the first person, privileging the protagonist as narrator. The convention in first-person narratives is that although the narrator might begin ignorant, the process of the tale is usually one of dawning (self-)knowledge. In addition, the fact of first-person narrative performs another, more ideological function: convincing the reader that the story *belongs* to the narrator; in some way the narrator will be central to the tale. The ownership of story is crucial to "The True State of Affairs." From the beginning it misdirects our attention: "I am still not sure how I come to be locked up here, but things are coming clearer, I shall find out in the end."[34] The tale, we have been informed, will be of the protagonist's capture, and presumably her eventual freedom. Yet the reality is quite other: Emily (the protagonist) is narrating not her tale but that of another. The first hint is in the introduction of "that bitch Hilda."[35] Emily's meeting with Hilda demonstrates the degree to which we need to keep an eye on Jones's allusions in all her work. The tale Emily tells is the classic one, of the princess who changes clothes with the beggar maid, but because Emily—disoriented by her arrival, where?—does not register this, she does not immediately realize that she is being drawn into someone else's story. The full consequence of this takes the whole story to work out. In the meantime, in the construction of her own story, she constructs the frame story, and frame-world, for the audience.

One of the conventions in the portal–quest fantasy is the degree to which the fantasy world is created through the intense eyes of the protagonist and the expository and distorting nature of description. Starved of other occupation, and with a mythical audience, Emily emulates this task.

> I thought I would describe my prison and perhaps what I can gather of this castle—or *stronghold* as they call it here—but paper is so very short that all I will say is that the walls are very thick, of very cold stone, and this window small and high.[36]

There are a number of aspects of this statement and its context to consider: first, the very denial of description in this quotation runs counter to the detail that is usually a given in portal fantasies; second, Emily's world is created not by surroundings but by the people—physically and literally.

Portal–quest fantasies rarely indicate the degree to which the protagonist's physical and emotional positions distort perspective, but in "The True State of Affairs," Jones uses Emily's descriptions to emphasize the constricted (and constructed) view of the stranger: "The living-room opens onto a courtyard with a shallow coping, high on the roof. I went out there as if it were freedom, but I could only see steep angles and corners of roofs and towers."[37] The visual carpet is not allowed to unroll in front of Emily; the intense detail of the impossible to see is missing. Only glimpses of the world allow her to build the pattern of the whole.

The protagonist in the portal–quest fantasy is almost always controlled by the figure of the guide, but usually this control is heavily disguised, and the passivity of the protagonist is explained by the almost instinctive knowledge of good and evil that all characters in these tales seem to own. In "The True State of Affairs," Jones draws attention to this construction, to its intensity, and to its perversity:

> One's relationship to one's jailor is an odd thing. One is at once a nuisance to him and of abiding interest. This one, at least, hangs about and questions my every action. And I am totally, if rebelliously, dependent on him for everything, including tastes of the outside world.[38]

Up to a point, Emily can manipulate this relationship. She creates for herself a character that will give her some leverage (that of a lady). It is a little thing, but it shifts the balance of power. This shift, in which Emily comes to control Wolfram's questions, is, however, double edged, as it breeds complacency. Wolfram is the guard; Emily is the prisoner. When she finally lets her guard down and trusts Wolfram as absolutely as his guide role demands, Wolfram discovers the paper strips she has cut to send notes to Asgrim. Dependency on the one who controls her view of the world proves lethal because it momentarily disguises her position as stranger.

However, it is from Wolfram's questions that Emily can build the partial version of the world outside. Every question directed at her allegiances contributes to the depiction of the civil war that rages; things emerge "sideways, in parenthesis and by implication,"[39] although it simultaneously reveals how little she knows. Occasionally Edwin, the underguard, leaks information: as he becomes complacent around Emily and the external situation, he can brag about the foolishness of Asgrim's ambitions to change the social structure of Dalemark. But even when Wolfram realizes that Emily's notes are wrong, based on hearsay and Edwin's misunderstandings of the real situation, there are no complete histories delivered around the guardroom fire. Wolfram still reveals only fragments. Unlike the traditional guide who manifests omniscience at these moments, Wolfram too is a prisoner, able to understand the situation only from one small corner.

The incompleteness of histories is emphasized when we discover the unreliability of the narrative. First-person narrative is generally seen as reliable (Agatha Christie's *The Murder of Roger Ackroyd* notwithstanding: that is a trick that can be played only once). But Jones renders the narrative unreliable—without the usual twist-in-the-tail approach—when Emily admits to the paper that she is keeping a secret. That the secret is her communication with Asgrim in the other tower, which will drive much of the rest of the narrative, is important but not as interesting as what this says about the structure of this kind of fantasy. Narrations in the first person are essentially conversations with the invisible reader. Emily's narration, however, is directed to the visible reader, to Wolfram who is almost certainly reading her papers, and to herself, so that the narrative functions simultaneously as truth, deception, and self-deception (the latter because Emily is reluctant to acknowledge the importance of this friendship). The text is destabilized: this is not a reverie, a seamless and truthful account of the past, but a product of censorship.

Torn out of context, the average protagonist in a portal–quest fantasy has few ways to make judgments. Fantasy literature is notoriously wedded to physiognomy and indicative features.[40] But this tradition, although transparent, is part of the self-deception that protagonists are frequently engaged with. Emily is fooling herself when she writes, "I won't have it that he [Asgrim] is a bloodthirsty seizer of power, or cold politician, as Uncle evidently is. He is not. You can see it in his bearing. If he was to be king, either he has a claim, or he is convinced the country needs a strong head."[41] Emily imputes character and motive simply from the way a man walks. But Emily's narrative is a translation:

> I see I am not rendering Edwin's peculiar dialect as it really is at all. I keep replacing his words and phrases by what I understand them to mean in my English. He would never use a word like *political*. The

words are *menward* and *landminding*. But when I think of what he says,
I think of it in translation.[42]

The power of translation and creation, the need to make some image out
of fragments, is Emily's anchor and the source of her eventual disillusion,
but what is crucial is that she is concurrently aware of what she is doing
and yet unaware of the degree to which she is accepting this as real so that
when she considers Asgrim's surroundings she can "imagine what it might
be like, but I will not let myself—I don't know why. Yet I have a clear
picture in my head of what his prison is. It is bound to be wrong, so I
won't dwell on it. I would much rather have it vague."[43] Emily is being
seduced by her own translation. Disillusion, when she discovers the luxury
that Asgrim enjoyed, is devastating because it implies much greater
misunderstanding elsewhere. The man who lived in the cold, grand rooms
could not truly fall in love with Emily.

The fallibility of translation serves multiple purposes in "The True
State of Affairs," not least serving to encode the messages passed between
Asgrim and Emily—by this I mean not that they are in code but that they
can never be revealing. Emily's attempts to respond to the cultural code
that Asgrim employs are the center of the tragedy of the tale, but it also
runs as an important element in the construction of place: Jones argues in
"The True State of Affairs" that the words one uses are fundamental: they
shape thought patterns and are shaped by political environment. It is
almost impossible for the guide figures to communicate the true state of
affairs to Emily because she will inevitably misprision what she hears.
Jones tells us this, up front, in the poem Asgrim writes to Emily:

> Unbounded truth is not a thing
> Cramped to Time and bound in place.
> It strangely changes space, Enlarging laws to loyalty
> And making words reality,
> And stones words or nothing.
> The boundaries containing me
> Are wider than the world, by grace
> Of truth, which is another thing.[44]

Another version of this poem appears in *Cart and Cwidder,* and
although that is in the future of the writing of "The True State of Affairs,"
it indicates the power of this poem as a cultural meme. Emily takes it as a

defense of the immutability of truth. It is in fact the opposite, an explanation that truth is a matter of context: Jones conducts this message in the behavior not just of Asgrim but of his son Kjartan, whose truth is shaped by his captivity, and Wolfram, whose behavior arises from his own social context as a bastard and by the position he occupies. Again, Emily does understand this—explains it to us even when she observes Kjartan and Wolfram but her estrangement from this society and her incomplete picture makes her vulnerable to willing misprision, as does her preference for truth to "manifest in particulars."[45] This is an interesting use of the conventions of the portal–quest fantasy in which codes and puzzles often are reducible to particulars (Susan Cooper's *The Dark Is Rising* sequence has riddles that prove to be instruction). Emily's instinct to do the same will send her in the wrong direction. Asgrim is burying abstract thought in abstract poetry. Later he sends a sequel:

> But truth, which is another thing
> Aside from laws or words or time,
> Has strangely entered space, Lifting the clod from under
> Moving men from asunder
> And only leaves us dying.
> Truth is the fire that fetches thunder,
> Kindled of itself, and only mine
> In the heart that has its fashioning.

I wish I knew what the hell it means. I get the feeling that it refers to a complete argument of which I am ignorant—terms, conclusions and all.[46] Yet it is attention to detail, to the concrete, that causes Emily first to question her misprision and then to rectify it; when Wolfram begins to "thee" and "thou" her she worries whether her social status has fallen. At the end, Emily must acknowledge that Asgrim never called her "thou": "It was all ceremonies and respectful and distant. And the verses he wrote made it clear, from the start, that what he wanted to feel was a something-else, metaphysical, large and abstract."[47] The only thing truth did not mean was the fidelity for which Emily hoped.

But "The True State of Affairs" is also about the seduction of a protagonist into the otherworld. In the majority of the portal–quest fantasies, this is automatic and rather sinister. In "The True State of Affairs," it is central to the tale. In a classic case of Stockholm syndrome. By the end of the story, Emily has come to identify with her captors. What happens to them is her fate too. Asgrim, in contrast, never makes this mistake: his hardness is the rigidity of one who insists in remaining at the center of his own story. In these terms, Emily must remain an object to him; full recognition would recenter the story.

"The True State of Affairs" denies the fulfillment of romance and subverts the conventional structures of the portal–quest fantasy. Jones takes every opportunity to defy the habits of the genre: this story reinforces the social order as it is. Wolfram the Bastard is not elevated—in fact his connection to Hrinkle condemns him; Hobby the drudge dies, he is a side note in this world; and Asgrim does not come back to liberate Emily or to destroy the citadel in vengeance. Instead he forgets, and causes to forget. Mark is abandoned to become a backwater unrepresented in the modern world. It is written out of the story that Hrinkle thought he controlled. Elsewhere, the story laughs at some of the conventions of fantasy: the gods of this world might exist, but few seem to care. "The Gods," says Wolfram, "Oh, the gods. I don't bother much with them. They don't bother much with men, thou knows."[48]

Most unusual is that this is a portal–quest fantasy in which we do not follow the quest. Emily is at the center of her own tale but not of the adventure. The adventure is a tale of high romance, of war, of politics, and of the prisoner Asgrim. The plot of the story is something we never actually get to see. The implied reader is led to expect that Emily will become a part of that, and she does not. She does not get swept up as an adjunct in a daring rescue. Emily does not appear on that map of fantasyland that structures the quest. The structure of the story absolutely breaches the rule that the protagonists who traverse the portal will make a difference to the world in such a way that their narrow description of it will distract us from the whole. Emily's attempts to construct a complete view of the outside consequently break the monosemic nature of the portal fantasy. This raises the question as to whether this internal narrative is intended to parallel the external narrative of exploration and observation. Can one have an internal quest that does not require the protagonist to move through a physical and internal landscape? There are very few portal fantasies that are not succeeded by journeys.[49]

CHAPTER 5
THE IMMERSIVE FANTASY

The construction of fantasy is, W.R. Irwin pointed out, the art of persuasion. The immersive fantasy requires the author to convince the reader of the existence of a whole world.[1] In the immersive or immersed fantasy, the magic just *is*. It is all around us, the protagonists are competent in their own world, and we ride invisible, picking up hints and clues. In *The Magicians of Caprona*, Chrestomanci can casually refer to the Court of Europe, and in *A Sudden Wild Magic*, Tod can take for granted that everyone understands what a gualdian is, because those who live in a world cannot predict what observers might wish to know. In the immersive fantasy it is possible for a good writer to construct a novel in which the reader position demanded is essentially one of interrogator: the reader will constantly ask, "Why?" and "What is that?" and "What does that mean?" The result can be something much more open than the portal fantasy.

However, the immersive fantasy is actually rather difficult to achieve: the temptation is always to give in to the desire to explain. A number of immersive fantasies have failed because they are overdidactically described. The immersive fantasy, at its most effective, is an ironic construction of the mimesis that we take for granted when we enter the strange world of the literary novel—*Pride and Prejudice*, for example. It relies on the construction of perspective within the fantastical world, that can be destroyed by excessive detail. For this reason, the immersive fantasy is not always synonymous with what is frequently referred to as otherworld fantasy. Otherworld fantasy is simply that kind of fantasy set in a different world. It moves the protagonists very quickly from their home base into an other world of adventure, often of a very different culture. Frodo Baggins, for example, moves speedily from the Shire to the strange world of Middle Earth in *Lord of the Rings:* the world portrayed soon becomes as strange to him as it is to the reader, and we are in the rhetoric of the portal–quest fantasy.

Unlike the portal–quest fantasies, which rarely seem to deviate from the trajectory of a goal sought out and a world saved, the immersive fantasy can hold almost any plot. It is not uncommon, for example, for the fully fantasticated world to be disrupted by an intrusion—as in *Howl's Moving Castle* or *The Magicians of Caprona,* in which an evil enters the world and must be defeated—and in these circumstances the author combines the acceptance of the fantasy world as it is with a sense of the new and disturbing of the intrusion, much as the writer of a modern horror novel combines our acceptance of quiet U.S. suburbia with the amazement at the intrusion of the supernatural. In both cases, the trajectory is the same—toward negotiation with, or defeat of, the intrusion.

Of Diana Wynne Jones's books only *The Magicians of Caprona, Witch Week, The Dark Lord of Derkholm,* and *Howl's Moving Castle* are fully immersive fantasies. Other apparently immersive fantasies are twisted so that the protagonist's apparent familiarity with the world becomes deceptive and misleading: as I discussed in chapter 4, *Hexwood* and *Fire and Hemlock* are constructed through tone and mood to signal the shifts between worlds and perspectives and to confuse the reader and the protagonists with regard to what is actually reality. The most taken for granted worlds and events in *Hexwood* are often the least real, whereas the most real in *Fire and Hemlock* (the discovery of Stowe-on-the-Water, for example) are the most metaphorized.

More obvious choices for this category, such as *Charmed Life* and *The Lives of Christopher Chant,* which take place in a fully otherworld, actually follow the form and trajectory of a portal fantasy because they are *Bildungsroman,* a form that is *transition;* from the world of childhood to the world of adults. Cat's and Christopher's portal fantasy perspective on the world of Chrestomanci Castle causes them seriously to misunderstand what is going on. Cat in particular is in denial, refusing to accept—from the moment of his parents' death—that this is his world and he must learn it. Only once the boys accept that this is their world do they function competently.

This chapter will consider how Jones achieves the sense of immersion through the casualization of the fantastic combined with the play on reader recognition, and through some of the grammatical tricks I first considered in chapter 4. Its major thrust will be to discuss how Jones uses the techniques of immersive fantasy to rework the way a quest can be written. That Jones has consciously considered what it takes to write a fully immersive fantasy is made quite clear in *The Merlin Conspiracy*. Roddy's grandfather has been writing murder mysteries set in his own Island of Blest and selling them in Britain. What are mimetic novels in one context are read as ironic mimesis in another.

The Dalemark novels stand apart from Jones's other work. They are much more threatening and intensely complex. Although there is a strong argument for all four novels to be considered as portal–quest fantasies, they are not written that way. With the exception of the final novel, *The Crown of Dalemark*, Jones refuses her protagonists an awareness of their quest and frequently allows them to presume their competence in a world that is not quite as they think it. In order to do this, it is not just fantasy Jones casualizes: it is also the process of world building and the construction, in particular, of the political depth of the novels that also functions as a critique of the political hand-waving that affects much genre fantasy. Whereas the portal–quest fantasy traditionally offers the detailed world of the pre-Raphaelites, Jones prefers impressionism, a world hinted at through what the protagonists find too common to comment on; complexity and depth created in casual remarks and brush strokes. Like Monet's *Haystacks* reality is constructed through multiple perspectives.

The Technique of Immersion

The Dark Lord of Derkholm, Witch Week, The Magicians of Caprona, and *Howl's Moving Castle* are Jones's most fully realized immersive fantasies. The first of these has already been discussed in chapter 4, for its subversion of the portal–quest fantasy, and I have pointed to the degree to which the reversed flow of information is crucial to this: an issue is first taken for granted and, only later, in another context, explained. This pattern begins on the opening pages of the text:

> "Will you all be quiet!" Hissed High Chancellor Querida. She pouched up her eyes and glared round the table.

> "I was only trying to say—" a king, an emperor and several wizards began.

> "At once," said Querida, "or the next person to speak spends the rest of his life as a snake!"

> This shut most of the University Emergency Committee up. Querida was the most powerful wizard in the world and she had a special feeling for snakes.[2]

The information we need takes us from detail to general context. This is precisely the reverse of the way we need to process the information: the result is that even with the direct explanation at the end of the passage, there is an assumed intimacy that clouds the degree to which we have been given only an impression of the world.

Even an apparent download (the science fiction term is *infodump*) can, in Jones's hands, be manipulated to convince us that we have been told more than we actually have. In that opening scene Querida goes on to list the complaints she has received from all over the world: " 'This pile is three letters signed by over a hundred female wizards, who claim they are being denied equal rights. They are accurate. Mr. Chesney does not think females can be wizards.'"[3] Without saying "...this is a world which values equality and distributes talents across the genders," Jones has made her point.

It is also important to note the kind of things about a world that Jones tells us. This and other descriptions are essentially political. Jones creates her worlds not through landscape but through economy. Querida continues,

> These letters are a selection of those I get from farmers and ordinary citizens. They all state that what with magical weather-conditions, armies marching over crops, soldiers rustling cattle, fires set by Dark Lord's Minions and other hazards, they are likely to starve for the foreseeable future. ... Almost the only people who seem to be prospering are the innkeepers and they complain that the lack of barley is making it hard to brew sufficient ale.[4]

Suddenly this is a full world, one that has an economy of its own. It is no longer a blank space on which adventure can be imposed—which is, of course, the plot of the novel. *The Dark Lord of Derkholm* does not just satirize the portal–quest fantasy; it reminds us that this type of fantasy is someone else's immersion. In *The Dark Lord of Derkholm*, Jones makes the portal–quest fantasy politically incorrect.

Impressionism as a world-building technique is developed to such a degree in *The Magicians of Caprona* that Jones uses it as the underpinning of the entire plot: in Caprona the two families of Montana and Petrocchi have been feuding for at least a century, the White Devil has entered the city, and the words to "The Angel of Caprona" have been lost. As we might by now expect of Jones, any theme she chooses appears at both the macro- and microcosmic levels, so that at every level of this novel, that which is taken for granted is the source of problems: the teacher who assumes that Tonino Montana cannot read; the families who assume that Tonino and Angelica cannot do magic because they cannot do it the family way; the families who assume that a feud just is and cannot be unpicked; the Duchess who assumes the Duke will flee and leave his city unguarded; Paolo who assumes that a cat who communicates will speak; the families of Montana and Petrocchi who assume that the words to the "Angel" are to be discovered by magic when they are in fact under their noses. Jones builds both plot and world in the words not uttered and the background assumed.

Describing an economy, or a family feud, in place of landscape is one method of creating immersion and a sense that there is more to the world than what is immediately before our eyes: Michael's sad comment in *Howl* on his parents' death—"nobody wants you when that happens"[5]—communicates volumes about this society and prevents it from being too nice, and this is the method that will be interrogated most deeply in this chapter's consideration of the Dalemark quartet. But another approach Jones develops is to describe the minds of the inhabitants. To quote once again the quite brilliant opening lines of *Howl's Moving Castle*:

> In the land of Ingary, where such things as seven-league boots and cloaks of invisibility really exist, it is quite a misfortune to be born the eldest of three. Everyone knows you are the one who will fail first, and worse, if the three of you set out to seek your fortunes.[6]

This is a novel that is about the mind of a country, about the way people think about themselves and their own worlds. What matters is not the magical objects but the tales with which people construct their lives. As an old lady Sophie has two encounters but notes, "not a scrap of magical gratitude from either."[7] In these terms Howl, the wizard of the moving castle, is actor and actant. In a land shaped by story, he and Sophie are on convergent trajectories: Sophie learns to reject the story line she has been handed, but Howl learns instead to accept the storyability of his life as expressed through the John Donne poem.[8] This acceptance allows Howl to become more fully immersed in Ingary: once he has accepted that this is a world constructed through story, he can follow the plots to break the Witch of the Waste's curse and Sophie's enchantment and to assist Sophie to break the tie between him and Calcifer.

In constructing an immersion, Jones applies rigorously her own dictum that the social ecology of a fantastic world must be complete.[9] For this to be the case, a truly fantastical world must have moments of mundanity. The Land of Ingary, however interesting, is ordinary. The ships of Porthaven and the cobbled streets of Kingsbury reference historical novels. They are fantastic only because we know them to be imaginary (although as Bristol is a port city one suspects a real reference), and fantastic also in the way in which these places are written. Kingsbury, for example, is not described. Jones refuses us the right to make exotic the worlds she creates. We are not going to be allowed to stare, mouth agape, at wondrous objects. Nor are we going to be able to use a protagonist as our eyes. Instead we see Kingsbury entirely through Sophie's sensations:

> Kingsbury was a long way south and it was a bakingly hot day there. The pavements shimmered. Sophie discovered another disadvantage to being old: you felt queer in hot weather. The elaborate buildings wavered in front of her eyes. She was annoyed because she wanted to look at the place, but all she had was the impression of a few golden domes and tall houses.[10]

A younger Sophie had been too terrified of crowds even to observe for us her own town of Market Chipping on a festival day. Jones reminds us that for those who live in a world, what it looks and feels like is essentially a function of perspective shaped by age, class, race, or even the level of stress a character is experiencing. We become fully immersed in her worlds because those worlds truly belong to someone. The most vivid example of this can be found in *Dogsbody*.

Dogsbody, a book that receives too little attention in this text, was first published in 1975, the same year as *Cart and Cwidder*, but its grammatical sophistication lies in different areas. *Dogsbody* could be considered a portal fantasy. Its opening scene is of the Dog Star confronting his accusers in court, and it takes the first three pages for Jones to show us Sirius's world, because it is told so vigorously from Sirius's perspective. *Dogsbody* can be studied as a literary exercise in how to restrict the writer's eye to only what the protagonist can know and understand. Take, for example, the scene in which Sirius and his brothers and sister are taken away to be drowned:

> To his terror, there was nothing to breathe but the cold stuff, and it choked him. ...

> Being dead seemed to mean floating out into a grey-green light. It was not a light he could see by, and it was stronger above him. ... Round bubbles, shining yellow, moved past his eyes and put him in mind of another life he could not quite remember. Then the light was like a silver lid, thick and solid looking overhead.[11]

Fred Inglis argues, "when we say of fine prose that it is vivid, we mean just that; it recreates the life of the event at the same time as it gives us a way of accommodating its meaning."[12] Jones does not mention either water or drowning; instead panic is created through sensation and the desperate attempt of Sirius to make sense of what is happening. And at the end of the book, when Sirius is readmitted to the firmament, he describes his world as something new, because he can, because it is somewhere he no longer takes for granted:

> "It was darker than he remembered, and the noises astonished him for a moment. Space sang. There were great slow notes, high sweet sounds—every note in human music and more beside, all winding, twining, combining and ringing. ... It was the sound the spheres made as they turned, and he had almost forgotten it."[13]

Having asserted that *Howl's Moving Castle* is a truly immersive fantasy, I now need to contradict this statement, because, of course, when Sophie steps into the castle, she steps through a portal into fantasyland. The usual equation of the portal fantasy runs as follows: go through the portal into a larger land and escape domesticity. In *Howl's Moving Castle* Sophie walks through the portal into the castle, which is actually a small "two up, two down" house of a kind familiar to working-class British families, into a much smaller land, where she becomes domestic. And although in the outside world we see the occasional seven-league boots and stranded mermaids, it is the inside of the castle and the events that take place there that are mostly depicted as fantastic, not the world around it.

Jones has consistently insisted that the fantastic takes place in the same realm as the domestic. Many of her novels take place indoors or are about the disputed safety of home. By the time of *Howl's Moving Castle*, it is the domestic space (the house) that is positioned in "the wood between the worlds" has become, in fact, fantastic. The depiction of the domestic demonstrates the way in which Jones naturalizes the fantastic, emphasizing the normality of magic within its own context, and removing the alienation of the protagonist endemic to the portal fantasy. One of the best examples is Sophie's first encounter with Calcifer. We are introduced to Calcifer through Sophie's description, but Jones prevents this from ejecting us from the immersion by contextualizing it. Sophie's description happens in her own head, in the context of her own thoughts and imaginings. It is not a description for us but an attempt to make sense in her own mind of the space around her.

> She turned back to the fire, which was now flaring up into blue and green flames. "Must be salt in that wood," Sophie murmured. She ... began dreamily considering what she ought to do in the morning. But she was sidetracked a little by imagining a face in the flames. "It would be a thin blue face," she murmured, "very long and thin, with a thin blue nose. But those curly green flames on top are most definitely your hair. Suppose I didn't go until Howl gets back? Wizards can lift spells, I suppose. And those purple flames near the bottom make the mouth—you have savage teeth, my friend. You have two green tufts of flame for eye-brows."[14]

Sophie moves from rationalizing to imagining, although, as we later learn that Sophie can talk life into things, there is also a chance that her speculation forced Calcifer into the open. But the real issue is that Sophie is not an outsider in this fantasyland. Indigenous to it, she is in dialogue with the world around her, and it is in this dialogue with the fantastic that Jones constructs the immersion. Sophie might be surprised to meet Calcifer, but she is not surprised to meet something like him.

> It was definitely the fire that spoke. ... "What are you?"

> "A fire demon," answered the purple mouth. There was more whine than spit to its voice as it said, "I'm bound to this hearth by contract. I can't move from this spot." Then its voice became brisk and crackling. "And what are *you*?" it asked. "I can see you're under a spell."

This roused Sophie from her dreamlike state. "You can see!" she exclaimed. "Can you take the spell off?"[15]

Sophie's reaction to Calcifer takes for granted the fact of Calcifer's existence, and the rapid turn to a mutual area of interest—enchantments—emphasizes this. Jones has written the kind of meeting that takes place in a cocktail party. Too often, this kind of meeting in fantasyland would include a statement that, if transferred into the real world, would be the equivalent of remarking to one of one's own species, "My, you're a *human*." In *Howl's Moving Castle* Jones remains careful throughout to distinguish the ways in which something might be strange to Sophie, rather than to assume that all strangeness is the same. The most obvious example of this—the trip to Wales—has already been discussed in chapter 4, but we can see it also in the description of the contents of Howl's bathroom cabinet:

> her main target was of course the shelf of packets, jars, and tubes. She took every one of them down, on the pretext of scrubbing the shelf, and spent most of a day carefully going through them to see if the ones labeled SKIN, EYES and HAIR were in fact pieces of girl. As far as she could tell, they were all just creams and powders and paint. If they had once been girls, then Sophie thought Howl had used the tube FOR DECAY on them and rotted them down the washbasin too thoroughly to recall. But she hoped they were only cosmetics in the packets.[16]

Sophie, like anyone in a world she knows, is confronted with items that are strange, contexts that are familiar and the reverse, and, as children do, she bootstraps the knowledge she needs from context. By writing this as process, the scene becomes a place lived in.

Finally, a brief consideration of *Witch Week*. Its uncompromising immersion is revealed in its opening scene. When a class teacher opens a note that reads, "Someone in this class is a witch," he plunges us directly into a world of witch burnings. We have to wait until the very end of the book before anyone questions the status quo of this world. Interestingly, when someone does it is the outsider, Chrestomanci. The children try to escape the witch burnings; only the outsider questions why they should exist. Immersion functions as both technique and ideology. Anyone sufficiently immersed in his or her world will find it very difficult to critique its premises, whether political, magical, or economic; yet for the reader, this very acceptance creates space for interrogation.[17] *Witch Week* is a very simple statement of this; the Dalemark quartet takes us into greater complexities.

A World Lived in: Politics, Economy, and Society in the Dalemark Quartet

Although there are actually more than four texts that form the Dalemark sequence, the novels *Cart and Cwidder, The Spellcoats, Drowned Ammet,* and *The Crown of Dalemark* form a coherent sequence that "speak to each other." Once one has read them all, later books illuminate earlier books, and this interaction deepens the immersion in the world.

Cart and Cwidder relates a small story set within a wider civil war. Moril travels with his Singer family through the North and South, entertaining for a living. Only when his father dies does he realize they have been smuggling messages between Southern rebels and their Northern supporters. The rest of the story is about his struggle to get back to the North with his passenger Kialan, who is an Earl's son, while simultaneously learning how to use the musical instrument he has inherited that might be a legacy from the great Singer Osfameron. The book ends with Moril's using the cwidder to bring down a mountain on the Southern soldiers. Unlike Moses and the Egyptians, however, Moril is consumed by remorse in ways that affect his actions in *The Crown of Dalemark.*[18]

The Spellcoats is rather different from the other books. It takes place in the prehistory of Dalemark and tells of an invasion and of a family driven from its home. As the two stories begin to cross, the invasion becomes less clear-cut, the invaders begin to look more like refugees, and the members of the family accused of connections to the supernatural powers begin to display such powers. Told through the medium of woven coats that have been translated, *The Spellcoats* is the story of the creation of the physical land of Dalemark. It is narrated from the point of view of a small family rather than through the eyes of the gods. In *Drowned Ammet* Mitt grows up in the oppressive South as a freedom fighter. When it all goes wrong, he flees the South, accidentally taking with him the children of the Earl's youngest son. On the way to safety, he meets Old Ammet and Libby Beer, the two Undying who seem to have the closest links to the land of Dalemark. The sequel, *The Crown of Dalemark,* is told from two points of view: as a portal fantasy by Maewen, daughter of the Curator of the Palace Museum in the future, and as an immersive fantasy by Mitt who has been sent on a mission to murder a woman who would be Queen. The only quest fantasy of the quartet, *The Crown of Dalemark,* will eventually see Mitt crowned as Amil, to become the Amil the Great, whom Maewen has seen depicted in murals.

Genre fantasy for adults and children has been a refuge for the reactionary. Although a number of fantasy writers—Michael Moorcock, M. John Harrison, Michael Swanwick, China Miéville, and most recently Steph Swainston—have tried to write left-wing fantasy, novel after novel within the genre revels in cod medievalism or early modernism and perpetuates an orientalist, static view of the past in which worlds exist in the period of history the author selects for them and in which major religious and political upheavals do little to change the industrial or economic landscape.

The Dalemark quartet forms probably Jones's most sustained fictional attack on this construction of otherworlds.[19] Each of the novels is a medieval fantasy, but even at the superficial level, this is a medieval of Geoffrey Trease's *Bows against the Barons* rather than Malory: it is not fun, people do not enjoy being medieval, and there are stresses and strains in the political system.

Dalemark changes. The early medieval Dalemark of *The Spellcoats* is noticeably different from the late medieval in appearance, but early modern in economy, Dalemark of *The Crown of Dalemark*. It seems ridiculous to regard this as a radical departure from the norm, but with only a few exceptions (Robin McKinley's Dammar sequence and lately Terry Pratchett's Discworld) fantasy series that concern themselves with an unfolding history (and most do) are written as if by the Venerable Bede or Geoffrey of Monmouth: kings and queens, dynasties, the doings of the great religions. Little attention is paid to changing structures.

Cart and Cwidder, the first of the Dalemark novels to be written, begins with this idea that Great Men is what history is really about. Moril, youngest son of Clennen the Singer, is obsessed with the legend of Osfameron, friend of the Adon. However, the way in which Jones restricts the download of legend extends the sense of a world known to the protagonists. There are no campfire tellings, no unquestionable club stories embedded in the text. Moril and his siblings know the stories of Osfameron, and when Clennen relates the tales, Moril records only that a tale is told; he does not need to narrate the tale, because in reality there are no naive listeners.

If Jones refuses us the tale, she leaves us with its tagline, "…there have been no kings in Dalemark. Nor will there be, until the sons of Manaliabrid return,"[20] as a nice distraction. It sounds as if we have just been given the prophetic line that will plot the novel. We have not. The hinted-at moment of prophecy never finds fulfillment. Although in some ways *Cart and Cwidder* feels like a quest fantasy, the promise of the quest narrative is withheld. The novel remains rhetorically and ideologically open; there is none of the monosemy of the quest or the sealed narrative. When Moril listens to the legend, he reacts with the complex disappointment of a real human being:

> The world had gone so ordinary. Compare the Adon, who lived such a splendid life, with the present-day Earl of Hannart, who could think of nothing better to do than to stir up a rebellion.[21]

Unlike the heroes of quest fantasies, his reaction to this story is less to be inspired than to be depressed; the world has thinned, it is no longer as fantastical as it once was. In each of these novels, adventure is like jam, adventure tomorrow and yesterday but never adventure today. Moril's realization that "legendary deeds always take place in a world of rain and anxiety and irritation. [That] Heroic deeds can only be performed in the material world,"[22] is an element of the reader's discovery that adventure in the fully immersed world, in a world that seeks to counterfeit mimesis, is something had, looked back on from the past; hence Moril's disgust when he learns that Kialan is the Adon (as his full name is the complementary Tanamoril Osfameron). They have been living the adventure he so desired, and it was not in the least bit fun or romantic.

As in the mimesis it ironizes, in the immersive fantasy the reader and protagonist must sift through an information-dense world. The way real people do this is rarely orderly. It is in depicting this that Jones demonstrates her skill. One of the greatest difficulties for the writer of immersive fantasy is how to deal with those things that one absolutely has to explain; Jones cannot always restrict us to what Moril notices.

Jones tackles this difficulty by stripping down the information she writes to the bare minimum—the best analogy is of removing vowels from a sentence, leaving something comprehensible to most readers—so on page 2 "Moril squeezed up to that end to change, very careful not to bang a cwidder or scrape the hand-organ. Each instrument was shiny with use and gleaming with care. Each had its special place. Everything in the cart did. Clennen insisted on it. He said that life in a small cart would otherwise become impossible."[23] Jones does not actually write that Moril lives in a cart. She shows us, slipping from authorial omniscience to internal monologue without signal. The information that Moril does live in the cart comes after he has entered it, reinforcing the sense that we know a place that we do not. Jones never does explain the cwidder as more than a stringed instrument, and it is mostly described by the actions of playing it. One way to think of the construction of immersive fantasy is that it is that form that most requires that the author show rather than tell. And the way in which the information is offered is grammatically interesting; when Moril steps outside to clean the cart, "he could have a good view of the cart that was his home." The object is the view, not the cart.

These techniques, combined with the sense of muddle and non sequitur that take place in the human mind, are similarly deployed to communicate political information. In the opening paragraph of *Cart and Cwidder*, Moril moves from the thought that the South is too physically hot in spring to the thought that it is also metaphorically hot: "The worst, to Moril's mind, was the need to be careful. You dared not put a foot, or a word, out of place for fear of being clapped in jail. ... Moril himself had been born in the North."[24] Jones takes us from the outside of a scene (the landscape) to the inside (Moril's mind). We have gone in reverse, from the detail of family to the generality of the world, but then back again to the personal. The trajectory of this paragraph is the trajectory in miniature of the novel, which will explore the place of a small family tragedy in a much larger rebellion. And also will be the Matter of the novel—the relationship of the family to a political crisis and to a sense of history. Perhaps the most illuminative piece of internal monologue is that which takes place in Moril's mind after Clennen is killed.

> He felt vividly and horribly attentive to everything, from the leaves in the hedge to the shape of Kialan's nose. Kialan's eagle-nose was so different from Dagner's, Brid's or Moril's that he was sure anyone could tell at a glance he was no relation. Why did he have to be a relation anyway? And had Clennen known he wanted to go to Hannart? Clennen would not have gone there, because he never went to Hannart. And why had the six men killed Clennen? Who were they, and what were they looking for in the wood? And why, why, why above all, had Clennen given Moril a cwidder he did not want in the least?[25]

Moril's thoughts spiral to what seems the most trivial but what is actually the most important issue of the book, but they create mimesis by insisting that humans cannot know what is important. The muddle of Moril's mind parallels that of the collective memory; the explanation of the civil war raging between North and South Dalemark remains unclear:

> The disagreement had begun so far in the past that not many people knew its cause: the North had one version, the South another. But it was

certain that three kings of Dalemark had died, one after another, without leaving a proper heir to the throne. ...

But the disagreement ran deeper than ever. The men of the North claimed that half the land was enslaved, and the earls of the South said the North was plotting against them. The year Brid was born, Keril, Earl of Hannart, had been proclaimed a public enemy by every earl and lord in the South.[26]

Instead of downloaded legend, what we get is gossip and current events set, and I think this is crucial, against something familiar and intimate: Moril does not take the tales of Southern cruelty as much more than shocking legends that define his own identity until first his brother Dagner is sentenced to death and then Kialan tells him about watching his own brother's hanging. Moril is confronted with the reality that the South is not just scenery; even tourists passing through are part of the world. In the Dalemark quartet all politics is mediated or filtered through the perceptions and positions of the principle characters.

The Spellcoats and *Cart and Cwidder* are told from a single viewpoint; *The Spellcoats* is told in the first person and *Cart and Cwidder* is told by the omniscient narrator. Realizing the real meaning of the world in these two novels is primarily about growing out of one's solipsism, but this solipsism is also used to deepen the sense of immersion. This is most vivid in the structure and grammar of *The Spellcoats.*

The Spellcoats is particularly interesting because of the way that Jones avoids the pitfalls of first-person retrospective. The critical problem with first-person narratives is that they frequently force us to imagine an auditory figure (the use of a diary only partially undercuts this), and too often the tension is undercut by apparent narrative omniscience. The story opens with Tanaqui's remembrance of Shelling and the news of strangers:

We are the children of Closti the Clam, and we lived all our lives in the village of Shelling, where a stream comes down to join the River, giving plentiful fishing and rich pasture.

This makes Shelling sound like a good place, but it is not. It is small and lonely, and the people here are dark and unpleasant, not excepting my Aunt Zara. They worship the River as a god. We know this is wrong. The only gods are the Undying.[27]

This section of the tale is told absolutely from the inside to an outsider, and at this stage the reader is hypothetical but justifies the extensive description without placing Tanaqui outside her own world. Jones can also bury a trick or two. Jones has an insider describe the world to us, but the insider—as her uncle Kestrel tells us later—feels herself to be an outsider, special, and apart from those she describes. At first this is described mostly in terms of looks: the children have fair curly hair, rather than dark straight hair. It seems superficial, but later it will be a source of estrangement—used to looking different from those around them, they will feel uncomfortable with the Heathen because they share their looks. It will feel unnatural.[28]

In the course of the book, however, we will be seduced by Tanaqui's air of knowledge and by her belief that she is a disinterested observer. This makes us more, not less, susceptible to the confusion of matter and meaning that Jones seems to want to create. The first trick Jones uses is the conceit of the spellcoats themselves; the narrative is being written, and although it takes a while to realize this for the first coat, we know that the second is being written for the Undying, and that in its narrative weaving is power.

The second trick is that by dividing the tale into two parts, or two coats, Jones can limit Tanaqui's understanding to a relatively small space of time: unlike many first-person narrators, Tanaqui does not know the outcome of the first tale, and the purpose of the second coat allows it (or her) to be ignorant of the second half, without the cliché of sudden death. Reinforcing these two devices is the epistemology of *The Spellcoats:* the absence (or reworking) of the figure and role of the guide, and a continual emphasis on the different perspectives and bodies of knowledge that each of the children owns.

Ways of knowing are crucial to the development of the text. Whatever Tanaqui initially thinks, the villagers are not stupid; they just know differently. In the end their understanding of the relationship between the river and the Undying will prove to be more accurate than Tanaqui's understanding. Along with the revelation that truth can come from those who appear ignorant is the growing awareness in the text, and by Tanaqui, that the children of Closti the Clam are not a single entity. Sharing a family is not here allowed to mean that each child understands or knows the family in the same way. One of the key differences between the way in which Jones confers gifts on people and the ways of many other fantasy writers is that Jones's gifts are almost always about ways of knowing things—*Power of Three* is the clearest statement of this, but the idea is repeated in *The Magicians of Caprona, Witch Week,* and *Fire and Hemlock,* among others. In *The Spellcoats* this becomes a major theme, tied to the way in which Jones refigures the role of the guide.

Jones's guide figure, Tanamil, tells the children very little. They have to figure out that he is one of the Undying, the tributary of the River and although he provides hints as to who he is (he uses the term *Heathens* for the invader, indicating he knows who they are, and it is clear that he knows that Duck has another name), the ways in which he is bound force him to provide help by providing the opportunity for questions. But the children do not ask the correct questions.

Tanamil is annoyingly oblique. Later we will come to understand that he is bound, that he cannot tell the children. But there is also the sense that by providing rather childish explanations, he allows the children to be the children they still are at this stage but are not by the end of the book. In this way Jones rather neatly illuminates the dependency syndrome at the heart of the guide–protagonist relationship.

Reflecting on the questions they asked is really the first time that Tanaqui acknowledges that her memory might be either faulty or incomplete:

> I have no memory of what was said. Duck says I do not remember because Robin was not there at the time. He says Tanamil came and asked each of us separately, and he says I do wrong to put it in here, because it happened right at the beginning of our stay. But I remember it almost at the end, and I am weaving this story.[29]

This is also the first indication not just that the children know different things but also that they might know them differently. As the tale moves on, we realize that Hern's rejection of magic, his grounding in the here and now, might actually be very powerful; that Duck might be the most conspicuously connected to the Undying through his rather uncanny ability to compose music; that Robin might be gifted by simply knowing; and that Tanaqui's talent is to record and interpret. Duck points this out to her when he refuses to explain what is happening: "You wouldn't believe me unless you'd worked it all out yourself anyway."[30] Jones rejects the idea that information given is the same thing as information learned or worked out for oneself: to understand the world, she seems to say, requires analysis. If we want to apply this for ourselves in this text, we can learn far more about the future of these characters than is actually told within the covers. Linking *The Crown of Dalemark* to *The Spellcoats*, we can work out that it was those members of the family with the longest and most vivid memories—Duck, Tanaqui, and possibly Gull—who inherited the most from the One and who might themselves be Undying.[31]

Ignorance, therefore, becomes a powerful tool in the creation of immersion. The reader moves from assuming that Tanaqui is omniscient, to the realization that the information we need is distributed among several characters and that we will be able to see them only from the outside, to the realization that a first-person narrative does not confer intimacy. The first-person narrative not only limits the perspective but also deliberately blocks the accumulation of perspective; there are things Tanaqui does not know that her siblings do, and there are also occasions when as narrator and despite her little lectures on the big issues, such as the need to put the One in the fire, she forgets to tell us what she does know, because it does not seem important. She goes to Duck and says, " 'And I want Mother. …' Duck had thought he was the only one who understood."[32] But she does not tell us what it was she had understood, until it manifests.

All of the devices discussed combine with a careful distinction between the world as it is known and the world unknown. To increase our identification with Tanaqui, Jones describes scenes that emphasize the alienness of things that Tanaqui would find alien. There is a distinct difference in the description of the familiar, usually very straightforward and plain (as with the description of Shelling), and the description of the unfamiliar.

> I do not think I like armies. They are about five hundred men, which is quite a large crowd of people, dressed in all sorts of old tough rugcoats, and some in fur or leather, so that they look as brown and scaly as River-mud. Each of these people carries bags and weapons and scythes and pitchforks, all in different ways, so that the army looks like an untidy pincushion, or a patch of dead grass … the army flows off like the River, brown, sluggish, and all one piece. As if people could become like water, all one thing![33]

Things unknown are described in metaphors of the familiar. And as ever with Jones, any description also conveys political information: as Tanaqui inadvertently makes clear, this is not a good army. Elsewhere, newness is frequently dampened rather than exoticized: floating along the swollen river, "All there was to see was tall bare trees, with the green just coming up to the upper boughs and water winding up against their trunks.

They had a chilly, slaty look. I confess I was disappointed. It is often the way when you dream of doing something new: it is not so new after all."[34] But the other trick is to make observation relevant.

> Among the trees and birds, we saw once a great stone house with a tower like a windmill and a few small windows.
>
> Hern was very interested. He said it looked easy to defend and, if it was empty, it would make a good place for us to live.[35]

What is noticed is something that can be used. However, sometimes the apparent perceptiveness is deceptive. Because Jones shows us the gaps in Tanaqui's knowledge, she traps us into assuming that what Tanaqui knows, she knows correctly and completely. But what Tanaqui remembers is not necessarily explanatory; it is simply presented as explanatory. Tanaqui cannot imagine a world in which the Undying have become meaningless, so it does not occur to her to explain precisely what they are or to consider that she does not really know. In these ways the immersion in *The Spellcoats* is built in the interstices of knowledge and assumption.

The idea that a world is created through perspectives is the fulcrum on which the immersion and plot of *Drowned Ammet* turns. The result is a novel that is about politics—in the sense of conspiracies and revolutions— and that is intensely political. Politics, which in the other books of the sequence is an undercurrent, here becomes a character.

Drowned Ammet has two primary strands: the story of Mitt, a child growing up in the streets of Holand, and that of Hildy and Ynen, the children of the youngest son of the heir to the Earldom. As a very young toddler, Mitt is tempted by a scent in the air, and he wanders off. He is brought back by Navis, youngest son of the Earl of Holand. His memories of childhood are good, but when the family bull attacks the rent collector, the family is forced off their land. Mitt, Al, and Milda move to the town, and Al joins the Free Holanders. Al disappears after a raid he arranged goes wrong, and Milda—a rather frivolous woman—brings Mitt up to believe he is a free soul, destined to bring down the Earl in revenge for the death of his father. To this end Mitt joins the Free Holanders with the intention of killing Hadd and blaming it on those members of the Free Holanders he thinks are responsible.

The Holand in which Mitt grows up is controlled by ruthless earls, an aristocracy that might be the result of an invasion (as told in *The*

Spellcoats). The description of Navis, the father of Ynen and Hildy, implies that the rulers look different from the people:

> [... the officer's face, which was very smooth and pale and narrow, with a nose that went out much more sharply than any noses Mitt had known before, and a mouth which Mitt somehow thought of as clean.[36]

Through Navis, Jones informs readers that this land still shows the scars of the invasion described in *The Spellcoats*. Jones refuses to clarify the situation, to tell us whether Kars Adon's people ever fully integrated. The implication is that they integrated in the north, while establishing themselves in the South. Or the North might have become their lands of settlement and the South their lands of fiefdom. Underneath the politics of this fantasy world is an archaeology of invasion forgotten, granting a greater quality of depth than do the recounted histories of so many fantasy novels.

Oppression, too, is described in ways that are small and intimate. After the rent collector is attacked by the bull, he raises Mitt's family's rent beyond their means to pay:

> Next quarter, they sold the mule. Then some furniture. And by that time they were in a vicious circle: the more things they sold from the farm to pay the rent, the less they had to make money with to pay the next quarter's rent, and the more things they had to sell.[37]

Oppression in the South is less a matter of ostentatious punishment than of ensuring ordinary people are too busy trying to survive to rebel. This awareness of the subtlety of oppression is extended to the nuances of revolutionary activity, resistance, and collaboration. The efforts of revolutionaries come in for some sharp comments:

> They [the Free Holanders] would sit in someone's shed or attic, often without a candle even, and Siriol would start by talking of tyranny and oppression. Then Didieo would say that the leaders of the future were coming from below. ... And, sooner or later, Ham would be thumping the table and saying, "We look to the North, we do. Let the North show its hand!"[38]

This is a group that sees itself as an elite yet needs the "ordinary people" to react, but it has little idea how to turn the might of the many into power against the few but well armed. Real resistance is made up of smaller, more practical gestures. When Mitt's assassination attempt on the Earl fails, he panics. As he had never intended to get away, he becomes completely lost in his own mind, and slowly the sense of being a free soul dissipates. As Mitt loses his rigid self-image, he can consider the nuances of behavior in the streets, the subtleties of resistance that do not rely on declaration. When the soldiers arrive, a woman who gives him the small Libby Beer made of wax admits she has seen him but says he has gone away.

> Other people had seen her talking to Mitt, and she dared not deny it. In the old days it used to make him amused and rather scornful, the way even respectable people like these went in dread of Harchad's soldiers.[39]

But the people on the street block the soldiers' view of him, allowing him a moment's respite even though he knows he could not ask them for greater assistance.

> Isn't that Holand people all over! He thought as he ran back round the corner and plunged downhill towards the harbour again. Where they could be, they were kind. But you could never count on it. Yesterday, this kindness had amused him. Now there did not seem to be anything left to laugh at.[40]

Quickly and relatively indirectly we have been given the structure of an oppressive society and a sense of how people survive, how they remain people in the face of attempts to make them slaves.

In the same way, Jones demonstrates the cruelty of Holand, not in the whip but in systems of injustice so embedded that it no longer occurs to people to question them. One of the more shocking stories in this book is the account of Kialan's landing in the South. In *Cart and Cwidder*, although the hanging of Kialan's brother is distressing, we are not asked to confront it directly. In *Drowned Ammet* Jones uses a range of techniques to force us up close. The first, oddly enough, is the dispassionate report.

> The prisoners were questioned. It came out that two of them were nobly born—and not only that, they were the sons of the Earl of Hannart himself. The excitement was feverish. The Earl of Hannart was a wanted man in the South. ...

> The fate of the Northermen was no longer in doubt. They were put on trial for their lives.

Now it is a fact that, if you are brought up to expect something, you expect it. Hildy and Ynen were used to people being tried and hanged almost daily. It did not worry them particularly that the Northmen were going to be hanged. Most of the Palace people said they had asked for it by putting into Holand anyway.[41]

The reportage, by placing it within the ordinariness of everyday journalism, intensifies the dissonance between Hildy and Ynen, and the reader. Hildy and Ynen's acceptance of this cruelty is the route through which Jones shakes the reader more than would a description of the incident—it certainly prevents the voyeurism of the horror novel, which is dependent in part on making death a commodity rather than, as here, a relationship. Jones forces the reader to consider observation as a role. Hildy and Ynen discover that to be a spectator of such events can make one as culpable as to be a participant. Watching Kialan and his brother dragged through the castle, Hildy discovers the terror of the terrorized:

when they were beside the archway, Harchad suddenly turned and kicked the earl's son. Instead of glaring or swearing at Harchad, as Hildy herself or any of the cousins would have done, the boy cringed away and put one arm over his head. "Don't!" he said. "Not any more!" …

She had thought that was the way common people behaved. But that an Earl's son should be brought to behave like that shook her to the core.[42]

When it comes to the hanging, Jones makes effective use of Greek off-stage horrors:

But in some ways a dreadful thing you do not see is more dreadful. Hildy tried not to watch the clock, but she knew the exact moment when the executions started. When a groaning sort of cheer came out of the court-yard, Ynen covered his ears. What made it seem all the more dreadful was that their cousin Irana was carried out screaming, their cousin Harilla actually fainted, and all the rest, boys and girls alike, were sick as dogs.[43]

Hildy learns that her own protests take place within a protected space. She can do and say things because of what she is, not because she is brave. Her reaction to the terrified Earl's son is a central element of Jones's polit-ical critique of fantasy; behavior in Jones's worlds is not determined by social position. Her characters are not permitted to be archetypes, yet at the same time Jones recognizes the power of such archetypes to shape people's expectations of themselves. Hildy has been promised in marriage to the Lord of the Holy Islands, and although she is furious that this has been done without her consent, this situation presents an appealing picture. When Hildy realizes Lithar is "a near imbecile,"

> It was as if her whole future, and her whole past too, fell away and left just herself—a small girl with untidy hair. … She seemed to have founded on them everything which made her into Hildrida and not one of her cousins. … And it was all unreal. It had not even gone: it had just never been.[44]

Hildy's recognition is of the fragility of high politics. Up until this moment her perspective has been that of conventional heroine of the fantasy tale, living on the surface of the world, part of the great events of high politics but relatively insulated from the complexities embodied in a Marxist perspective. In *Drowned Ammet* Jones constructs her world by paying attention to these different layers of politics and contrasting the stories that people tell themselves, with the choices they make each day.

As Hildy rests on the surface of the world, and its high politics, Mitt moves through its political levels and ideological layers and is told and tells different tales of the world, and politics is written on his features and in his actions. When he tastes the water in Ynen's boat, "Mitt … remarked that it was some of the sweetest-tasting water he had ever drunk. Hildy and Ynen were both shuddering at its musty wooden taste."[45] Fishing makes him strong and wiry, but "He did not grow much—probably because he had to work so hard."[46] When he dresses as a palace boy, "he had rather a shock. He looked good, it was true. But there were things in his face one never saw in the smooth faces of wealthy boys—lines which made it look old and shrewd. It was the knowing face of the poor city boys who ran about in the streets, fending for themselves."[47] Poverty has physical consequences; the idea of an unknown king growing fit and strong in poverty is rubbished. This is a portrayal of a political world, not a fantasyland in which poverty happens to caricatures whose role is to demonstrate pity in the hearts of the truly noble or to demonstrate the true worthiness of the child of destiny.

The portrayals of Moril, Hildy, and Mitt rework the idea that a child can be used to comment on an adult world. Nina Bawden reminded readers that one can use "a child's eyes, his innocence and fresh susceptibilities, to challenge accepted assumptions."[48] Jones does use her child characters to challenge the accepted narratives of fantasy, but her children are not wholly innocent. Each has been corrupted by his or her own context, and until those contexts change they are unquestioning of their own culture's assumptions. The more drastic the shift in their experience, the more they are antagonists within the tale, increasingly resisting their culturally "intended" narrative.

Mitt, the individual with the most extreme trajectory, moves from a fairy-tale narrative of the world to one that has been cut and shaped by maturity and experience. Mitt is at first dependent—like most children—on his mother's interpretation of the world. Milda's understanding, however, is romantic and muddled:

> "No, there's no kings anymore," she said. "I've heard they have earls in the North just like we do, only the earls there are all freedom fighters like your Dad was."

> Mitt could not understand how an earl could be anything of the sort. Nor could Milda explain.

> "All I can say is I wish there *were* kings again," she told Mitt. "Earls are no good. Look at Hadd—us poor people are just rent on two legs to him."[49]

One of the most common fallacies of the fantasy is that tyranny can be replaced by a king and that a king magically confers freedom. Milda is given to espouse the illogicality of the argument because it is an illogicality that holds sway in the minds of many. However, the trajectory on which Mitt has been placed is not simply to discover truth or a truth teller but also to acquire critical faculties and discernment.

In *Drowned Ammet* the tension is between those who have a critical sense of the world and those who have a romantic sense. Most of the people Mitt likes have an extremely distorted understanding of the world around them. Only his resented stepfather—Hobin—and his unpleasant father—Al—present him with anything like a useful picture of either the South or the North. Yet Mitt is not a blank slate; he is bright and thoughtful, and he has that inner voice that cannot help but question, even when he is consumed by youthful desire for revolution. This is quite unlike the way genre fantasy—and particularly children's fantasy—is usually written. Within the genre good people give truthful information and bad people lie. Guide figures are often deemed trustworthy because they have told the protagonist they are or because they appear mysterious. Neither Harry Potter (J.K. Rowling), Arthur Penhaligon (Garth Nix), or Taran Wanderer (Lloyd Alexander) ever question his guides' common sense. In contrast, by the end of the novel, Mitt has become critically aware, enough that when the gods (Poor Old Ammet and Libby Beer) do appear, he does not accept their direction without careful thought. As a corollary, if we have been paying attention to Jones's work in general, and to the series in particular, then by *The Crown of Dalemark* we have learned to distrust the voice that speaks to Maewen in that book, because it is the only voice that speaks of prophecy and grandeur.

Thanks to Milda, Mitt begins the adventure with a very distorted sense of self, which has at least two levels. His belief that he is keeping secrets and is training for a special mission allows him to hold himself apart from "the herd" and assume greater knowledge than he actually has. This sense of the inner self is very common in fantasy, and it is usually used to grant the protagonist special intuitive powers. Jones has no truck with this: when Mitt chooses a boat, "he thought he was weighing each one up as he looked at it, but, in fact, all he was doing was comparing them to that blue beauty ten yards away and finding them trash in comparison."[50] Intuition is based on knowledge and learning, and Mitt has enough to recognize a good boat but not enough to consider whether the nicest boat might not also be the one most valued and missed. The other element is Milda's insistence that he is a free soul destined to bring down the Earl and gain revenge for the betrayal of his father; Milda's definition of a free soul is a person with recklessness and an ignorance of fear. The result is that when Mitt does feel fear, he panics, and his sense of freedom slips away as he becomes more fearful and more aware of himself as a person rather than an actor in Milda's fantasy.

> Get hold of yourself! He thought angrily. You're on the run, that's all. People go on the run all the time in this place, I don't know how it keeps happening, but it's like I can't help myself from running. What's gone wrong with me?[51]

The loss of goal and the failure to think beyond the goal has left Mitt without direction. Into that space has come fear and doubt. He now knows that he cannot sell out his fellow Free Holanders, because they have become friends. Mitt begins to recover himself only when he starts to act despite fear, confronting a storm into which the boat has sailed:

He was blind with panic. It was as if he had run away from himself and left the inside of his head empty. ... He had to run after himself, inside his head, and bring himself back with one arm twisted up his back, before he was able to pick up an armful of soaking sail and stagger with it to the hatch.[52]

At the very moment Mitt decides that there is nothing left of his fear-lessness, he begins to learn what bravery is actually about. Later, when he discovers that Al is his father, he also abandons his dreams of glorious revolution and merciless killing, recognizing this freedom for the evil it actually is. But there is little external acknowledgment of this in the book. If anything, we continue to receive indications of the low value that Mitt places on his own life. Mitt has swallowed a status system of deserving-ness. He readily accepts—although resentfully—the rescued Al's domina-tion of the boat and the rewriting of Mitt's adventure first as Al's, then as Hildy and Ynen's. It is thus a surprise when the Islanders leave him a better suit of clothes than they grant Ynen. The change in Mitt takes place inside him. In *The Crown of Dalemark*, this change will help him ascend to greatness, but in *Drowned Ammet* Jones leaves it as an internal, personal issue, increasing the sense of layers within the book. In this way, Mitt is an exemplar of the dialogue that created the reader immersion in the world, moving the reader through different levels of politics as Mitt is told and tells different tales. The world that is Dalemark is built in the sifting of perspectives and the mixing of complexities.

Drowned Ammet and *The Crown of Dalemark* are both told from multiple viewpoints, but the purpose and achievement are different. In *The Crown of Dalemark*, the two viewpoints, Mitt's and Maewen's, contrast the understandings of the world that can be constructed by an insider and an outsider, contrasting in turn the immersive and the portal fantasy narra-tives that run parallel to create the story. However, even that dichotomy does not quite describe the situation, because Mitt also begins the book as an outsider. Both Mitt and Maewen are liminal figures: Maewen because she is from the future, Mitt because he is from the South.

At the beginning of *The Crown of Dalemark*, Mitt is living in the North, a pensioner in the household of Aberath. Navis is living elsewhere —also dependent on the kindness of strangers—while Hildy and Ynen have been sent away to school. Mitt is grateful for the treatment he has received until Earl Keril (father of Kialan) tells him that in return he is to kill a young woman called Noreth. Noreth is believed to be the One's daughter and has declared that she is on a mission to reunite Dalemark, to ride the King's Road to become queen. Keril and his allies are afraid for their own power and of the disturbance this will cause in the South.

Approximately two hundred years in the future, Maewen is sent to spend the summer with her father, Curator of the Palace Museum at Kernsberg. On the journey, an elderly man on the train tries to suborn her, and she is rescued by Wend, who turns out to be her father's assistant. Once in the palace, and having got to know many of the portraits of the age of Amil the Great, Maewen is persuaded (or tricked) by Wend to travel into the past to find out what happened to Noreth, who never reached the end of the King's Road, and who was supplanted in history by Amil. It is history, and the nature of history, that becomes the crux of this novel, as perspective was for *Drowned Ammet*.

Jones has understood that history is about memory. It is not the past; it is the stories we tell about the past. *The Crown of Dalemark* is about the writing of those stories. One of the most revealing moments of the book is the glossary at the very end. Jones does not usually provide glossaries: such things spoil the immersion of a novel by their insistence on explaining, but if one reads the glossary at the back of *The Crown of Dalemark* carefully, it becomes evident that this is not, strictly speaking, Jones's glossary: it is a glossary written from within the world of the novel, reflecting the same gaps in knowledge demonstrated by Maewen's father. Returning briefly to *The Spellcoats*, we can see the same technique used in the penultimate note. *The Spellcoats*, the note tells us, is an unreliable text, for it is a translation of the coats by someone in the present of *The Crown of Dalemark*. The glossary in *The Crown of Dalemark* shares this delicate status.

But within the main text are other places where comments about the historical process serve to deepen the immersion. As Mitt strolls through Aberath, the evidence of rapid change forms a background to his thoughts:

> Mitt trailed his fingers across the cargo hoist and then across the steam plough, and the thing that Alk hoped might one day drive a ship. None of them worked very well, but Alk kept trying. ... Mitt dragged his fingertips across the wet and greasy bolts of the newest machine and shuddered as he imagined himself pushing a knife into a young woman.[53]

As usual with Jones the element of the paragraph that drives the plot is at the end, but it is the offering of landscape that is becoming marvelous, yet is also familiar enough to form a background to anxious thoughts, that constructs the immersion. Elsewhere Jones uses her sense that the societies are complex to create dissonance and estrangement and to rethink what traveling through a portal might really be like. Maewen's focus is rather different from the description of buildings that usually build the lands of portal fantasy:

> Everyone who crowded the street here seemed to have more lines on their faces—or fewer—as if they all worried about different things from those that concerned people in Maewen's own time. This set their faces into quite another shape, like people who spoke a foreign language.[54]

Unlike the heroine of Penelope Lively's *A Stitch in Time*, who sees that "People aren't different on the outside. ... But the inside of their heads must be, because of everything all around them,"[55] Maewen sees the world written on the faces of its inhabitants. Maewen's observations fix her as an outsider, but Jones can use Maewen's status to allow her to notice what Mitt does not because he is part of the scene. The sense of people as different yet understandable assists the creation of the past as a real place. By acknowledging that Maewen can judge only surfaces, Jones knit her contributions tighter into the immersion. Because Maewen questions what she sees, she is actually more, not less reliable.[56]

The world Jones creates is a function of its interacting politics, economics, religion, and culture. As Patrick O'Donovan has observed, "The language of realism and politics is simply a process of mimesis."[57] Magic then becomes one more thread in the weave.

Magic and Meaning in the Dalemark Quartet

The Dalemark quartet might be built in part through its politics and economy, but the way in which Jones argues for the fantastic is also vital. In *Cart and Cwidder*, where magic fits in, the world is central to Moril's growing self-awareness. Similarly, in *The Crown of Dalemark*, Mitt comes to realize that he might live in a world aligned in ways other than those that are understood by his friends and colleagues.

There is a sense that these books are precisely about the state of being that is immersion in the world. *Cart and Cwidder* states this most forcefully with its dialogic plot. At stake in *Cart and Cwidder* is less whether Kialan will get home or whether the North will defeat the South than how Moril will negotiate his place in a world that is both magical and brutally real. Clennen treats the world like a portal fantasy, entering into the persona of The Porter, moving through the surface of the world. Although Clennen is serious about revolution, it still remains a performance. It is only when Moril uses the cwidder to state the truth that the cwidder can bring the world of magic and the world of here and now together.

Central to the construction of Dalemark are the tales of Osfameron and with them a confirmation of the outside–inside structure of the world that runs through its politics. Dalemark has a secret history. One of the fascinating decisions that Jones has made is to retell not the legendary periods of Dalemark's history but to tell that which is prelegendary or postlegendary, so that it is the tale of Amil before Amil is on the throne that we are told, and not the explanation for this "greatness." This is extremely unusual: most authors cannot resist filling in the gaps of their tales even if they choose to make the reality they write a little different from the legend that has been narrated. Jones constructs her legends in the spaces between historical time, which is not unlike the idea of stable and unstable eras in *A Tale of Time City,* in which the unstable eras are defined by the stable ones around them. As we have already seen, this structure is repeated like a Russian doll down to the ground level of Jones's work: the thing we must notice is frequently identified by what is not described or told or explained. The same is true with the way in which the magical enters the text of *The Spellcoats.*

Rather rashly, given that the term is as much a geographical as generic description, I want to suggest that *The Spellcoats* can be read as a magic realist novel, both in the way the magic is handled and in the content and the trajectory of the novel. Although it is difficult to sum up magic realism, three elements can be perceived as intertwining: that magic and one's vulnerability to the supernatural is taken for granted; that civil society is declining, in disorder, or at war; and that the thinning of magic—its possible disappearance from the world—runs parallel to the collapse of that order. Teya Rosenberg uses a slightly different definition in her study of *Black Maria* but agrees that *The Spellcoats* fits the bill.[58] These are stories that do not end with the healing or restoration of the classic novel or the classic genre fantasy. If *The Spellcoats* were an Arthurian fantasy, it would not be about the crowned Arthur and the Round Table but be about the moment when invaders and invasions meet—Rosemary Sutcliff, rather than Thomas Malory. The loss of the fabulous is accompanied with the loss of a civil golden age.

The fabulous in *The Spellcoats* manifests in a range of different ways, but all are in some way casualized. Meetings with fabulous people become part of the everyday. When Robin, Tanaqui, Hern, and Duck meet Tanamil, he seems a part of the world:

> He seemed—how shall I say?—wet with haste or damp with the open air. His skin was ruddier than ours. Otherwise, he was not so different, except that he was grown up and four of us were not. ... His rugcoat was an old, faded red one, not unlike the one my father went to war in, very plain and wet with dew.[59]

Tanamil is ordinary, and the more so because the way he turns the war-traumatized Gull into a small statue emphasizes he is a powerful magician. Magicians fit within the worldview of Tanaqui and her siblings. They are not extraordinary, not to be marveled at. The explanation that Tanamil gives, that Gull's soul could be used to "drain off the souls of his soul, as it were and draw through it the soul of his forebears,"[60] is also relentlessly of their world. Only Hern rejects this acceptance of the (super)natural, and it is he who will eventually be in charge of the new world order, the thinned world in which the Undying are Unbound and retreat further from the world.

The presence of gods is similarly absorbed into the texture of Tanaqui's world; the burning of the One is normal, "It is a peculiar habit, but he is the One, and not like the other Undying,"[61] yet it emphasizes its importance to a greater degree than pomposity might. The same is true in Jones's creation of the supernatural mood:

> The gulls followed us. They made a noise like a sharp misery, and I was afraid of them. ... When they floated on the River, they seemed lighter than was natural. I was not sure they were really birds. There was a new light in the air, bleached and chalky, like bones or Hern's eyes when he is angry, and the gulls wheeled about in it.[62]

In fantasy there is a tradition that one can sense evil, but here Jones leaves it open; there is a chance that it is simply the stillness after a flood that is unnerving Tanaqui. The possibility of the dual reading intensifies the sense of the fantastic inherent in every element of the world. Later the possibility of the mundane makes the moment of recognition more frightening:

We saw what seemed to be a small boat being poled across in front of the obstruction, just at the limit of what we could see. It went slowly, but we could barely see it all the same. We saw the fair heads of Heathens in it. One was poling, the other stooping and flinging things from the water into the boat. They had gone, slowly to the right, before we could see more.

We knew—though I do not know how—that we had seen something terrible.[63]

Tanaqui, Hern, and Duck recognize less what is happening—that souls are being captured—than that there is something different about them, about the way they perceive the world. This realization is repeated for all of them individually, but each time described to the reader in incomplete terms. Duck pipes them through the soul net and reveals, "Everything goes away when I play. ... You know, I think I shall be a magician when I grow up. I shall be a better one than Kankredin."[64] The insouciance of the child emphasizes the naturalness of being a magic worker.

The real power of Jones's style is revealed at the end: so often, having invested the landscape with grandeur, the writers of fantasy have nowhere to go. Because *The Spellcoats* depicts magic as everyday, Jones has left herself room to indicate the impact of something else. When Kankredin marshals his power and draws on the One,

The wave is not transparent, nor yet quite solid. It is green-black, stinking of River rottenness, with trees and beams and the greater part of a bridge, and many other things, carried along in it and glimpsed from time to time. But inside it, gleaming out through the dark water, we could see terrible shapes, staring eyes and glances of bared teeth.[65]

The novel ends with the shadow of the One leaning across the loom and giving the first direct order of the novel: "Weave this, Granddaughter," he seems to say, "and use the thread I gave you. It was Cenblith's."[66] Jones argues for the power of the quiet voice, in the restrained depictions of the One in contrast with the roar and rage of the pretender.

One of the oddities of the Dalemark sequence is that with the exception of *The Spellcoats*, there is not much magic. *Cart and Cwidder* has only one incidence of clear magic (the other events can be described as hypnosis), whereas many of the events of *The Crown of Dalemark* (the Undying, the time traveling, the genetically keyed magical items) have a scientific explanation. The result is a world in which the possibility of magic is accepted but not expected; the world of Dalemark is essentially secular and unbelieving. As Al comments in *Drowned Ammet,*

> "When I was in Waywold, they had a saying there that Holanders kept gods they didn't own to. And that's true. I bet you didn't know they were gods one time."[67]

Al has a point; the gods in Dalemark seem to exist at the subconscious level. Absent are the formal priesthoods or continual genuflecting of genre fantasy. But the gods are real, and the Undying fear being known too well. Hern of *The Spellcoats* avoids having his image rendered, and we finally come to understand that so too did Amil, choosing instead to be represented in the form we might recognize as "Old Ammet in summer." Although doubt exists, it is a doubt that depends on belief. It is this construction that allows Jones to write such apparently smooth segues into a magical world, taking us from a description of a storm to the presence of a god in barely a breath.

> Great lumps of water loomed and fell, smashing across the bows, banging down on the cabin, thundering over Hildy and Mitt, until they were as bruised as they were wet, and went fizzing and boiling away behind.

> The man in the bows with the flying fair hair understood their danger and leant into the wave, dragging at *Wind's Road's* forward rigging. *Wind's Road* did not want to come, but Mitt thought the man dragged her round by main force.[68]

Important here is the definite article at the beginning of the second paragraph and the way in which none of the children question his presence during the incident, but do question that of the horses:

> He and Hildy got quite used to seeing him, up there in the bows. ... But the horses bothered them both. ...They knew they were imagining things. Sailors told stories of horses playing round doomed ships, frolicking at the death of mortals.[69]

Libby Beer appears too, a red-gold-haired woman kneeling at the stern, who appears to be handing Hildy rope at the same time as assisting Mitt on the tiller and pointing Ynen to the locker where the pump was kept.

Only, when it is all over, do they discuss what has happened and acknowledge that they were caught in the moment of the fantastic.

> "Hey, look," said Mitt. "We haven't all run mad, have we?"

> "Of course not," said Ynen. "Libby Beer was sitting behind you, helping you sail her, and Old Ammet was standing in the bows stopping her sinking and keeping the horses off. I saw both of them."[70]

In *The Crown of Dalemark,* Jones manipulates Mitt's acceptance of the gods to accentuate his sense that the North is strange. At least in the early sections of the novel, Jones positions Mitt so that he segues into the fantastic almost without noticing; it is the return to reality that is the shock.

> It was a fine big river, wider than any Mitt had seen, and the way it rolled quietly among all those reeds and willow trees suggested that it might be pretty deep. Mitt hoped Rith knew what he was talking about when he said they could ford it.[71]

But two pages later, "There was no wide rolling river any more. Rith was on his way down to a sunken crater in the hillside that was choked with small oak trees. Mitt could hear water rushing among the trees."[72] Repeatedly, Mitt experiences the magical first, the mundane second. It is the real that surprises Mitt. One consequence is that despite Mitt's natural skepticism, he increasingly assumes the supernatural. As a shadow advances on the gates at the ceremony of the Midsummer festival, Mitt jumps to the conclusion that something really is coming in, and he is disappointed when he sees is the singer Hestefan. One clue to the change in Mitt's position is the affect of Moril's playing. When Noreth calls for people to accompany her on the King's Road, Moril plays Osfameron's cwidder. The next day Moril reveals he did it to put off those without serious intent. What Mitt does not recognize is not just that he does not seem to have been affected but also that he was vividly aware of the cwidder's power at work. Like Moril, he was inside the power, not outside it. When the power does affect Mitt, it sweeps up Moril too, taking them to an island in a River that no longer is. The others can see the river, but cannot enter it. In turn, Mitt and Moril are barely conscious of their watching companions.

Mitt and Moril get out of the river by working out the truth of what they want: first their crushes on Maewen, and then their feelings about the South and the North, Moril's fear and hatred, and Mitt's awareness that the North is poor and that what is needed is unity. "Noreth wants to do that, so I'm for her. Very dull and political."[73] Moril also likes the idea that Singers should have a royal academy. In other words, neither of these two is inspired in the conventional quest context; instead, each has a desire that is contiguous with Noreth's mission. Part of these realizations, however, connects to where they are; Moril works out that they have not time traveled. Rather they are in "the place in the stories where the One really is. 'I *think*,' Moril said doubtfully. 'It's hard to explain, but the other world the cwidder moves in is the place where the stories are.' "[74]

This sense that fantasy is in story and in the tale telling ripples through the book. Mitt sees

> the green roads ... winding away into the past ... the way they turned back and forth through history, up to the present, into the place where he lay in such danger, and then went winding and snaking on into the far future. The Undying went walking on, taking the roads through time, and history went with them, ignoring them, forgetting the Undying were making history.[75]

When the group encounters Cennoreth the Weaver, once Tanaqui, sister of Duck/Mallard/Wend and mother of Manaliabrid, Maewen's deception is discovered because she is not a part of the story being told.[76]

The fantastic in the Dalemark quartet is always grounded in a bringing together of what is with what might be. The archaeology of Dalemark is created through the overlaying of cities and times in Kernsberg, continually emphasizing that a fully immersed world is holographic. To feel real, it must have layers we never see to support those we do. When Moril, Maewen, Mitt, and Kialan go in search of the crown, Moril uses the tales of the old Kernsburg, the presence of the small waystone in the "here and now" and the truth of the great waystone in Maewen's time, to create a route to a pocket universe in which Hern, King of Kernsberg, sits waiting like King Arthur, not to rescue the land but to crown a new king. Hern's magic too is tied to story. The story he asked for was to present the crown to the new king,[77] but as with all stories, that which is not asked for precisely can be interpreted in many ways, and Hern, who had been careful to avoid all image making in case he should prove to be of the Undying, has been trapped by his carelessly worded request.

The penultimate story that is then told is one of magic and honor (the final story is Maewen's defeat of Kankredin in her "present"). Unable to work out who should be king, Hern asks instead, "Who will be Amil?"[78] Who, in effect, will play the role in a story that has already been written? Hern forces them to consider the advice they might give a king, allowing Mitt to tell his own story of kingship and so talk himself into the role. And as with all narratives within this text, this is then embedded in the larger, as Mitt chooses to take the name Amil and with it the responsibility to seek out the pieces of Kankredin (the evil mage of *The Spellcoats*) that have floated through space and time. Mitt, the outsider, has become the ultimate insider, moving through the concentric circles that construct the world. As with Jamie in *The Homeward Bounders,* one reading of this novel is that Mitt eventually uses his outsider–portal status to construct a safe world in which others can remain immersed.

CHAPTER 6
MAKING THE MUNDANE FANTASTIC, OR LIMINAL FANTASY

In chapter 1 I discussed the degree to which *Wilkins' Tooth* (*Witch's Business* in the United States) demonstrated a compromise with a number of forms, in particular the attempt to accede to the demands of the 1970s and 1980s that children's books be more realistic. These demands did not go away, and Diana Wynne Jones responded by producing such books as *The Ogre Downstairs* and *Dogsbody*, which took on current issues such as blended families, racism, and bullying. However, in later books the ostentatious issues disappear from view. In search of a compromise with realism, Jones turned instead to technique, and to making the mundane fantastical.

Introducing fantasy into the real world in a demotic, matter-of-fact voice is a technique pioneered by Edith Nesbit, the author with whom Jones is most frequently compared. Nesbit, and imitators such as Edward Eager, sought to make magic only as strange as the world is strange to children, and it was to be dealt with in the same matter-of-fact way. Jones clearly works in this tradition, but she adds an extra twist. Although Nesbit's and Eager's children accept magic coolly and calmly—reflecting the curiosity, wonder, and acceptance that is the child's take on the unfamiliar world he or she is growing into[1]—they are clearly aware that magic is something unusual and not of this world. In many of Jones's books, the status of the world and of the magic are held in doubt for substantial periods of time, while the child characters reinforce this doubt by their often bizarre choice of what to believe.[2] In Jones's worlds the dividing line between magic and reality is deliberately blurred, unassailable by logic. Charles Butler puts it best: "It is more like mapping a complicated sea-coast, full of inlets and pools and crags, increasing in complexity the more closely one looks."[3]

The intrusion of the fantastic into the mundane world can leave the real world looking bleached. In Jones's work the much more contentious relationship of the mundane and the fantastical results in an enhancement of the mundane. The fantastic does not so much intrude in these books as act as the butter in puff pastry that creates the complex texture of the whole. "The back of the mind, the corner of the eye, the tip of the tongue: these are the places that fascinate her."[4] Fantasy that holds the fantastic in doubt, which leaves us uncertain as to the status of the fantastic, I have described elsewhere as *liminal* fantasy.[5] The liminal fantasy relies on one of two techniques deployed either separately or in conjunction: *irony* and *equipoise*. Each relies on a sense of unease and estrangement that permeates its text, and each gives the ordinary an air of the fantastical.

Equipoise is that moment of balance between mimesis and the fantastic. What is happening, and whether it is magical, is held in doubt. The mundane is made fantastical as the reader is taken repeatedly to the edge of the portal without ever being allowed to cross. We gain glimpses of the fantastic without ever quite seeing it in focus. In the story of equipoise, we are held in that moment of expectation, waiting for magic to happen, but the moment of doubt relies in part on our knowledge of possibilities.[6] The reason that this is not synonymous with Todorov's notion of the uncanny is because the reader expects the fantastic.[7] *Irony* is about what we actually do see, and the distance between how the protagonist and reader choose to interpret this. In the mode of liminal fantasy, although the fantastic permeates the book the establishing shots insist that this is our world: a superficial reading suggests that this is a fairly standard intrusive fantasy in which magic intrudes to cause chaos. What distinguishes it from the intrusive fantasy is that our identification of what is wrong or fantastical can differ from that of the protagonist. It is a form of fantasy that estranges the reader from the fantastic as understood by the protagonist.

Although none of Jones's novels are fully liminal in that all her work—even *Fire and Hemlock*—eventually resolves in favor of a shared reader–protagonist understanding of the fantastic, many of them manipulate irony and equipoise to challenge the presumptions behind the concept of realist fiction and to reverse some of the conventional patterns of fantasy.[8] For example, in *Eight Days of Luke, Black Maria,* and *Archer's Goon,* the children do not use the knowledge they gain dealing with the fantastic to resolve their family problems; instead they use their knowledge of the family to negotiate with the fantastic.

Although these three books manipulate the moment of equipoise and doubt, each moves toward an acknowledgment that magic does exist and resolves this moment in clear favor of the fantastic. In these books magic is clearly happening: Luke is a god, Aunt Maria can turn people into wolves, and there really are seven powerful beings farming Howard's town. The books stand out, however, for the degree to which Jones normalizes the fantastic within the everyday. This allows her to focus on the ways in which magic is manipulated rather than on its existence.

Each of the three books has an urban(ish) everyday setting (small town rather than city) and can be encompassed by the label "urban fantasy." Typically this label has been used to imply that an author rejects Tolkien as a model and has some claim to making fantasy relevant. Brian Attebery characterized the form as constructing "settings that seem to be real, familiar, present day places, except that they contain the magical characters and impossible events of fantasy."[9] But in these three books, place is more significant than Attebery's statement implies, because place emphasizes the permeability of the world. Jones uses her everyday settings as maps of fantasyland within which are marked off territories and safe spaces, while the simultaneous interlocking of the mundane and the magical seeps through into the hindbrain of the reader.

Jones begins *Eight Days of Luke* with a reversal: challenging all the conventions of children's fiction, and fantasy fiction in particular. *Eight Days of Luke* begins not with a going away but with a coming home, which offers a direct challenge to the increasing sense in post-1970 children's fiction that danger lies in the outside world.[10] Although there are a number of movements through portals into clearly fantastical worlds in this novel, the most significant transition has already taken place, from the normal world of school to the disorienting and dissonant world of a dysfunctional home life.[11] This reversal is repeated in *Archer's Goon,* in which Howard returns from school to find that the sanctuary of home has been invaded. There is a Goon sitting at the kitchen table. In addition, in *Archer's Goon* what is on the other side of the portal frequently looks more normal than what is happening in our own world. *Black Maria* works differently, as

Mig, Chris, and their mother Betty travel to Cranbury to look after their father's Aunt Maria after his death, but at stake in *Black Maria* is where home is. One of Aunt Maria's aims is to assimilate the family into Cranbury: the "home" as defined by Aunt Maria is an unsafe space.

In all three novels the geography of the land in which the characters exist turns out to be more complicated than is at first apparent. David in *Eight Days of Luke* releases a god within the nowhere space at the end of the garden (mapping onto the nowhere space of the gods' prison). Mig realizes that Cranbury is constrained within a supernormality that renders the place both less and more magical than the outside world, and Howard discovers that his town is divided into *ancien régime* fiefdoms. In each case normality is undercut with dissonance that must be accepted at face value if the characters are to negotiate the problems that surround them.

Jones takes advantage of the extent to which we expect fantasy to have rules, and yet be able to live calmly in a world in which the rules are forever being broken. *Eight Days of Luke, Black Maria,* and *Archer's Goon* are ironic because the fantastic is often portrayed as the most sensible and logical aspect of the character's situation, while in contrast the mundane, everyday world is described as if from afar, noticed for the first time and in often baroque detail. As the rules of the everyday break down, the rules of the fantastical become more evident or understandable.

The awareness of the fantastic builds slowly in *Eight Days of Luke,* but the construction of the fantastic world within the mundane is there from the beginning. The story is straightforward: David is miserable because he has to live with cousins who do not care for him. David's home is described in ways familiar to the fairy-tale reader:

> Unlike most boys, David dreaded the holidays. His parents were dead and he lived with his Great-Aunt Dot, Great Uncle Bernard, their son Cousin Ronald and Cousin Ronald's wife Astrid; and all these four people insisted that he should be grateful for the way they looked after him.[12]

The paragraph presents David's emotional position, the familial relationships that will be at the heart of the novel, and the sense of wrongness that John Clute identified as the starting point of the fantasy novel, the sense that the world has thinned and that things are not as they should be. In *Eight Days of Luke,* this wrongness is centered on the thinning of the family and of what family means. This is David's real family, but none of the adults care for David, and in the final analysis only Astrid, not a blood relation, loves him. This small but telling subversion of the political assumptions of the fairy tale provides a sense of the weird, a cutting across of our expectations. But we are never told that this family is peculiar. David is aware that they are different, but he is only dimly aware of this difference from the stories of his school friends. He is so fully immersed in his world that his understanding of the wider world and himself is utterly bound by the rules of the pocket universe that is his home life.

The construction of the strange in *Eight Days of Luke* continues to play on our expectations of what is, or is not, safe and, paralleling that, what is or is not vulnerable to the fantastic. In *Eight Days of Luke,* David's home life is awful not precisely because it is cruel but because the rules are arbitrary and obey a quite different code from the real world. In the house he must wear a suit, his hair must be short, he must demonstrate a gratitude he does not feel, and what he says is continually questioned. Instead of the outside world functioning as the strange place to be negotiated, it is the inside world in which he is the intruder. Compounding the problem is that everything that David does is imbued with a motive by others. This is not unlike the dissonance Alice experiences in her conversations with the Cheshire Cat or the Red Queen and is written with a similar intention, to demonstrate the alienness of the adult world to the child. The mundane issue of time spent at home is also placed in doubt, the expectations reversed. In children's fantasy novels time goes faster in the otherworld than it does in ours, and when David returns from school he discovers that no one is expecting him. Time has run at a different rate: it is not yet the school holidays in the minds of his guardians, and David should not have grown. In contrast to all this, the outside, when David finally reaches it, is refreshingly normal.

> There was a tall hedge there. Behind the hedge was a steamy compost heap with baby marrows growing on it and a spade stuck in the compost, and a strip of gravely ground where Cousin Ronald always meant to have a carpentry shed.[13]

Yet this normality is described in detail as if David has never seen it before. It is not simply a place, it is a polder,[14] a patch of ground that feels safe, shielded from malevolence. And it is against this background of perceived normality in chapter 2 that David, miserable with the realization that he is unwanted, experiments with cursing.

> For the next twenty minutes or so, David walked up and down the hot gravel, from compost to wall and back, muttering words and mouthing what he hoped were strange oaths. When he found a combination that sounded good, he stood still and recited it aloud. Each time he felt secretly a little foolish, because he knew perfectly well it had made no difference to his relations at all.[15]

This is magic as a game of pretend, and the inference is quite deliberate because for at least a third of the book, David will insist that there is a real or metaphorical explanation for everything that then happens, and Jones, the narrator, colludes in this. Chapter 2 ends with David's throwing a handful of compost at the wall: "As soon as he did that, the wall started to fall down."[16] Chapter three begins, "It was like an earthquake. ... The wavering and heaving were to some extent under David's feet, and the compost shifted and quivered like quicksand."[17] The three sentences signal moments of transfiguration at which we cross the boundaries from the mundane world in which things are *like* earthquakes to one in which we accept that this *is* an earthquake. And it is because this transmutation takes place over something relatively mundane, and in the apparently safe and shielded space of the garden, that we accept the two events of this chapter—the appearance of the snakes and the appearance of Luke—as of equal fantastical import.

As the wall falls it is described in intense, almost baroque detail: "He could hear the bricks grinding as they swayed up and down. The top of the wall made a crazy outline against the blue sky, wagging up and down, with bricks coming loose and lifting, then banging back into place again."[18] In contrast the snakes are described in a flatter style: "a very large snake indeed," "with a head as flat as Mrs. Thirsk's feet, a forked flicking tongue, and yellow eyes which seemed to be made of skin."[19] The concentration on the actualities of the snake make it more real than the undulating motions of the wall, and under the cover of this false air of reality, Jones sneaks in Luke. David, distracted from the snakes by Luke and from the origin of Luke by the snakes, and from both by the "hideous mess" that is the wall, accepts Luke as a part of his world. Even Luke's attempt to explain and his cheerful chatter about his captivity are viewed with skepticism by David, who "after all, had been there to see nothing but flames and snakes."[20] We are continually presented with the recognizable fantastic, only for the protagonist to attempt to encompass it within a mundane understanding.

Elsewhere, the preservation of the mundane world is achieved by burying crucial information. David takes the bus up Wednesday Hill, but only at the conclusion of the novel are we sure that the threatening Mr. Wedding is Woden, the titular god.[21] David comments on the oddness of Mr. Chew's appearing on a Tuesday, and Luke mutters that it would be odd if he had not appeared.[22] And David resolutely ignores the hints with which he is provided: the indeterminacy of Luke's age and the burn that heals rapidly, the scorched creeper and the power of a flame to summon Luke. David refuses the fantastic because he depends on Luke's presence fitting into but changing his boring, ordinary life. His success at summoning Luke while shopping with Astrid is the moment of transition, and it is important to the form of the book because it is not marked. There is no moment of awe, wonder, or surprise. One moment Luke is not there, and the next he is strolling beside David, for whom "Life was suddenly quite different."[23] That David does not comment on this is a moment of irony. This time David acknowledges to himself that what is happening is magical, but he shows no surprise that it is possible. He has accepted the fantastic into his worldview and what proceeds, proceeds from this position.

By refusing to mark the moments of magic, redirecting our gaze with either rival events or the insouciance of David or Luke, Jones constructs doubt and unease and makes the boundaries of the fantastic indistinct. When she does fix our interpretation, and makes a moment that is recognized by David as fantastical (when Luke starts a fire), the boundaries of the real and unreal worlds become clearer and more permeable. Increasingly, Jones allows a segue between the mundane and the fantastical and demands that the reader accept that David has encompassed both within one frame of reference, while seeming to exist within our world, a world in which the fantastic should be commented on and marveled at. Karen Sands O'Connor describes these moments in *Eight Days of Luke* as "jarring."[24] But it is precisely the way in which these elements do not jar and how Jones achieves this that is so notable about the book and the techniques Jones develops.

Three scenes are particularly telling—the trip to Wallsey with Mr. Wedding, the visit of the false Mr. and Mrs. Fry, and the scene in Valhalla—all of which succeed in maintaining visual metaphors while resisting the full move into fantasy (as in the confrontation with the three crones or the retrieval of Thor's hammer). This results in scenes in which the mundane and the fantastical occupy the same imaginative space.

Mr. Wedding appears as a friend of the despised family yet at the same time wears "the kind of face he [David] could not help liking."[25] David's family is one that has denied him anything pleasurable yet is willing to see him taken out for lunch by a stranger. Inclined to protest whatever his family directs, David is baffled that he wishes to go. Jones buries the initial dissonance of the fantastic in David's conflicted feelings—his unease at the sense of the lurking magic is transmuted here into unease at the social scenario. The trip to Wallsey is shaped by the ordinary and the urban. Mr. Wedding drives David through the streets of Ashbury, and both he and we are circumscribed by the fact that he "had heard of the place, of course, but he had no real idea where it was or what it was like."[26] As in his judgment of Mr. Wedding, David's ability to be suspicious is limited by his ignorance and by his companion's supernatural influence, that is exerted by appealing to what Luke has already indicated is David's weak point: his response to friendliness. It is within the time frame of this friendliness, in "transitions so subtle that the characters could not say at what instant the shift had happened,"[27] that the transition into a fantasy-land takes place.

> While he was describing the fifth wicket, which had really been something of an accident, David noticed that the countryside he could see from the windows of the car was strange and wild. There were steep hills, very green grass and waterfalls dashing down past pine-trees. It reminded him a little of Norway.[28]

But before David can ask where they are, he is distracted partly by Mr. Wedding and partly by the sight of the bridge. The bridge is a liminal object: is it made of iron, or are the rainbows a function not of sun refraction but of magic? The image is wondrous, "a spider web of girders," but any close reading of that text reveals that this is an utterly mundane place. It is the language that makes the bridge seem magical. We are told nothing other than what it is. The magic, if it is there, is in part a function of how we choose to read the placing of words such as "misty" and "green island in a lake."[29] Jones here is playing to our emotional resonance with fantasy and myth, and also with the wonders of the manufactured world. Francis Spufford remembers the delight of discovering that "the borders between the worlds could be vested in modern stuff: that the green and white signs on motorways counting down the miles to London could suddenly show the distance to Gramarye or Logres."[30] But Jones does not actually describe anything fantastical; it is all done by implication. Neither did she do so when Mr. Wedding threatens David with the news that although he is in Wallsey, it is not where David thinks it is. We the readers and David, the protagonist can make guesses, but we are not told, and the possibility remains open that this is simply not Wallsey, that Mr. Wedding is lying, or that the reason David will not be found is that Mr. Wedding did not tell the family where they were going (the decision was taken in the car).[31§] Jones loads her prose to incline us to the fantastical interpretation. Not until the raven speaks on page 79—and before Mr. Wedding makes the statement about Wallsey—can we be sure that there is truly something fantastical occurring, and it is the speech of the raven that is the first fantastic incident fully acknowledged by David. By the time it is introduced, however, the fantasticating of the mundane makes it less surprising to the reader than it is to David. We, after all, have read that descriptive language of his surroundings that induces the expectation of magic. He has not.

By the time the Frys arrive, David has accepted that magic will happen, and he and we know that we are in a fantasy. But even so, Jones is determined to present magic as something that jars because of its impression on the mundane rather than because of its effect. Like the bridge, the Frys stand out because of their intensity and the way in which the light and people's attention refract in their presence. Jones links their impression on the family with that of a movie star, and because it is explainable, it can be encompassed within the day-to-day. Only very slowly does David notice that they have slid into a fantastic space, that once the family is gone and the Frys have captured Luke, "he had a feeling that they were no longer in Uncle Bernard's dining room but somewhere high up and out of doors."[32] Jones refuses to clarify the position: are we elsewhere or aren't we? But as Luke is interrogated and his potential punishment is made more specific, again the real and the unreal appear to exist side by side. For the next two pages the conversation around Luke's alleged crime refuses to state the myth in which the book is rooted. Jones forces us to recreate the story; no one explains to us the correspondences between Mr. Wedding and Wodin, between Chew and Tiu or the Frys, Frey and Freya, or even between Luke and Loki the god of fire. Luke's identity is permanently withheld. For a few readers all of this is recognizable; they will know more than David. For most readers, however, Jones's act of refusal lends the tension of ambiguity; the continual sense that there is more to the tale than is being spoken.

This refusal to speak myth out loud is crucial to the most ironic of the three scenes: when David descends into a Valhalla that seems to be located in an amusement arcade at the end of the pier.[33] David has been sent to find the clue to the location of an object, the nature of which he is not allowed to know—it is actually Thor's hammer. The scene on the pier, in Valhalla, insists that the magic and the mundane coexist. The amusement arcade is Valhalla, as Valhalla is simultaneously the amusement arcade; this overlaid location is reinforced by such mundane matters as the amusement arcade's male-only space paralleling the hall of the heroes. Like the room at home, the presence of magic is indicated primarily by the shift in proportions. In place of the pier, David sees "carved pillars, painted recesses and the glitter of golden things on either side,"[34] but the end of the hall is "still opened into the fairground."[35] The magic retains its connection to the mundane world, and the scene in which David, his friend Allan, and Cousin Ronald run the gauntlet gains its resonance from the parallels in the real world of school and in the treatment meted out to David by the family.

With each of these scenes we are taken slightly further into the fantasy world and the idea that the fantastic is, at root, normal and relevant. The result is that the sequences with the crones and later with Brunhilda do not jar because we have been taught to accept that the fantastic is around the corner, not separate from us but living alongside us. However, one very unusual element of this book is that although David participates in the magic, he is never fully part of it—even his eventual recapture of the hammer is essentially mundane. David, in all of this, is a tool or sidekick. It is actually Loki's story.

In *Black Maria* the balance shifts. *Black Maria* moves us much closer to the ironic fantasy. Mig, Chris, and their mother Betty find themselves in the town of Cranbury, forced to care for their dead father's Aunt Maria. As the plot unfolds we discover that the town of Cranbury is divided along sex lines, with different powers held by men and women. Currently the women led by Aunt Maria are in charge, the men seem curiously helpless, and there are no children, except for those in the orphanage on the hill. The perspective is rather different from the one we occupied in *Eight Days of Luke*. *Black Maria* is told in the first person through Mig's diary. This device is deployed in children's fiction mostly to confer omniscience, but instead Jones uses Mig and the first-person position to shape the way we perceive Cranbury, the events of the book, and the fantastic.

Overt manifestations of the fantastic are relatively rare in *Black Maria*—the people turned into wolves, the enchanted cats, and the burying of Anthony Green—and as seen through Mig's eyes they are encompassed within the ordinary. Chris and Mig easily accept the appearance of magic, and they are mostly interested in its rules or whom it has been worked on. So although Chris and Mig react to the appearance of a ghost in Chris's room, neither Chris nor Mig are surprised that ghosts exist. They are interested in the effect of a ghost. Mig notes that Chris has at least four versions of when he registered that the presence in his room was a manifestation: that there is something about ghosts that makes them hard to pin down, mentally as well as physically. Miss Phelps, Aunt Maria's enemy, is able to argue that the manifestation is not a ghost because it does not act like one (it behaves differently each time). Shock and dissonance is reserved for the discovery that Mig and Chris's father is alive. This threatens to disrupt their lives far more than magic.

Irony in *Black Maria* is centered on what people will and will not acknowledge both in the reality of the world and in its magic. People are willing to acknowledge that power is there and that some people wield it. They are even willing to acknowledge that it is used to punish people, but they do not acknowledge what precisely is done or to whom it is done, and most of all they frequently refuse to recognize the consequences of what has been done. Thus, after Aunt Maria turns Chris into a wolf, her colleagues (the Mrs. Urs) conspire to act as if he never had been there, just as Mig's father is similarly written out of the family story and is himself willing to write out of his own story the existence of his family. This affects even our heroes. Mig, and therefore to a degree the reader, accepts completely that Aunt Maria has the capacity to turn people into animals, but Mig is horrified that it is Chris who has been so turned. This shapes the way in which the other wolf's death is described: no one pities Naomi-wolf; they express only relief that it is Naomi-not-Chris-wolf. That Mig is aware of, and disconcerted by, this insouciant acceptance is part of the dynamic of the family and power relationships within the novel.

Mig's retelling of the story is in part structured around her failure to get her mother's attention and the dissonance between what she sees and knows, and what Betty will allow to be knowable. Betty displays two distinct reactions. The first reaction is part of Aunt Maria's spell casting. Betty continually rationalizes the fantastic events around her and is encouraged to believe (by Aunt Maria) that Chris was left behind in London rather than that he is missing. As is discussed further in chapter 7, this kind of magic rests on the cusp of what might be ordinary coercion, or, as Charles Butler argues, "We have been unsure whether we are dealing with a metaphor (magic standing in for manipulative behaviour) or a metonym (talk of magic being a representative *aspect* of manipulative behaviour)."[36]

The result of Aunt Maria's talk spell is that Mig is isolated as if her mother were not there, recreating the common trope of the fantastic that deprives children of the physical presence of adults. But it is how Betty reacts when she is released from the spell that is particularly interesting, because even then Betty proceeds in a way that normalizes the magic. Faced with the possibility of time travel, she chooses to focus her concerns on its logic rather than its existence, in a way not dissimilar to Mig's reaction to the ghost. Both Betty and Mig, in fact, seem determined to make the magic mundane and comprehensible, subject to rules.

This desire to make magic mundane is part of the divide between men and women in Cranbury. The wild magic of Anthony Green argues that there is no such thing as normal or that, if there is, it cannot exist as a standard alongside freedom. It also reverses the conventional structures of fantasy that assume women's magic to be wild and men's ordered. In *Black Maria* men and women are both subject to the desire to control that which should permeate the landscape.

It is the insistence on normality that is most disruptive and threatening. Cranbury is relentlessly normal. The village has no chip shop and no entertainment, the men are dull, and the children in the orphanage are dull. Men and women have been completely separated.[37] What is fantastical about this place is the way it has been drained of the magic of the everyday. In contrast the weirdness of Loupe wood comes to be reassuring: its strangeness indicates its safety and its status as a place of power and protection.

Aunt Maria's spell-casting is designed to drain the wildness, the mystique, and the glamour from the fantastic. Aunt Maria wields her power through conversation. The main spell is "just talk," but it is talk that bores into the head, "working away underneath the talk, putting all sorts of things into people's minds and tying their thoughts into the right shape."[38] This means of spell-casting is reliant on compliance, on people's wanting to be normal and wanting their lives to be mundane. This is made particularly clear when Betty explains why she does not regret the end of her marriage to Greg. Both Greg and Nathaniel Phelps prefer the comfort of rules to a consideration of consequences and are therefore susceptible to the power of the fantastic as constructed in *Black Maria*. But even Betty, whose rejection of a rule-bound existence is a source of conflict with Greg, can be controlled by the desire that events be explicable. When Mig tries to tell her mother about Chris, each line of response is perfectly logical as a reply to Meg's immediate comment. I repeat here only the speech:

Mig: *Chris-is-a-wolf.* Understand? That's why he's not here. He hasn't been here since yesterday afternoon.

Mum: Don't be silly Mig. ... He took a packed lunch and went out.

Mig: When did he take a packed lunch?

Mum: It must have been while we were getting Auntie dressed. ... He used all the white bread up.

Mig: No. *We* finished the white loaf at breakfast.

Mum: Then he must have taken brown bread.[39]

Betty's logic works fine for any two consecutive phrases. Once they are collated, however, we are in a fantasy world in which the chain of logic running through the conversation has been severed. Disruption and dissonance are embedded within the conversation. This kind of double-dealing of belief and logic switch underpins *Black Maria*, because if there is a moment of recognition in this novel, it is Mig's recognition that Aunt Maria's trick is to allow people to find their own means of reconciling the distasteful. The fantastic is about what we can allow ourselves to believe from the mass of illogical evidence: it is the tension between what Mig sees, what is emotionally acceptable to see, and what she is told she sees that is the fulcrum on which *Black Maria* balances. Here it is not just that the fantastic exists within the mundane setting of a rather boring village but also that the mundane becomes the very quality of the fantastic that is most prized.

So far we have seen two different relations of the mundane to the fantastical, both of which depend on the absorption into the everyday of elements that are clearly fantastical. In *Eight Days of Luke,* the magic is around us but is unperceived and is met either as an intruder or through a portal; in *Black Maria* the fantastic is something extra in the landscape. In *Archer's Goon* the fantastic is what makes the buses run on time.

As ever with Jones's work, the initial plot is deceptively simple: Howard comes home to find a Goon at the kitchen table threatening his father Quentin if he does not deliver the "two thousand" to Archer. As Howard tries to find out who Archer is, he discovers that the town in which he lives is ruled by seven siblings, each with the power to control different aspects of the town and one of whom is apparently using his father's words to keep all of them confined to the town. Howard must work out which sibling is responsible and how to break the spell without releasing these rather unsavory wizards out to rule the world.

Archer's Goon is one of the most complex and sophisticated of Jones's novels. As Suzanne Rahn pointed out, the novel is structured in part around ten apparently nonsensical theses, each of which receives its due care and attention. What begins as a mystery and proceeds as a detective novel turns into a voyage of self-discovery and change.[40] If rational mysteries involve an explanation of the mystery, and supernatural mysteries demand that we accept mystery as an inexplicable part of human life,[41] then *Archer's Goon* demonstrates how it is possible to nestle one within the other and to turn a treasure hunt into a complex discussion of the abuse of power.[42] Eventually, Howard will discover that he is Venturus, the youngest sibling, and the one responsible for the chain of events in which he is entangled.

As Brian Attebery has observed *Archer's Goon* has one of the most complex time narrations of any of Jones's books: there is a twelve-year cycle of repetition, but different characters have differing levels of access to the memory, and as this cycle is not yet completed, these memories can function as prophecies, with the caveat that "like all prophecies, a memory may bring about its own fulfillment or, in Jones's less deterministic universe, invalidate itself because it changes the balance of forces."[43] Consequently, it is difficult to know where to begin, but given the usual definition of urban fantasy as fantasy that takes place in the here and now, and Rahn's assertion that what Jones does is to bring the fantastic into the world of children, it is worth considering where *Archer's Goon* exists in place and time, for much of the irony in this novel is in the dissonance between where we think we are and where we actually are.

Jones pointed out in *The Tough Guide to Fantasyland* that if a map is provided at the beginning of a fantasy novel, we just know we will visit every place on it, and until we have done this, the fantasy cannot be resolved. Jones cheats, in that she provides two maps: one physical, but toward the end of the book rather than—as is conventional—at the start, and one cognitive, at the beginning of the novel.

The cognitive map is dealt with superbly by Rahn, who points out that the ten sayings that comprise the author's note at the beginning of *Archer's Goon* all manifest within the book.[44] Some of the meanings are literalized:

"3. All power corrupts but we need electricity" resolves when we discover that Archer, the eldest of the siblings, is in charge of the power supply. Others are more obviously imbued with the fantastical implications that overlay the novel: "9. Space is the final frontier, and so is the sewage farm" turns out to be literally true, as none of the siblings can pass the sewage farm and at the end of the book space is the furthest away they can be sent. Even "Pigs have wings, making them hard to catch," which Jones says no one (including this critic) seems to get, is played out metonymically: "It refers to Dillian as farmer of the police, and her ability to make her house disappear."[45] Each of the propositions in the author's note is visited in the order in which it is presented; each proposition formalizes a moment in the development of Howard's understanding of the world about him.

But what of that world? I have said that Jones cheats; this is because her second map detailing the physical places that must be visited appears quite late, when Howard considers the model of the town built by the second-year students. Rahn notes that the clue is in the appearance of the new Polytechnic building, which is shaped as a temple. Howard assumes that it must be associated with Torquil, who is in charge of music and entertainment, and ignores for the moment that he has already been told that Venturus, the last of the seven siblings, is in charge of education. But this is a double clue because, as in all of her work, Jones is playing not just with logic but also with what she expects the readers to know of fantasy. The temple is one of two places on the map not yet visited, and it is the one that Howard ignores, therefore it must be the final destination of the quest.

The model has a second function, however: with its clear edges and existence on a table surrounded by space, it provokes the question, "What is outside the town?" The answer might well be "nothing."[46] There is a problem with the placement of this town: if time has repeated itself twice, what is happening outside? Has time there repeated itself? If not, has no one outside the town noticed anything odd? Jones is too clever a writer for this to be a mere oversight. The town has no name; it simply is. This is not uncommon in the liminal fantasy. Steve Cockayne's recent novel *Wanderers and Islanders* takes place in somewhere called simply "the Land," while John Crowley's *Little, Big* is in part set in The City. The town in *Archer's Goon* might not be connected to anything outside during the twenty six years in which Howard has held it apart from time. Unlike in *Eight Days of Luke* or *Black Maria*, the boundaries of the enchanted space seem closed: once the thirteen-year cycle is in place, no one with a name (apart from Erskine) comes into the town and no one goes out (it is not clear whether the workers at the sewage works can cross the boundary or what is beyond the sewage works, since Erskine cannot go there and only the bus drivers are seen to cross), and yet this is never questioned by the characters. We know from what Howard knows of his parents that some people have come in during the thirteen years, but there are only the buses to indicate that there has been any intercourse with the outside world in that time.

One difficulty critics sometimes find with fantasy is that when one pushes the walls of the construct, the internal logic collapses. But in this case, if I am correct, there is a cohesive rationale that supports this interpretation. By the end of the novel we know that Catriona and Quentin are as much held by the injunction to protect Venturus as are the siblings. And we also know, because Hathaway has told us, that Hathaway is the ancestor of many of the town's inhabitants. At the end of the novel, there are many "interferences" that protect Venturus (Howard) from Erskine's anger. These are understood as by the direction of the siblings, but it is quite plausible that the individuals at the wheels of the various vehicles are also motivated by the injunction to protect Howard. In this context Ginger Hind's change of sides might not be quite such a result of revelatory free will as it is presented as being.

There are two ramifications of my closed-world theory. The first is speculative but connects to the second. What if there is no outside, no world? What if the town is a construct in which the siblings play? This solution is hinted at by Rahn, when she refers us to the myths of the Greek gods, the youngest of whom was also the most powerful: "They don't age as we do … they're bigger than we are, they inhabit huge spaces in separate realms." And Venturus, like Zeus, is the youngest of the pantheon.[47] And if either this or the utter disconnection of the town from the outside world is the case, it creates a logical substructure for the placement of the fantastic in this novel, because it is not simply, as Rahn argues, that the fantasy intrudes into the urban landscape, into children's everyday world[48] but that the fantastic overlays the nonfantastical urban landscape metaphorized in Archer's network of electric lines or Erskine's drains and imbues the ordinary with double meanings. It cannot be otherwise. Without physical context for the town, there is nowhere else for the magic to be.

Let us now examine more closely the ways in which Jones creates this multiple overlay. The first element, and one already explored in *Eight*

Days of Luke and *Black Maria,* is the way in which characters rationalize the fantastic in what they see and hear. The very first example of this takes place early, on page 3. The Goon throws his knife at Awful:

> At least that was what seemed to happen. Something certainly zipped past Awful's screaming face. Awful ducked and stopped screaming at once. Something certainly flew on past Awful and landed *thuk* in Howard's bag on the table. After it had, the Goon went placidly back to cleaning his nails with what was obviously the self same knife.[49]

Although immediately wondering, by page 6, Howard can consider, "That knife … must be made of something most unusual, which could cut china and come back to you when it was thrown."[50] Later, "very sane and severe" Catriona declares that the carving in the china mug cannot have been done with a knife, because the marks are glazed over. When Quentin accepts the fact of the carving but jokes about what is carved, Howard knows that Quentin does not intend to take the matter seriously. Both parents reach the same point from different angles; Catriona by ignoring the evidence of the fantastic, Quentin by regarding reality (in this case the fantastic) as something to joke about. Howard himself is at a liminal point. He chooses not to worry because his parents are not worried: adolescence changes that positioning, but this decision and the way it is framed is a metaphor for much of what happens next and for the outcome of the novel. It encapsulates one of the meanings of *Archer's Goon,* which is that adulthood is something one chooses to embrace.

Catriona and Quentin will be forced to shift position by the end of the novel, but more important to *Archer's Goon* is the degree to which the fantastic is used to demonstrate the essential dissonance of the real world and in turn the extent to which the real world becomes a metaphor for the operation of the fantastic.

Marilynn Olson has argued that Jones produces work that captures the postmodern condition of life in Britain's cities, where few know why they are doing certain things, where elected authorities have merely the illusion of power, and where magicians (central government) appoint quangos to make disruptive magic in our streets. Olson's analysis of the sound and rhythms of the city and the modes of living, which demand precisely the kind of passivity Howard comes to despise, is a convincing part and parcel of this whole argument.[51] That Howard's father can control a world with his words and chooses not to stands, for Olson, for the alienation of the citizen from the postmodern world. That at the end Quentin finds a new relevance to the words "It pays to increase your word power" is indicative that the world can be understood if we see its connections as irrational.

Jones's arguments about the way in which we live in the modern world are, as usual, made in reverse. Maisie Potter is in search of ideas to live by, but rather than think for herself she quotes other scholars in class and Dillian (the second oldest of the siblings) out of class. Behavior in the nonfantastical world shapes behavior in the fantastic. Quentin's decision to embrace reality (owning up to the tax demand) enables him to manipulate superreality.

This reversal is most vivid in the ways in which the fantastic and the urban mundane are interwoven. This is the element of *Archer's Goon* that typically draws most attention. Throughout the novel, as Butler, Olson, and Rahn have all pointed out, the siblings exercise their power by exaggerating the impact that the modern world can have on an individual's quality of life.[52] When the siblings attack the Sykes family they do so through the power of the modern world: Hathaway—superficially the gentlest of the siblings—digs up the road, creating a moat; Archer switches off the power; and Torquil plagues the family with music and ensures that they cannot shop. The last straw is when Erskine calls in Quentin's back taxes. There is no need for anything visibly supernatural while the fantastic can be one extreme on a continuum of the discordance and irrationality of the everyday. Erskine's drains, Shine's closed circuit television and Archer's power crisscross the town; the fantastic is both endemic and intrinsic to the workings of the town.

But paying attention to this very visible manifestation of the urban fantastic—the clothing of fantasy in modern tools and techniques—disguises the degree to which the fabric of the mundane and of fantasy are crosshatched. The permeability of the world of *Archer's Goon* is extreme: the map of the fantasy world is overlaid visibly with that of the real. Each place has multiple resonance, multiple meaning. Our first indication of this is the initial visit of Fifi, Howard, Awful, and the Goon to the Polytechnic: "There were a lot of people about, students hurrying home and men working on the site. It should have felt safe. But the Goon still had hold of Awful's hand and none of them felt safe."[53] Causality here is implied, not stated. By making an apparently obvious link, Jones disguises the fact that the link is not obvious. What is unsafe is less the presence of the Goon—so far his behavior has been fairly benign—but the sense that something has gone awry, that the world has been twisted. The Poly is transfigured, now not just a place in the world but an element of the geography of the fantastic, a place where something can happen.

Once the Poly acquires this element of fantasy space, Howard begins to notice that other locations within the town do not just hint at the fantastic but also offer portals into other worlds and other times (what Maria Nikolajeva terms *chronotopes*).[54] The first of these is the town hall. Although Mountjoy is not one of the siblings and the town hall does not offer a direct route to Archer, Jones writes it in ways that imbue the place with the air of the fantastic rather than the mundane. The search for Mountjoy is presented as a quest, each room is tested and checked, and the exploration serves to emphasize that this is an adventure that is taking place in the fantastic spaces of bureaucracy. But it is in the writing of their departure from the town hall that Jones begins to hint at the doubled nature of the town. The scene is written as if the escape were from a portal into the fantastic:

> They kept galloping down past other wide-and-glass doors, and some of these were bumping open and shut. Howard could see the dark shapes of people milling about behind them, and at least twice he heard some of the things they said. "Walked straight through the highwayboard!"[55]

It is as if there are real people in the town to whom Howard and his companions are ghosts. If Howard and his friends are real, then the security guards lurk around the exit-portal to trap them as if they were wraiths.

The second portal is Dillian's house. Like the town hall, the implications of normality are defied by the relentless creation of a sense of dissonance in Jones's language and the heightened sensibilities she accords Howard and Awful. Maisie Potter's house is the first problem. It exists in a relentless pastiche of the ordinary:

> Even the ordinary houses were beautifully painted and very neat. Most of the houses were more like red-brick castles than ordinary houses, and they got bigger and redder and more castle like. ... It was quite a surprise to find Woodland Terrace was a row of small houses.[56]

In this configuration, suburbia is something alien, whereas Dillian's residence, further up the hill, exaggerates that sense that this is a kind of lifestyle somehow at variance to the real. Dillian's house has a large glass porch around a "mighty studded door,"[57] and from the outside it looks like a castle.

Light blazed from crystal chandeliers onto an acre of shiny floor made of different woods put together in patterns. The light gleamed off the gilding of elegant little armchairs and winked in the drops of a small fountain near the stairs. There were banks of flowers across the fountain and here and there in the rest of the space. … Golden statues held more lights at the foot of the stairs, which swept around the far side of the room in a grand curve.[58]

The wrongness that Awful suspects is based not solely on Dillian's dyed hair and apparent age or even the disappearance of the house, but also on this sense that all of this is a fake, neither a real castle nor real suburbia. The dissonance is in the recognition that this lifestyle is intended by Dillian to be seen as desirable. It is suburbia, as much as Dillian is, which is under attack, but the concept of suburbia is used to attack the person that is Dillian; the manifestation of the mundane tells us about her fantastical nature, rather than the other way around. Howard later muses that one can judge a person by the home he or she creates.

Dillian lives at the edge of town. The most integrated portal, present at the heart of both story and map, is that of Archer. Archer's hanger is accessed through the bank. To get to it Howard goes through a safe, the walls lined with pigeonholes, bending down through a small door that only Awful is small enough to go through. The image makes modern and mundane Alice's fall down the tunnel (similarly lined with niches) and her difficulty in getting through the door into the garden.

Once through into the aircraft hanger–laboratory, Howard is disoriented, and because Dillian and Mountjoy have both been visited within the compass of the town—although Dillian's house is no longer there when they try to revisit it—it does not occur to Howard or Awful to question where they actually are. It is very unclear whether Archer's lair is under the bank, next door, or in a different world altogether. Given my earlier thoughts about the placement of the town, one suspects that the last might be the case, and we are in yet another pocket universe. Either way, Archer's hanger exists in potentially the same space as something else, because there is nowhere else for it to be. The interpretation is corroborated by Torquil's and Shine's residences. Although Hathaway and Venturus clearly live in the same geographical space as other elements of the town, they are displaced by time and consequently the overlap is not complete. But Torquil and Shine occupy already occupied buildings. Torquil hangs out in the Bishop's Lane disco and the cathedral, but so does Shine.

In each case the place in which the characters live is a mundane(ish) manifestation of themselves and their powers. Archer's power is the machines in his life, which allow him to "tamper with anything in town." He does not control people directly, but he can watch people through the TV or through the lightbulb, every bit the modern totalitarian. Worst of all, Archer is a well-meaning despot, convinced that he will be the best ruler and is therefore the rightful ruler. He is aloof and uninvolved with the people he rules, and even in his hangar his office is elevated in a cream leather car.

The extent and understanding of Torquil's power is similarly revealed: Torquil lives in the disco and the cathedral, both places of music, but only one of them (the cathedral) is a place of fear and coercion. When in chapter 6 he attempts coercion through music, Jones contrasts him with Catriona (his niece many times removed, of course, removing any coincidence in this scene) who gentles Howard's school orchestra into a semblance of effectiveness that is accompanied by enjoyment and pleasure. In contrast Torquil can create only cacophony or prevent pleasure (such as when he closes the shops to the Sykes family). Only when he refuses to exert his power do the elements of life, which are apparently his to influence, reach their potential. Torquil's real powers, like Catriona's, are to facilitate, not to force, but to learn this he has to accept that he does not like his own behavior or that of his siblings.

Only Hathaway has a home life that Howard recognizes as good. Hathaway's home life is integrated, and it is in the integration that Jones places the fantastic. In *Archer's Goon* Jones rejects both the configuration of the fantastic as antique and the assumption that the fantastic is something separate from the real world. Hathaway resides not in an antique shop but in a vibrant past, living a very ordinary life. Similarly, this rejection of the quaint explains why Hathaway's house is presented as a manifestation of modernity: "it shone with newness. The thick oak of the open door was yellow with newness."[59] This is the past as lived, not as remembered. Hathaway's place is presented as part of a layered urban landscape, not as history.

The landscape of *Archer's Goon* is mapped three ways. On the surface is the mundane world of tax offices, schools, and colleges. Underneath is the mysterious world of power, in its mundane, fantastical, and irrational bureaucracy. Swimming through this is an argument about people and families. What Jones demands is that Howard learn to see not one as a metaphor for the other but the ways in which they interrelate so that techniques learned in one environment are transferred effortlessly to the other. At the end of *Archer's Goon,* it is worth taking a step back and considering that it is coming to terms with the fantastic that has taught Quentin to face the real world, that Erskine (the Goon) has decided that the real world is more worth exploring than the fantastical, and that sometime in the future a Polytechnic building with four caryatids with Howard's face on them are going to appear. The fantastic and the real continue to vie for attention, for the occupation of real space and for significance.

It is becoming quite clear that although Jones makes use of irony to create a fantasy world that permeates ours (rather than sitting alongside it), one that relies absolutely on the recognition of the conventions of genre fantasy, elsewhere the sense that the worlds are permeable is achieved by holding the very presence of magic in doubt. In the *Eight Days of Luke, Black Maria,* and even to an extent in *Archer's Goon,* this is a functional tool. In *Fire and Hemlock* and in *The Spellcoats,* it is the maintenance of equipoise that structures the meaning and depiction of the fantastic.

The Spellcoats, and to an extent the whole of the Dalemark quartet, makes extensive use of this sense of doubt, although as Charles Butler has remarked it is always resolved in favor of magic. *The Spellcoats* has at least three systems of doubt shaping its structure and the way we can read it. Even the ending is left in doubt, as Tanaqui's narrative ends with her dream of a possible outcome, but without the reality fully resolved. At the end of the tale, we discover that what we are reading is a historical text, a lost book that might recount a fantasy or explain some of the legends of Dalemark. The placement of this short (fewer than two pages) explanation is interesting because it comes at the end of a text that has operated to convince us of the existence of real magic within the narrated world. Had it been a prologue, we would have been forewarned that we need to judge. Acting as epilogue the historical explanation functions instead to challenge what we think we have come to believe. It adds an extra tension to a work that has consistently balanced metaphor and competing beliefs to keep the characters and the reader off balance. The project that is *The Spellcoats,* and later the whole Dalemark quartet, is liminal to the degree that its subject is the relationship between history and story. This will be taken up in much greater detail in the next chapter.

Fire and Hemlock, which followed *Archer's Goon,* is another of the more complicated of Jones's novels. It is also the most deliberately liminal. Jones has declared that her intention was to see how long she could go without confirming the magic. The story's drive rests precisely on the ability of children (and specifically Polly) to blur the distinction between the rational and the logical, so that the narrative a child writes between them can fuse two worlds.

While staying with her Granny, Polly becomes separated from her friend Nina and wanders into Hunsdon House, where there is a funeral. Tom rescues and entertains her, shows her the vases with Nowhere written on them, and encourages her to tell him her imaginings. At the end he gets her to help him choose six paintings gifted to him before he escorts her home. Over the next few years they communicate sporadically; Tom sends her books, and she sends him her ideas for fantasy. Each time they meet, strange but relatively explicable things happen, until Polly's late teens when the events become more obviously supernatural. All of this remains linked to Hunsdon House, to Laurel and her new husband Morton Leroy, to his son Seb Leroy and to a family of Perries and Leroys, and in an odd way to the narrative of Polly's own family that has been fractured in two generations. But the story begins when Polly realizes that she has parallel memories for a period from the age of eight up to four years before (she is now eighteen). The realization is triggered by a photograph on Polly's wall, of figures emerging from flames,[60] and by a book, *Time Out of Mind*, which seems to have changed but still contains one story, of a man with two memories, which she does remember.

There are three obvious frames provided for *Fire and Hemlock*: the pictures Tom chooses, the lines from Tam Lin, and the relationships between Polly, her mother, and Granny and between the Leroys and Perries. The role of Tam Lin and of other captives of the fairy queen sharing the name Thomas, a series of musicians whom she has pulled into her orbit for nine years, each in order to provide a substitute for her consort when his life is forfeit to hell, is the most acknowledged and the most easily understood of the frames of the novel. Even so, Diana Wynne Jones has asserted in conversation that Tom o' Bedlam, for all he does not appear within the text, should also be considered as a fore-runner of Thomas Lynn. In some cases such young men have escaped but been cursed by the Queen for their refusal to play out their allotted role; some, as in the case of Tam Lin, have been rescued by a young woman. Tam Lin's example is the template for the plot in which Polly finds herself caught up. In the interstices of these tales, Polly redeems Tom. As I discussed in the introduction, *Fire and Hemlock* is a fantastically complex overlay of myths, legends, and fictions. In her essay "The Heroic Ideal—A Personal Odyssey," Jones references Homer, Spenser, Chaucer, Malory, European romance cycles and Norse legends, and finally T.S. Eliot's *Four Quartets*. All of these are fed into the skeleton of the story and into Polly's education and become the framework for her actions.[61]

The role of the pictures has been discussed by Martha P. Hixon, who points out that the pictures Polly chooses will define the totemic events in Tom's life—a rearing horse, a group of violinists, an unhappy harlequin, a picnic, a fairground, and the enlarged photograph that gives the book its title.[62] She also points to the role of T.S. Eliot's *Four Quartets*, which perhaps more than any other single element underpins the liminal in this novel. If we return just a moment to the discussion of time in chapter 3, we can see—as Hixon argues—that the liminality of *Fire and Hemlock* rests on an extreme, A-series–relative time scheme, "the belief that although our everyday lives are predicated on the concepts of Past, Present, and Future, in actuality these divisions of time are artificial."[63] In *Fire and Hemlock,* as Hixon points out, the linear narrative is disrupted by the dual time-stream (Polly's two sets of memories) but also by the ordinary timescale of her life juxtaposed against the immortality of faerie, "the fluid reality of entities such as Edna, Mr. Piper, and Leslie,"[64] to which I would add the creation of seasons in the ritual of nine years for men and eighty-one years for women.

The permeability of the world in *Fire and Hemlock* is extreme, and vital to this permeability are the relationships within the novel and the construction of a range of archetypes: it is here, rather than in the Tam Lin tale, that Jones seems to have inserted a good part of the power. Polly is not the only one acting within a framework. Tom is Tam Lin and Thomas the Rhymer, but he is also Odysseus trying to escape Calypso, Leander, Kay kidnapped by the Snow Queen, the Knight of the Moon, Artegall, Harlequin, Orpheus: the full list can be found in Jones's article.

This use of parallels and doubles in the novels extends throughout: when Jones indulges in indicative naming, it is worth taking notice. Jones has written that "Polly" was selected because *poly* means "more than one; many or much," and Polly takes on a range of roles throughout the book. Polly's mother is called Ivy. An innocent enough name, but one that partners too comfortably with Laurel, the owner of Hunsdon House. Polly's relationship with Ivy is interesting. Ivy is a very difficult woman. Polly is less a daughter than a courtier whose role it is to soothe and flatter, fetch and carry, and who can fall easily out of favor. At first we think Ivy's complaints about her husband are in some way justified, there is another woman after all, but as the novel unfolds we realise that Ivy is a miser. She holds her love tight like tadpoles in a jar, and the tighter she holds, the more slips away from her. Constantly searching for her "little bit of happiness," she is consumed with a sense of entitlement that does little but make her miserable. Ivy's behavior, however, parallels that of Laurel, the faerie queen, and provides a warning to Polly.

What Polly learns from Ivy is to see the grasping nature of Laurel which she can then identify as weakness. Although Laurel does not wish to release what is hers, underlying such sense of possession is an indifference to individuality. For Laurel and Ivy any man will do as long as he submits to rule. This is a powerful lesson on the mundane level, but it operates magically too, for Polly is being guided throughout by the tales she reads. The tale, "East of the Sun and West of the Moon" warns her about the desire for too much control, whereas the ballad of Tam Lin demands she hold on tight. Only by studying the consequences of such action in real life is she able to work out where to steer, and she gets it wrong. Enraged by Tom's girlfriend Mary, Polly uses the magic she has worked out from the fairy tales to spy on him. But we have already been told that Polly would get this wrong. Polly has not been able to find the "one true fact" in "East of the Sun, and West of the Moon": "The girl had only herself to blame for her troubles. She was told not to do a thing and she did. And she cried so much. Polly despised her."[65]

Fire and Hemlock is constructed of *mise en abyme,* in which each element of intertextuality—the ballads, the pictures, the doubling—reflects, reproduces, or comments on aspects of what we might call the primary narrative or story. Charles Butler, in his superb analysis of *Fire and Hemlock,*[66] has pointed out even the techniques of refusal such as the refusal to name what Laurel is, "while this may be perfectly good sense for an author not wishing to put off otherwise streetwise teenagers, it is also quite in keeping with the traditional propitiatory practice of referring to fairies by indirect epithets such as 'the good neighbours.' "[67]

Because there are so many *mise en abyme* elements, *Fire and Hemlock* is told on a continuous feedback loop: each new element as it is introduced parallels, reflects, or mirrors the story as told so far, to build the kind of coda that "reflects partly back on the movement just completed, and partly forwards to what is to come," which Jones identified as an innovation of Tolkien.[68] This is in turn built into the plot because it is Polly who is constructing the story, and deliberately (if incomprehendingly) creating the connections between the world of faerie and the world of humans, so that all exist together and function as colored filters over spotlights to create a stage that is both somewhere—all places at once—and also nowhere—none of those places—so that each person can have many facets and many avatars according to which filter—or combination of filters—shines on them.

In *Fire and Hemlock* the fantastic is frequently narrated as a thread we are to understand and relate to, rather than itself appearing and changing events. We can see this in the positioning of Tom's friend Ann, who appears to know things, recognizes the supernatural, and is, it turns out, a Perry on her mother's side. Ann understands that Tom is under supernatural threat, and she appears to recognize Polly's role. Granny is a bit of an enigma. At the very end of the book we discover that Granny has always suspected that Tom is using Polly and has always known what the house is, because in her youth she lost her own husband to Laurel; on rereading it becomes obvious that Granny has sought to use her understanding of this to shape the final outcome.

Granny's very first question to Mr. Lynn is rather peculiar. After expressing her gratitude that Mr. Lynn kept Polly out of mischief, she asks, "but what were *you* up to there?" Mr. Lynn is flustered but does not challenge the oddness of the question. A more conventional form would be, "and are you related to the family?" Granny has signaled an awareness of the house.[69] Similarly, when Polly calls her in desperation because Mr. Lynn has invited her out and her one good dress is too small, Granny says two things: first she asks for reassurance that the invitation is genuine, that Mr. Lynn asked Polly. Then she says, "But be wary of what he gives you. Keep that to yourself, understand?"[70]

It becomes clear that Granny knows—she is both Fate and Wisdom—and that we are being told that she knows. But what Granny understands best, and what both she and Tom succeed in communicating to Polly, is that power in the land of faerie is structured around equivalence. This is depicted—as I have already described—in the real-world relationships and in the fantasy: once more, it is the ability to negotiate the real world that assists a hero in deconstructing fantasy, rather than the other way around.

In these terms Ivy is a failed faerie queen, and Reg seems doomed to follow in the footsteps of his father, even if at a more mundane level. Granny blames herself for spoiling him, but his decision to allow his girlfriend, Joanna, to take over his life is essentially no different from that of any of the men (with the exception perhaps of Seb) in the novel. And

Joanna is just as jealous of her prerogatives as is Laurel. Polly's parents have each constructed fantasies and required Polly to live in the borderlands. Morton Leroy, although clearly of faerie, is trapped with Laurel. Leslie has enslaved himself to Laurel, and it is important to understand that Tom's relationship with Polly is structured, at least in his mind, within the same paradigm. Polly's power to imagine things that he can make come true (thanks to Laurel's barbed gift) places Tom's life in her hands—and it is the rejection of this paradigm that is crucial to the conclusion of the novel.

But before we get to that point, Polly must learn the playing out of equivalences in the fantastical world, for it is Polly's ability to understand the world as fantasy rather than the fantasy itself that maintains the liminality. The magic is to be read in the pattern, in the weft and weave of the tale. The story is less told than it is framed. If you do not understand the frame, you (and Polly) are in trouble.

Early descriptions of Polly lay emphasis on her imagination: although Nina is the wild one who eggs Polly on, it is Polly who actually comes up with the ideas. But she can do this only when Nina threatens her. When Tom tries encouragement, she dries up. Yet the lack of threat from Mr. Lynn also leads Polly to imagine something ordinary, which gives Mr. Lynn his first link to a firmer truth. Rather than wild imagination, Polly gives Mr. Lynn a life as a very ordinary shopkeeper, with a sister and nephew, yet hidden within that is a fantasy life as a superhero. The imaginary world holds its own equivalences—the lack of character complexity is made up for by the dual nature of each character. There seems also to be a parallel between the threat structure that shapes Polly's inventiveness and the threats that keep Mr. Lynn in line. Whereas Polly learns to dispense with threats as a stimulus to the imagination, and eventually to ignore them, Lynn needs to learn to work around them.

Equivalence exists elsewhere in the rules of the game that Tom and Polly must play. Some they control: Polly, having decided to be a hero in her game, trains to be a hero in real life, running to and from school and joining the athletic club. Others seem merely coincidence: Tom buys the car by selling the horse that appeared in one of the pictures. As the book proceeds the equivalences move from the incidental to the spooky. When Polly finds Thomas Piper Hardware in Stow-on-the-Water, we share the cold sweats as Mr. Piper turns out to have a nephew called Leslie and a sister-in-law called Edna. They do not actually meet Thomas Piper, or the issue might be resolved. Instead Tom and Polly are overwhelmed with the sense that their words have created this reality (although these are not the people they created: Leslie is nice and Edna is much younger than they had envisaged). As with the horse and the car, the overlap is not complete. But it is enough that from this point onward Polly begins consciously to notice the equivalences that exist. In the third and fourth parts of the novel, Polly shapes her understanding of what is happening in terms of the moral universe of fantasy. Nothing can happen without reason; an equivalence must always be reached. In case we miss the point, Polly's reading material on the way to Bristol is *The Golden Bough*, full of sacrificial kings and sympathetic magic. When she sees Leroy on the Bristol suspension bridge, she is already primed to understand the situation.

And it is here, at this point of recognition, that Polly first experiences real magic. Until this point most of what she has understood is about juxtaposition or disorientation. But in Bristol, rescued by Tom, she and Tom are chased down the streets:

> In the middle of the dark little street, the pattering rubbish was slowly piling upon itself, floating slowly and deliberately into a nightmare shape. It could have been a trick of the wind, but it was not. It was too deliberate. Plastic cups, peanut packets, leaves, and old wrappers were winding upward, putting themselves in place as parts of a huge, bear-like shape. As Polly watched, a piece of newspaper rose like a slow ghost to make the creature a staring face. Tom seized her wrist while she stared and pulled her away, among the tower buildings.[71]

The creature acquires a "staring face" of newspaper as it chases them, and Polly and Tom know they are being chased. This is magic, this is the fantastic, but what we see is the normal made unreal, and as they drive through the monster, Tom hits Sam–Tam Hanivar. Tom keeps driving.

> "Was it Sam and Ed all along?" she said as they roared along a huge, orange-lit road. "Not paper at all?"

> "I don't know," Tom said. "I just don't know." Polly thought he was going to run into silence then, but he went on, "what is it about us?" and roared through some traffic lights just as they turned red. Cold air whistled in Polly's hair. "We make things up, and then they go and happen. I wrote you a letter something very like this."[72]

Yet the switch in the book, the element that allows Tom to use Polly, is that Polly's equivalences lead to her creation of the hero team who resolve as Ann, Sam, and Ed, and the doubt over whether Polly is recognizing or creating these patterns is what makes her so dangerous to the Leroys. The problem is that Polly's own recognition of this brings her downfall. Angry with Tom for his involvement with Mary and his insistence (in manner rather than deed) that she is too young, she uses what she has learned of equivalence (through the miniature of him she has taken from the House the year before) to contact him. In doing so she alerts Laurel, who turns Polly's own powers against her: faced with the story that Tom will die soon—a story that is actually true in a very different way—Polly forgets because she agrees to forget. As she realizes much later, the lesson she had discarded was that the real hero was the one who could cope with feeling silly.

The final part of *Fire and Hemlock* is intense. As the story coheres Polly brings together the emotional and literary education she has received to understand the fantastic. Just as she has been constantly pushed into the margins of memory, of people's lives, and of faerie, she discovers that many of the answers she needs lie in her borderlands. Fiona, a friend from the single-track memory of her life, still remembers Tom, because she was too marginal to Polly at the time to have attracted Leroy's gaze. Granny has no memory of Tom, but Mr. Leroy has failed to erase Granny's own experience of Laurel. Even without immediate memory, she has knowledge.

Rereading the two ballads of Tam Lin and Thomas the Rhymer that have structured the novel *we* have read, Polly is struck by the two stories, about Thomas the Rhymer, who is turned out with a poisoned gift—to speak true—and Tam Lin, who is rescued by his Janet.[73] So with Granny's help, she heads down to Miles Cross at 11 p.m. and watches until the Leroy Perrys arrive. And when the lads (with Leslie) and the family (with Seb) have gone into the station, last of all arrive the musicians, the Dumas Quartet. Polly follows them in while Tom is distracted by the appearance of Mr. Piper, buys a ticket, and boards a train—an ordinary, modern train, but as Jones notes, a nice pun on "entourage."[74] Nothing that takes place in the final pages is ordinary, but as always, the landscape of fantasy in this book is kept relentlessly mundane. While the train takes them to a strange place, in day rather than night, the scene they arrive at—Laurel's garden party—is marked by its ordinariness. This is a text in which the ordinary is more threatening than the obviously fantastical.

When Polly finally challenges Laurel, it is on a point of the ordinary: Laurel has broken the rules of the game. Polly's challenge is that Leroy was not supposed to hurt Tom, and in his attacks on Polly, Leroy has hurt Tom twice.

The conclusion to *Fire and Hemlock* is one of the most disturbing scenes in Jones's books. To begin with, Polly quite deliberately acts knowing that Seb, who although not as nice as Tom is not bad, will die if she wins. Second, the terms and act of the challenge uncover some unpleasant truths about Tom's relationship to Polly.

The challenge places Leroy and Tom in the pool that Polly noticed on her very first visit:

> The sun reached the dry pool. For just a flickering part of a second some trick of the light filled the pool deep with transparent water. The sun made bright, curved wrinkles on the bottom, and the leaves, Polly could have sworn, instead of rolling on the bottom, were, just for an instant, floating, green and growing. Then the sunbeam traveled on, and there was just a dry oblong of concrete again.[75]

But this time the pool is full. Each man must depend on only what is his; the balance of equivalence is kept. But when Tom calls his cello, he sinks further into the pool, and Polly realizes that anything else he calls, his horse or her, will only make it worse. Dorian Grey has suggested that this is part of the twist in Laurel's curse, that anything Tom makes up will hurt him.[76] Tom must believe that nothing and no one will come to rescue him. Polly sets out to alienate him.

What is startling is that Polly's accusations are the absolute truth. He has used her; he has manipulated a child and put her in danger to save his own skin. Nicki Humble points out that this also defuses "the dodgiest aspect of the narrative," a relationship between a little girl and a grown man.[77] But it is at the point that Polly screams this that the scene ends. We turn over the page and the Coda has begun.

It is very difficult to tell from the Coda precisely what has happened, how Tom has won, or what the outcome of that victory will be. Pressed by an audience at the International Board on Books (IBBY) conference in 2004, I suggested that one possibility (a possibility supported, I think, by arguments in chapter 7) is that what Polly gives up is not love but romance. Much earlier in the novel, Polly is taught that romance does not make for good writing. All of the images Tom tries to use but discovers are not really his are intensely romantic and symbolic. What he and Polly are left with is the day-to-day reality of love. Jones rarely uses an argument only once, so it is worth considering if there is another instance of giving up the romance of life for its reality. The answer lies in *The Time of the Ghost*. At the end of this novel, Imogen gives up a romantic career as a concert pianist in favor of what she really wants (we do not find out what that is). More obviously Zillah and Herrel, and Maureen and Joe in *A Sudden Wild Magic* must all accept the complexities of their partners. In her essay "The Heroic Ideal," Jones points out that Tom's last role is as Cupid, "although few people seem to notice."[78] For Polly and Tom to have a future together, Tom must acquire clearer vision than his avatar.

So for Polly and Tom, there is no "happily ever after." Polly knows that she must keep meaning what she said: she must be willing to let him go forever. Any hope that might exist for her and Tom as a couple lies in the liminal spaces of Nowhere and Now Here, in the bargain that they seem to have struck with Laurel.

The chapter ends with the following lines:

> "If two people can't get together anywhere—"

> "You think?" Tom said with a shivery laugh. "Nowhere?"

> "Yes, and if it's not true nowhere, it has to be somewhere." Polly laughed and held out her hands. "We've got her, either way."[79]

The possibility of a happy ending lies in the same borderland as does the fantastic, on the portico of the world.

CHAPTER 7
A MAD KIND OF REASONABLENESS

"What is it? A call for help?" panted Paolo.

"Must be," gasped Renata. "Angelica's spells—always—mad kind of reasonableness." (*The Magicians of Caprona*, 187)

Although there are many themes that one can pick up and discuss in Diana Wynne Jones's work, the overriding issues that shape her fantasies are a concern with the power of words, the creation of story, and a sense that the writer is a real and constant presence within the fiction. Jones's work is simultaneously metafictive and an argument for the metafictive. Buried in her metaphors, in the instructions she gives to readers about how to read, in her construction of magic and of context, and eventually in four books—*Hexwood, Fire and Hemlock, Archer's Goon,* and *The Spellcoats,* all of which make the creation of story and the writing of story fundamental elements of the plot—Jones talks about how to write and what writing is for. Many of her stories are conscious of being written: we are intended to remain conscious of this as a narrated story, a fiction within a fiction. The text we read, over the shoulder of Mig of *Black Maria* or Tanaqui of *The Spellcoats*, has been revised and rethought. Many of these stories are very subtle instauration fantasies in which the aim is to replace a false or defective story or understanding with a true one.[1] *The Homeward*

Bounders, *Deep Secret*, and *The Merlin Conspiracy* are all reported tales, but each has a reason for being told and a justification for the manner of the narration. The presence of the writer as a figure in these texts is not incidental but draws attention to writing as a deliberate process, a manipulation of a constructed mimesis. At the center of all of this is the mad reasonableness first unleashed in *Wilkins' Tooth* that imparts to her writing a rambunctiousness that spirals out from the extension of the rigorously logical, whether in the construction of magic or the consequences of setting.

One of the first issues to tackle, which should not actually be necessary, is the extent to which Jones's choice to be a fantasy writer matters. Most of this book has dealt with the ways in which Jones has tackled the problems of writing fantasy. However, at least one critic, Maria Nikolajeva, sees the fantastic in Jones's work as essentially metaphoric: "Unlike the majority of fantasy and science fiction novels, Jones's works are character oriented rather than plot oriented. The multitude of worlds is not merely a backdrop for adventure but a reflection of the young protagonists' split and distorted picture of the reality in which they are living."[2] Consequently she "regard[s] fantasy in Jones's books as a narrative device rather than an objective in itself and view[s] her works primarily as novels of adolescence." The choice to set *Deep Secret* at a fantasy convention (and not a conference, as she suggests) is simply an "additional postmodern trait of the novel," or in Charles Butler's elegant coinage, "just a kind of stunt double for the everyday."[3] The implication is that Jones's interest in metafantasy is incidental or parasitic upon her work as a storyteller. However if, as I have argued in this book, Jones is a writer concerned to show what writing can achieve, and specifically what writing within the fantastic can achieve, then we cannot exclude her settings from this thesis.

Nikolajeva's arguments rest on the idea that because fantasy is a metaphoric mode, it can be a genre in itself, but it cannot be a genre for itself.[4] Clare Bradford expresses the common sense of limitations within the fantastic in this way: "fantasy as a metaphoric mode and realism as a metonymic mode, which may employ metaphor but which works metonymically through representing aspects of story and discourse as part of larger signifying patterns."[5] The result is that fantasy is denied the flexibility and duality of realism. For critics and writers in the fantastic, this limitation is an arbitrary construction. The assumption that all aspects of the fantastic are metaphoric—that horror is about a fear of contamination, that the quest is the *Bildungsroman* (the story of growing up)—is an imposition that limits the understanding of the fantastic and renders it impossible to consider fantasy qua fantasy, or fantasy as technique. It is not wrong, or uninteresting, but it treats fantasy fiction as medicine rather than a creative act. Butler wrote of fantasy generally, and Jones specifically,

> To think of it [fantasy] as a disposable husk, to be discarded once the enabling work has been done would imply a naïve conception of the experience of reading. In Jones's case, it would also miss the point. One of the attractions of Jones's magical literature is its ability to convey the sense that "normal" life (or the etiolated version of it available to the inactive imagination) is partial and illusory. In her books magic can also function metonymically as well as metaphorically.[6]

If metonymy is a figure of speech in which something stands for the whole by means of an overlap of literal and figurative function, then the fantastic offers greater resources than does the realistic mode. Jones uses certain settings precisely because of the fantastic possibilities they permit. This is as true of the over-crowded suburban house of *The Ogre Downstairs* as it is of the trade-marked fantasyland of *The Dark Lord of Derkholm*. Running throughout *The Ogre Downstairs* is a very simple analogy made real: that when two chemicals mix there will be an effect. As the chosen chemicals mix, so do the two families in a variety of permutations. The absurdity of the analogy is played out until it becomes reasonable, an extension into the carnivalesque, but the setting is coincidental only if one does not recognize the analogy and sees this book simply as a "social issues" book, typical of its time but for the trappings of magic. It is metaphoric only if one ignores the experiment to write the fantastic precisely as an exercise in metonymy.

In *The Ogre Downstairs* there are the first hints of what we might describe as "setting as character." This is not unique to Jones by any means: one of the aspects of science fiction and fantasy that make it—as a genre—distinct from much literary fiction but that often connect it to the detective genre is the degree to which a place can shape the course of events as if it had its own lines in the script. The best example of this in Jones's work is *Deep Secret*, the very novel of which Nikolajeva dismissed the setting as postmodern.

Deep Secret tells two stories, one in which Rupert Venables sets out to find someone to fill the space opened up among the Magids by the death of his friend Stan, and another in which Rupert tries to help out in the Koryfos Empire that is falling apart after someone has assassinated the Emperor and his entire court, leaving only one hassled General and a High Lady to search for the hidden heir. Both of these stories are traditional fantasy plots—find the missing person of power, and find the missing heir—and are much more traditional, as it happens, than is common in Jones's work. This is not coincidental, as in *Deep Secret* the recognizability of story is where the fantastic is embedded. The background work of the Magids is less to right injustice than to push Earth "ayewards," along the figure eight of infinity, to make the world more receptive to magic. This is done precisely by building the recognition of story into everyday culture.

Stan takes most pride in the changed receptivity of Earth during his tenure: "When I was a lad, no one even considered there might be other universes, let alone talking of *going* to them. But now people write books about that, and they talk about working magic and having former lives, and nobody thinks you're a nutcase for mentioning it."[7] And much later, we discover Rupert's speculations about Lewis Carroll were correct. Alice's traverse of the chessboard looks so much like the movement between universes because Charles Dodgson was a Magid. In what we might call a postmodern manner, just for a moment we can imagine that Dodgson was influenced by Jones.

The two plotlines of *Deep Secret* very quickly become entangled. Maree Mallory turns out to be ranked the highest on Rupert's list of potential Magids—although her wildness appalls him—and Maree and her "cousin" Nick (he is actually her half-brother) are eventually revealed to be two of the Emperor's three missing heirs. The third heir is a centaur, and two others die because Rupert does not realize that he is dealing with not only the sick machinations of the Emperor but also a struggle for the Empire.

Nick's mother is a consort of the Emperor—Maree's mother is never revealed—and is plotting with a magician called Gram White and the centaur Knarros, who is the Uncle of the centaur heir Rob, to ensure that Nick ascends to the throne. In the process Maree is stripped, her soul broken into two, and half of it destroyed in a volcano. The only chance of making things right is for Maree to walk to Babylon. Just as, buried in *Alice through the Looking Glass*, are the instructions to move through universes, a child's rhyme "How Many Miles to Babylon" holds a secret, a deep secret:

How many miles to Babylon?
Three score miles and ten.
Can I get there by candle-light?
Yes, and back again.
If your feet are speedy and light
You can get there by candle-light.[8]

This verse is the well-known part of the secret. As a spell, it contains its own instructions. With the aid of four other verses,[9] Nick, Maree, and Rob are able to negotiate a journey to somewhere and something else, and return rather different. But the point here is why it is necessary for the setting to be fantasy. First, we can learn something from the fact that Jones does not tell the trip to Babylon until the very end of the story (Nick relates it to the Upper Room). In terms of narrative tension, Rupert's waiting at the edge of a row of candles, desperately trying to make sure they last until Maree returns, is much more stressful to the reader than accompanying Maree on the journey might have been, because this audience, the fantasy audience, can fill the gap with its own expectations. In *Deep Secret,* more even perhaps than in *The Dark Lord of Derkholm,* Jones is writing to her most dedicated audience, and because of this she can rely on something that she knows her audience believes: that there is truth in story and that play-oriented activities are a route to deeper learning. *Deep Secret* is part of an argument that extends as far back as *Wilkins' Tooth* (and to her nonfantastical adult novel *Changeover,* in which belief makes "mark changeover" into Mark Changeover).

The difference between the core audience factor for *Dark Lord* and that of *Deep Secret* is that *Dark Lord* is recognizable to anyone who has read any of the emulators of Tolkien,[10] whereas *Deep Secret* focuses on the core of the core, the few thousand fans who turn up each year to one of the several science fiction conventions that take place across the English-speaking world, Europe, and Japan. Some of what Jones uses this for is simply that moment of identification. Rather than providing a tabula rasa for her readers, she gives instead a distinct type of person, and Maree Mallory, standing in for Jones's preferred reader, responds appropriately:

> I know what *really* struck me: the hall was full of people I'd like to get to know. An unusual feeling for sulky, solitary me, that. This feeling extended to the large sprinkling of shy-looking, middle-aged ladies (much to my surprise).[11]

The description of this and of the large number of T-shirts, beards, glasses, paunches, achingly glamorous women (not all of whom are women), and overweight women is a crucial part of the atmosphere of this book. It places the fantastic in an environment that is seriously weird, yet very mundane. Jones parallels this with Rupert Venables's self-perception of the role of Magid: special yet ordinary. Strangeness in *Deep Secret* is not merely limited to the fantastic; the ordinary life of the convention can make much of the magic, the waiting around for things to happen, seem pretty mundane.

But if Jones uses the atmosphere of a science fiction convention as a counterpoint to the fantastic, she uses familiar space to launch the fantastic in ways that rework the pattern of disruption common to intrusion fantasies. In the intrusion fantasy the strange breaks into the world, disrupts it, is negotiated with or defeated, but is always recognized and typed as alien. In the space of a science fiction convention Jones can play a variation. The intrusion passes unrecognized by most and is absorbed by and absorbs the craziness of the context; while for those not familiar with science fiction conventions the craziness becomes all of a piece.

To those for whom con-going is a habit, the descriptions of the convention space itself are worryingly familiar. "Everyone sits in the Grand Lobby. It is pretty big, but it looks *enormous,* because there are mirrors in one wall reflecting large windows in the wall opposite. It is full of armchairs and tables and small children running about in little cloaks or small-scale batman gear, and all the adults sitting around in bundles."[12] The hotel in Wantchester is a composite. A very well-known fan wrote,

> The hotel in *Deep Secret* is by no means exclusively the Adelphi, though the mirrored ceiling in the foyer is taken from that hotel. The five-sides-to-a-square hotel is near the railway station ... [later notes say it was Wolverhampton] and was the site of a filk con DWJ attended in 1992, on which occasion she *did* walk round five sides of a square to find the lifts on her way down to breakfast on the first morning. The lifts themselves, and their unco-operative nature, are borrowed from a hotel in Glasgow that shall remain nameless. ... In fact DWJ made a certain effort *not* to draw a portrait of any one hotel.[13]

All this, however, is mere trappings, and if it stopped there, Nikolajeva would be correct: Jones could set her stories in realistic settings and it would not matter, but this collection of images is precisely how Jones describes her creative imagination—these anecdotes are those Germans in

Twyford again, the attempt to make rational an irrational world. And Jones uses settings and the behavioral conventions associated with these settings to provide her characters with amazing leeway.

In a science fiction and fantasy convention, much that would other-wise shock passes without comment: this extends from bizarre cos-tumes in the bar (although a Klingon costume might bring accusations of tackiness), a great deal of seminaked flesh, and sexual behaviour that in other contexts would be considered improper. Science fiction conventions exist—at least in theory—in a metaphorical space-time bubble. Anything can happen and pass as normal. The appearance of an injured centaur in the lobby mostly attracts comment about the quality of the costume. Ironically, this infuriates Nick. Like Maree, he has identified with the other attenders, in part because they had struck him as smarter than the average, but he is baffled at the way they absorb the event into their understanding of the world. This is not Douglas Adams's Someone Else's Problem; both the absorption of the event and Nick's reaction are location specific.

But much that is odd is absorbed into the whole. The hotel in which the convention takes place is rather odd. There seem to be five right-angled turns in the corridor. In the bedrooms, one cannot hear one's neighbors but one can hear the disco four floors below. Mirrors create endless reflections: is it any wonder a harassed Magid might not notice that some of those reflections are not right, particularly when what they show is your neighbor in costumes that are not a million miles away from the aesthetic taste of the other convention goers?

Jones has taken us, step-by-step, from the normal to the fantastic, so that the road to Babylon does not open up arbitrarily. When Rupert attempts to tangle the fate lines of his potential Magids, he ends up choosing Wantchester because it is a node of power, of access to other-worlds both in reality and metaphorically. Stan has already hinted to us that those who read science fiction and fantasy are more aware of the possibility of such nodes of power than are others, so that in turn, the choice of Wantchester for a convention is linked to this overlaying of worlds.

The very strangeness of reality at the convention helps to create the casual quality that makes Rupert's vigil on the edge of the road to Babylon more interesting than accompanying Nick and Maree on the trip might have been. Although Jones builds plenty of jokes around the setting she chooses, it is the way she uses an entire convention as a liminal place between the mundane and the fantastic that is really interesting. The missing selves of Andrew (Rupert's neighbor) can appear in the mirrors in part because it is the convention as character that is taking a hand in the proceedings.

Deep Secret is full of in-jokes, but it is essentially a book about the meaning of words, and a sense that the world is storied, through either the Deep Secret of creation myths—something we see also in *The Spellcoats*—or the surface myths of destinarianism that plague the Empire and the Magids. It does not, however, demonstrate much of the mad reasonableness of this chapter's title, although Maree with her luck dance is one of the characters who embodies it.

The books that begin to explain this title are those that play on words, beginning from a casual joke—such as Chris and Mig's jokes about the Cranbury men's being zombies and their Aunt Maria's being a queen bee[14]—and extending it as a prolonged metaphor that runs throughout a tale, becoming increasingly more real as the story proceeds. In this, Jones seems to be purposefully challenging the belief that children want humor that is "simple and spontaneous."[15] Instead, Jones's humor is scented with dark, made more frightening because it lurks in the innocuous. A friend commented to her, "There was nothing … that inspired him with more fear than a polite tea-party given by a dear old lady."[16] From here it spirals, Escher-like, into absurdity. *Archer's Goon*, as we have already seen, delivers this structure with greatest intensity—Jones wrote that *Archer's Goon* "is founded on a dire pun: 'urban gorilla' "[17]—but the joke that explains the family feud in *The Magicians of Caprona* is perhaps the most unsubtle: a Montana invites a Petrocchi to a dinner made of long strips of pasta magicked from the shreds of an offensive letter. As eating one's own words always disagrees, Old Petrocchi leaves with indigestion. This one joke is not extended per se, but it indicates that magic in *The Magicians of Caprona* is essentially sympathetic or metaphorical magic. When Tonino gets the better of the Duchess at the end of chapter 9, it is because he turns her metaphor against her, forcing her to feel the noose around the hangman's neck. This is particularly apt, because it works with the traditional script of Punch and Judy, in which the hanging of the policeman or hangman is a matter of guile, of the use of words to convince.

The ultimate in this mad extension of reasonableness is the curse that Laurel places on Tom in *Fire and Hemlock*, in which imagination becomes true, magnified, and wilder, so that an imagined fiery steed becomes a bucking, terrified circus horse in the middle of the high street. In Jones's worlds magic is frequently conducted in that liminal space that exists between intention and meaning, literal and metaphorical interpretation, what Mary Norton once identified as "real" story.[18] But then Jones is a writer who says something in her books always comes true on her.[19]

If metaphor is so powerful, then precision becomes essential. Casual metaphor, Jones tells her audience repeatedly, is literally dangerous. As Deborah Kaplan has pointed out, throughout *Witch Week* where words are used with precision the spell works, but incidents of ambiguity, such as Charles's generalized call for shoes or Nan's spell for clothes, result, respectively, in a cascade of footwear and an inappropriate ballet frock.[20] More seriously, in *Fire and Hemlock* Tom has been cursed with a link between his words and the world. What he says will come true and hurt him, so that the difference between metaphor and mimetic description becomes vital. When Tom tells Polly to take a look at what backs really look like, to consider "backs bulging, and backs with ingrained dirt,"[21] the lesson is for both the writer and the magic worker. If you cannot see and describe properly, you cannot enchant. In *Dogsbody* Jones provides a superb example of the problem of careless or romantic metaphor:

> Basil went sullen. "I was festering furious. ... I was going to stay out all night and scare them properly. I've read hundreds of books where people are up all night. Only ... they none of them warn you how boring it is. And they say you get tired—but you don't. You just get a sick, hungry sort of feeling and keep on wanting to sit down, and all the cafes close so you can't get anything to eat.[22]

At these moments Jones's attention seems to be on what we might call the writer's eye. Only when one understands the power of reality, Jones seems to say, can one use metaphor consciously, deliberately and effectively. This, of course, is the deep secret in *Witch Week*.

Witch Week has more to say about the mechanisms of prejudice than does *Dogsbody* in part because its emphasis is on the power of words. Toward the end Charles has a moment of recognition that they are all fearful of the inquisitor because they have swallowed the illusion of power that he is peddling. They have persuaded, by words, to accept a certain structure of things. I will come back to this issue when I consider the power of words to coerce in Jones's works, but underlying Charles's realization has been a growing sense throughout the novel that words are tools that must be wielded with precision. The most vivid example is the

"Simon Says" spell, cast by Charles to humiliate Simon. Simon discovers quite quickly that he needs to think carefully not just about what he says but also the precise words he uses to create meaning. Ambiguity such as "You haven't got one golden hand" leaves Theresa with a space where her hand should be.[23] Nirupam, the cleverest of the five children at the center of the story, gets Simon to say, "Nothing I say is going to come true in the future,"[24] which we only much later realize has reversed, rather than cancelled, the spell. We are given a clue, however. When Brian is discovered to be missing, Simon takes charge.

> "We're not going to panic," he said. "Someone get the master on duty."
>
> There was instant emergency. Voices jabbered, rumours roared. Charles fetched Mr. Crossley since everyone else seemed too astonished to think.[25]

Charles, of course, is immune to the effect because he cast the spell. The rigor of the magic, the precision with which Jones displays the consequences of Nirupam's intervention, is slipped into a logical response to a crisis, in a way similar to the reverse ellipse discussed in chapter 3.[26]

Jones's ability to make magic and the effects of magic seem casual—often thereby disguising the dramatic consequences, as we saw with the Simon Says spell— is constructed precisely by this extension of significance into the past of the incident, as well as the future, and also by what John Stephens described as "conversational discourse."[27] This comes into its own in *Howl's Moving Castle,* in which Sophie Hatter, as one of the chapter titles indicates, talks to hats. Sophie can talk life into things. She can charm a suit of clothing into a girl attractor, talk life into the fire demon Calcifer, and, in *Castle in the Air,* beckon the air to come closer so that she and Abdullah can breathe.

> "Really, air!" she said. "This is disgraceful!! You are going to have to let us breathe a bit better than this or we won't last out. Gather round and let us breathe you!"[28]

Stephens argues that Sophie uses "randomly selected signifiers" that function as "a comic reversal of the usual convention that a spell must be exact and precise in its wording."[29] But this elides the point that Sophie—unlike the spell-casters of Caprona—is precisely not about being either exact or precise; her magic is about enlarging and magnifying and generating reality from metaphor (replicating the work of the writer perhaps). Sophie's magic (like that of Nan in *Witch Week*) is a subtle form of coercion or flattery (Stephens suggested "polite heavying"),[30] a magical version, as Abdullah notes, of Abdullah's floral politeness in *Castle in the Air*. Although Sophie's abilities are crucial to the salvation of both Howl and Calcifer, it is the technique which is really important to the plot of *Witch Week*. As we have already seen, almost all the magic worked is a magic of conversation. But the importance of words as words has been made clear before any magic occurs. The most powerful speakers in the book are Simon, who is not actually a witch, and Theresa, who is only "a very small, third-grade sort of witch."[31] As Nan writes in her journal, "SS is so certain he is the real boy he has managed to convince Brian too."[32] Jones is reminding the reader that we can decide how much power we let others have over us. The trajectory of this and other Jones novels, as Deborah Kaplan has pointed out, is for the underdog to regain control over reality by gaining control of narrative.[33]

What all of this conversational discourse constructs is a form of magic that is essentially about persuasion. The difficulty, as Jones argues in almost every book, is how to distinguish persuasion from coercion. In *Dogsbody* Duffie coerces through insult. Similarly in *Witch Week* Nan is belittled by the words used to describe her, as Charles is both enraged and marginalized.[34] This particular power of words, to manipulate, to force people to accept untrue stories about themselves to gain economic or emotional power, is explored most extensively in *Black Maria*.

Aunt Maria coerces by denying her needs. Whether this is for silver-ware, homemade cake, or gardening, she "not-asks." Mig tests it out on her brother Chris: " 'You don't need to bother bringing the cases in from the car. ... We're camping on the floor in our clothes,' "[35] and discovers that he jumps up to collect them before he realizes that Mig is laughing.

This kind of coercion controls people by imposing a narrative upon them, and is most successful when they can be coerced not just into acquiescing to the story line but also into extending it.[36] By the time Chris is transformed into a wolf, Mig has become intellectually dependent on Chris because "everyone here takes for granted that having ideas is not women's work and not nice somehow."[37] As Jones argues, it is from the pressure of conformity that Mig (like Polly) must rescue her heroic self.

Imposed narratives are not necessarily applied with ill intent—emotional carelessness is the issue in *Time of the Ghost* and Jones's memoirs[38]—but if elsewhere Jones has suggested that a good deed can be soured by the wrong motives, in *Black Maria* the most fundamental of all motives, the desire for a happy ending, is regarded with extreme suspicion. There is a constant refrain from her parents, and from her brother, that Mig is too keen on happy endings. The trajectory of the book brings into question not just whether such an ending is possible but also what is meant by a "happy ending". Each of the protagonists—Mig, Dad, Mr. Phelps, Aunt Maria—wants to make a nice, tight story within Cranbury. Aunt Maria's happy ending requires rigid control and a respect for hierarchy. Mr. Phelps wants to restore men's power and is obsessed with control of the little green box; his happy ending is merely a reversal of Aunt Maria's. Mig's Dad wants life to follow rules, and he actually regards happiness as somehow unreal. Chris, both as boy and anarchic wolf, understands that the way to fight back is to wreck the story, and that story is malleable. As Mig observes, he revises his story of the ghost at least four times, a strategy that leaves what he has seen open to interpretation.

It is Miss Phelps and Anthony Green who insist that life cannot be made into a story. Miss Phelps sees it all as "stupid melodrama" and, interestingly, counters the idea of story with the idea of history. The orphanage is there to bring up perfect little citizens of Cranbury, divided by sex. "But don't imagine that's the only time that's been tried. Some of the men holding the green box went even further in the attempt and tried to breed a whole race of obedient folk."[39] To Anthony Green the imposition of narrative goes deeper: those who are not "main characters" " 'seem to think they're not proper people … and then they have to go to hideous lengths to prove they *are*.'"[40] Jones, who clearly values story, uses *Black Maria* to express her suspicion of many of the ideas that she has set out in *Fire and Hemlock*. Margaret Mahy's argument that "there is a code to your lives … something which gives form to your political responses,"[41] is here and elsewhere rendered sinister.

By the time Mig works out that the gray cat is Aunt Maria's assistant Lavinia, she can think sadly, " 'I wish this really was a story I was writing! I'd write in a happy ending this moment. But it isn't, it's real and it goes on and on.'"[42] It is astonishing when one considers it, but there are actually very few truly happy endings in Jones's work. In *Dogsbody* and *Eight Days of Luke*, Katherine and David will never see their best friends ever again. Janet loses her parents in *Charmed Life*, and Vivien Smith loses her world in *A Tale of Time City*. In *Archer's Goon* and the Dalemark quartet, we are left not at the end of adventures but at the beginning of history.

Consideration of the later of Jones's books produce similar results, and it might be the clearly happy endings that render *Power of Three* and *Year of the Griffin* Jones's least successful books.

In *Black Maria* the lesson is less that happy endings are unrealistic but that they are not necessarily narratively interesting. Aunt Maria's ending is neat—the parents reunited, Mig as one of the thirteen—but it is an ending with nowhere else to go. Mig ends up able to write a much more fascinating ending, which is loose and open. The Stepford husbands are liberated, the orphanage children are adopted, Chris is no longer a wolf but is still dealing with the claustrophobia it has gifted him, and Mig's mother is involved with someone who is interesting, complex, and a real adult with a life of his own. Mig's Dad ends up with an ending that is acceptable to him, but not necessarily happy, while she looks on it with scorn but understanding.

What makes *Black Maria* unnerving is what we learn about Aunt Maria's methods: "The main spell is just talk, and that's quite easy, but of course you are working away underneath the talk, putting all sorts of things into people's minds and tying their thoughts into the right shape."[43] This is, of course, precisely the art of the writer, to persuade the reader into the right shape to understand the message. Jones, however, wants to tie her reader's minds into shapes that will in turn question what they read and hear.

If words plus certainty confer power, then for Jones it is words plus certainty plus analysis that can confront this power. This is where Nan in *Witch Week* comes in again. By the end of the book, we have learned that although Nan has power—she can conjure new clothing when the need is there—her habit is to reach for words not magic. But it is Nan, not one of the strongest witches, who emerges as the most powerful figure in the story, because she is the only one who can break away from the stories that are being written by authority figures (teachers, peers, inquisitors). Nan uses her journal to write what she really believes and what she really sees, even though she knows it will be read. The metaphors she spins create a version of truth: "The tongue-test proves that the yellow stuff has a strong taste of armpits, combined with—yes—just a touch of old drains. It comes from the bottom of a dustbin. ... It's like the gift of tongues! she thought. Only in my case it's the gift of foul-mouth."[44] In Nan, Jones can let her imagination run riot but also demonstrate that analysis, the reframing of what is seen, can breach consensus reality. It is Nan's inability to dissemble, combined with her powers of analysis, that allows Chrestomanci to put the worlds together again. Although her classmates avoid villains when Chrestomanci demands the names of historical figures, Nan blurts out Guy Fawkes and then, as Chrestomanci has promised, she gets "one really good opportunity to describe things."[45]

> In it, this whole stripe of the rainbow, where we are now, and all the magic anywhere near, got blown out of the rest of the world, like a sort of long coloured splinter. But it wasn't blown quite free.[46]

Charles forces Simon to say that Guy Fawkes blew up the Houses of Parliament, and, with the spell still on him, Simon unravels history, and it never happened. The two worlds meld. The crucial intervention is Nan's analysis of the story.

The demands Jones makes on her readers, and her decision to work all sorts of things into their minds, is evident in unexpected places and unexpected moments of ruthlessness, not necessarily relevant to the plot but often providing counterpoint to the humor and lightheartedness. Jones continually reminds us—as in Nan's diary—that truth might not be nice. In *A Sudden Wild Magic,* Mark and Gladys, members of the Inner Circle of the Witches of Britain, visit a hospital:

> Hospitals always bothered him acutely. They were so full of pain, and of pain's obverse, cheerful insensitivity—or was cruelty the word...here were wrung faces on pillows. Women here and there sat up and, in the concentrated egotism of mortal sickness, greedily ate chocolates or stared while visitors harangued them.[47]

There is in this description that mad reasonableness again, the "concentrated egotism of mortal sickness" that gets beyond the clichés and focuses on the improper as the real center of meaning.[48] This runs through many of the books but reaches its apogee in *A Sudden Wild Magic,* a book (written for adults) that rollicks along while slipping in comments about adultery, vicious relationships, and exploitation of various kinds, and kills a number of its characters very early on. Even the plot of *A Sudden Wild Magic* is absurd, and it is presented as if we should regard it as such. It begins when Mark, the only man in the Inner Circle of the Witches of Britain, runs a computer program and comes to some startling conclusions. These he takes to Gladys, one of his colleagues and an older woman who might regard purple as a rather sedate color for clothing. Gladys is one of Jones's maddeningly reasonable but outrageous characters, and the author has the wit to demonstrate just how annoying a mother she would be.

What Mark takes to Gladys is his belief that there is a conspiracy to destabilize the Earth. And in the time honored tradition of conspiracy narratives, it is not responsible for small matters, but it " 'distracted you with the bombing of Libya ... cause World War Two, or the Cold War, AIDS, drugs, ... the greenhouse effect? Who isn't interested in our having a space program?' "[49] This immense overkill renders the entire plot ludicrous, but as we eventually discover, rendering things ludicrous is the solution to the problem—a projection of balance that also appears in other ways in the novel because Jones uses reactions in the same way as she uses themes. A reaction delivered for one purpose runs through the novel as a whole.

The Inner Circle works out that the attacks are coming from a Blishian city (a city that floats above its planet) in another universe and sends a crack team, mostly of women but some men (although all of the men and some of the women die on arrival), to find out what is happening. What they find there is a neomonastic order dedicated to studying Earth in order to find solutions for Arth's problems. From the first Jones renders the neomonastery laughable: its head is called High Head, the oath is over the top, and the food is terrible. The surviving members of the team set about trying to destroy the city by undermining the rigidity and discipline of the order, accepting High Head's word that the city can be kept in balance only by calm and quiet. It is Zillah, herself another one of the disturbing and madly reasonable women Jones loves, who dissents.

Zillah's presence on the trip is unplanned. Zillah's life is unplanned. Sister to the remarkably well-organized Amanda, she has spent an entire life avoiding being organized by anyone, preferring low-paying jobs to careers. Sometime in the recent past she had an affair with a married man, and when she became pregnant she refused to tell either him, or to tell Amanda who he was. Now with a two-year-old son, Zillah seems the epitome of the uncontrolled, and this is manifested also in her magic, for which she has refused training. At the time the story starts, she is living with Amanda, but unbeknownst to any of them, the High Head has been using Amanda's children as a source of information. When he tries it in Zillah's presence, he "found himself confronted with a sudden wild magic, passionate and strong ... it flung fluctuations all over the Wheel with a force that a full-blooded gualdian could hardly have equaled."[50]

Zillah is a stowaway on the trip; her main aim is to get away from the pain she feels over her lover and her sense that there is something incomplete about him. It is this sense that is the key. Zillah makes up in empathy what she lacks in actual knowledge, and this allows her to see past the information provided by the High Head, which the rest of the team accepts unquestioningly. Instead, Zillah tries to match what she sees with what she feels, and she finds incongruity:

> Not a trace of decoration anywhere. It was, to look at, a serious, clinical place. The cells they were to sleep in were monastic. Yet—this was what was muddling Zillah—for no reason she could see, the fortress was not cold or joyless. If the place were a person, Zillah would have said it was itching to spring up and do a mad dance, because it was full of health and delighting in that health, but it seemed to have been too well trained or severely brought up to do anything so frivolous.[51]

Zillah is Jones's questioning reader, and, like Nan in *Witch Week*, it is the analysis that Zillah offers to Judy and Flan and Helen that eventually allows them to collapse the Order—in a wonderfully wild conga scene—without bringing down the citadel.

Zillah's wild power is disguised in a meek and humble outer casing, much like Nan's when we first meet her. Maree Mallory in *Deep Secret* gets to wear her wildness on the outside and to celebrate it publicly. Whereas Zillah's magic is mostly performed for an audience of only a few, or sneaks itself cunningly into the magic of others—as when she uses Tod's powers against the High Head—Maree stands on the Bristol suspension bridge and dances. One of Rupert's problems throughout this book is that he keeps trying to hang on to his dignity. As the youngest of three brothers and the youngest Magid, he has confused his dignity with getting the job done. Maree drives a coach and horses through this because she is much more need-and-end driven; she has no dignity to lose.

> She was a small, unlovely woman in glasses, with a figure like a sack of straw with a string tied round it. And she danced. She bent her knees, she hopped, she cavorted. Her ragbag skirt swirled, her untidy hair flew and her spectacles slid on her barely-existent nose.[52]

If we have any doubt that Jones is on the side of the wild, the undisciplined, and the imaginative, she clears up this point when she uses Maree's Uncle Ted as the voice of the writer: "Uncle Ted won't talk about his work at home, it's a job 'I like to come home from the office and put my feet up, as it were.' (He works at home of course.)."[53] It gets even worse when Ted and Janine begin talking about Ted's work in terms of what it bought for them: "Nick's basement came out of *The Curse on the Cottage;* and he retorted with the fitted bookcases out of *Surrender, You Devil.*"[54] And the final straw for Maree is the wavy glass in the windows:

> It waves and wobbles. … From some shapes and angles, the houses bend and stretch into weird shapes, and you might really believe they were sliding into a different set of dimensions. …

> I knew Uncle Ted was going to destroy all the strangeness by saying something dreary about the windows, and I terribly didn't want him to. I almost prayed at him not to. But he did. He said, "It's genuine wartime glass from World War Two, you know. It dates from when Hitler bombed the docks here. …" So we leave the panes, whatever else we do. The glass is historic. It adds quite a bit to the value of the house.[55]

Ted Mallory's's mistake is to create a rigid division between work and fun: "You can't afford to get carried away, or your book becomes a dangerous, out-of-hand thing and it may not sell."[56] Even in earlier novels, Jones keeps telling us this is wrong. When Christopher in *The Lives of Christopher Chant* finally gets to run Chrestomanci Castle, he ruminates that despite everyone's demand for discipline, he is at his best when most bumptious. Jones's work can be interpreted as an attempt to combine precisely these elements, the disciplined, and the rambunctious.

We come at last to those texts that can be seen as being precisely about writing: in effect, forming a short course in how (and why) to write. The most obvious is "Carol Oneir's Hundreth Dream," which is a response to the standard author quip "my characters just got the better of me" and to the innumerable saccharine interviews with popular authors which appear every year. In a speech delivered at the Children's Literature New England summer institute, published as "Birthing a Book" in *The Horn Book Magazine,* Jones discusses how the story was a response to an earlier paper (discussed in the introduction) in which she wrote about the construction of *Fire and Hemlock.* "Very nice, Diana, but writers don't work like that," one of her editors responded.[57]

> As soon as I thought, I realized that the book had *not* been written in at all the analytical way I had tried to describe. The *second* draft might have

been, when I was trying to make clear all the various elements that went into it ... but the *first* draft had been written at white heat, in a state where I was unable to put it down.[58]

As Jones went on to explain, "Carol Oneir's Hundredth Dream" was explicitly about the traps for the young writer. Carol Oneir is a dreamer. She goes to sleep, and her dreams are recorded, packaged in pink, and sold. As a small child, she is a prodigy, celebrated for as much for her as for the quality of her dreams. Since she is a child, she has almost never had to deal with critics, because for critics to take on a child is jut not done.[59] However Carol has found it impossible to dream her one hundredth dream. She has writer's block and does not know why. When the specialists have been exhausted, Carol's father arranges for her to see Chrestomanci, who takes her into her dreams where she finds her characters have gone on strike for the right to be real people.

In the course of the story, we learn a number of things. Chrestomanci refuses to accept the saccharine and rehearsed account of Being a Writer that Carol delivers. He points out to Carol that although Janet loves her work, the boys and Julia think they are slush and samish, knocking down the idea that children do not have critical faculties.[60] Chrestomanci recognizes very quickly that there are only five or six real characters in Carol's dreams. When Carol goes into her dream, she discovers a cast of thousands resentful that they have no identity—the first she meets has "a dull, unfinished look."[61] Her main characters are fed up with playing the same roles, time after time. When Lucy—who plays heroines to Francis's heroes and "hated being forced to wear frilly dresses and simper at Francis"—fell in love with Norman, "they began complaining they never got a chance to become real people."[62] But Jones is too good a critic to allow us to accept this superficially. This is not so much about the characters' running away with the story as demanding that Carol take on the responsibilities of a real author. Chrestomanci asks Melville what he thinks of Carol's dreams, and reluctantly he replies,

> She has tremendous talent, of course ... but I do sometimes feel that she—well—she repeats herself. Put it like this: I think maybe Carol doesn't give herself a chance to be herself any more than she gives us.[63]

What Carol is being rescued from is the curse of the serial writer. Elsewhere, in the much more complex *Fire and Hemlock,* Polly is liberated from the curse of the clichéd writer in ways that I have already described, and we get to see what Jones might require of a course in creative writing. One of Carol's problems is that she has become hooked on the idea that imagination is essentially internal, that it comes from within, without external stimulus. In *Fire and Hemlock* Jones argues that creativity is much more antagonistic and responsive.

When we first meet Polly, she is dependent on Nina, because Nina, with her habit of daring and demanding Polly's ideas, forces her to be creative. When she first meets Tom, his passivity dampens her: "Without any prodding, Polly's invention went dead on her."[64] Once Tom starts to ask questions, Polly's imagination begins to flow, and her creativity stimulates his flow of questions. The antagonistic nature of creativity then manifests itself in the reading with which Tom supplies Polly.

Polly's reading almost always coincides with the moral or character or literary issue that has come up between them. The Christmas parcel contains *The Wonderful Wizard of Oz, Five Children and It, The Treasure Seekers,* and *The Wolves of Willoughby Chase,* all of which have things to say about the nature of courage, which chime with Tom's discovery that courage relates mostly to the willingness to put up with embarrassment. The first parcel of books included *The Lion, the Witch and the Wardrobe, A Box of Delights,* and *The Sword in the Stone,* as well as *One Hundred and One Dalmatians* and *Henrietta's House.* Each of these contains discussions about the relation of the real world to the fantasy world. Teaching through story is inferential, not instructional.

The relationship between the fiction and the real world is one that bothers writers, and *Fire and Hemlock* can be read as an argument about this relationship. Early in the story, Polly's imagination leads her to provide the counterfactual Tom with a wife:

> "No there isn't," Mr. Lynn said. He said it quietly and calmly, as if someone had asked him if there was any butter and he had opened the fridge and found none. But Polly could tell he meant it absolutely.[65]

Tom's absolute rejection of this implies that he fully understands the curse—something that is not always clear—but in a manifestation of the power of words, when we meet Tom Piper the ironmonger, we discover that both Polly's statement and Tom's refutation are true: Mr. Piper claims not to have a wife, and the woman we meet is presented as his sister (as Polly had suggested), but she is in fact married to him. More directly, Tom asks Polly how his hero nature and their adventures relate to reality.

"But I still don't understand about Tan Coul," he said thoughtfully, with his big hands clasped round his knees. ... "Where is he when he—or I—do his deeds? Are the dragons and giants and so forth here and now, or are they somewhere else entirely?" ...

"Sort of both," she said. "The other place they come from and where you do your deeds *is* here—but it's not here too. It's—Oh bother you! I just can't explain!" ...

She saw in her mind two stone vases spinning, one slowly, the other fast, and stopping to show half a word each. ... "It's like those vases. Now-here and Nowhere."[66]

Polly never explains further, but if there is a spell cast, this is the moment. Polly challenges the notion that the boundary between the created world and the real world is impermeable. In this small quotation Polly also, for the first time, begins to become a writer. The incident of the rippling backs is part of a larger schema in which Polly first makes an attempt to write a novel. In *Witch Week* uncontrolled invention is lauded, and when Polly first attempts a novel the same note of congratulation seems evident. She writes it almost until her fourteenth birthday, using Shakespeare's use of others' plots as an excuse to raid everything she has read. She becomes fascinated with ways to describe people (those rippling muscles again), and she writes obsessively. The result, as Tom points out, is sentimental rubbish. Only when she rereads it with some distance between her and her product does Polly see what Tom is getting at.

She found she knew exactly what Tom meant. She writhed. Oddly enough, it was all the bits she had been most pleased with that now made her writhe hardest.[67]

Polly learns that control of one's narrative is as important as one's free imagination; the point is reiterated in *Archer's Goon* when Quentin loses control of his characters in the last act. She also learns that fantasy does not mean a complete divorce from reality and that the writer should be self-critical. All of these ideas are repeated and extended in *The Spellcoats*, a second book that is also told from the perspective of a writer, but this time one with a greater awareness of the degree to which her actions are shaping the story.

The Spellcoats is, to state the obvious, written in two parts, each a story written in the weaving of a coat. It is a metafiction in which the story of making the story is as important as the tale itself, in which there "is the story actually being told, a series of events that compose the *histoire* … [and] the story of the telling."[68]

As Tanaqui moves from the first coat to the second coat, she contemplates how to write, how to create expression, and how to make her words more powerful. In part the transition occurs simply because Tanaqui has learned through her observations of Kankredin's mages that her weaving can be understood as magic through prediction. Weaving here operates as itself and as analogy. Tanaqui's weaving is close and fine, and her threads are as tight as the intricacies of plot. To weave quickly, "I set the first part of the pattern and cast the threads, there and back, and then the row to hold it, and while I do that, I am thinking of the next line. By the time I have finished that band of words, I often have the next three or four ready in my head."[69] Meaning builds on sense; creativity, imagination, and narrative have an internal rhythm and structure that accumulates.

But *The Spellcoats* is also a book that is shaped by an argument about structure. The first coat and the second coat do not tell the same kinds of stories or narrate them in the same way. Both are internal monologues, but the first coat is an account of a narrative history, and the second coat is a diary, a narrative as it occurs. The result is two rather different voices. The first coat opens with, "I want to tell of our journey down the River. We are five,"[70] whereas the second coat opens with, "I am Tanaqui. I must begin on a second rugcoat, because understanding has come to me at last, and maybe I no longer need to blame myself."[71] The first coat closes with a transition to the immediacy of the second coat.

> I am now at the back hem of my rugcoat. All I have space to say is that we are at a stand. Gull is still a clay figure. Robin is ill. I am afraid she will die … all I can do is weave, and hope for understanding. The meaning of our journey is now in this rugcoat. I am Tanaqui and I end my weaving.[72]

The difference this change in voice makes is that the first coat is far less of a process. With the exception perhaps of the consideration of Tanamil, it is a relatively naive story in which description is assumed to carry the weight of analysis. The second coat, in contrast and in part because describes the previous coat, is a book of commentary, as the following example illustrates:

I thought this was just his joke at the time, but it has now become clear to me that our King has indeed no intention of fighting the Heathen again. He enquires daily about the Heathen, but this is in order to avoid them.[73]

Although the second coat does have story of its own to tell, this story is a comment on events: the first coat told of the invasion: the second coat told of the consequences for the land. The first coat is story; the second coat is criticism. It is in this analysis and argument that Tanaqui will hand her full power to the One to unbind him, suggesting that analysis, the shaping of story, is more powerful than the mere telling; a story is a whole in which the argument is the shape it makes. When Tanaqui—angry with Duck and anxious to prove him wrong—reads the rugcoat, she sees not just words but also shapes.

> In the front, the gloomy colours gather up the centre into a shape, and that shape is the same shadow with a long nose and a bent head that I saw when Uncle Kestrel came. ... There is a lightness on the back, that begins from the time we met Tanamil. ... Across the neck of the long-nosed shadow, near the hem, runs a band woven in that expressive twist which Tanamil showed me. It expresses my terror of Kankredin and his soulnet.[74]

It is the overall shape of the narrative that tells Tanaqui which are the important events in the morass of happenings (even her father's death is "put into perspective" by its place within the overall pattern of the coat). And in addition, by having Tanaqui weave rather than write the words, Jones uses her to capture the sense that many readers and printers have—but few reading specialists ever mention—that the words on a page form shapes as they cluster together and that a book and the reading of it is more than simply the sum of its words.[75]

The lessons of *The Spellcoats* are essentially about writing in a medium that is linear. After the meeting with Tanamil, Tanaqui is muddled as to what happened. She discusses it with Duck, but she is still not sure she has it in the right order:

> "That's the trouble with you Tanaqui," Duck said to me. "You always have to have things in *order*. You're as bad as Hern." I think Duck is right, though I did not realise it before. If I cannot get a thing straight in my head, it offends me, like a piece of weaving that has one wrong. ...

> This is why Hern and I are so much more horrified than Duck by our
> strange time with Tanamil.[76]

Later they argue about how and when Tanamil got them to question him:
"he says I do wrong to put it in here, because it happened right at the
beginning of our stay. But I remember it almost at the end, and I am
weaving this story."[77] Where there are disputes as to what has happened,
the maintenance of the linear narrative, and of a unity, takes precedence
over creating perspective. This is very different from the structure of
Hexwood, a novel that seems modeled after the interactive game books
popular (particularly among boys) in the 1980s.

In *Hexwood* Jones signaled her intentions very early on, first with the
letter to the Reigners, which informs us that some sort of role-playing
game is getting out of hand, then again almost immediately when Ann
tells us that her brother Martin likes books about dinosaurs or those based
on role-playing games. In *Hexwood* Jones produced a book that is precisely about control of the tale. The Bannus has set in train a series of
events designed to see who is the strongest writer, so that, for example,
when Reigner Three enters the game, we get a very different story within
the castle from the one previously played out—instead of rivalries around
the court, we see a plot to marry the King and take control that way.

But *Hexwood* is also one of the books, like *The Spellcoats,* that is about
writing as editing (or editing as a creative process). The Bannus has
clearly been taking tips from Jones's "Hints about Writing a Story."[78] The
Bannus is not merely a Dungeonmaster: it aims everything toward one
outcome—"I wish you to know that every one of my six hundred and
ninety-seven plans of action was designed to end in your death."[79] The
Bannus keeps working out scenes, such as Mordion's encounters with
Ann and his dealings with Hume, until Mordion's character is edited in
such a way that he can react the way the Bannus wants him to. Each character pulled in provides another set of possibilities to the Bannus as
writer; the library in the center provides new ideas; and in the end some of
the characters become rival writers. Whereas Tanaqui sought to keep
argument and multiple perspectives out of her writing, the Bannus and
the novel *Hexwood* constructs the story in the consensus space created by
these multiple perspectives.

Archer's Goon includes many of the themes about writing that have been
explored in other books. With a writer—Quentin—as a main character
and a plot that revolves around whether or not words have power, this

seems rather obvious. The book deals with what we might think of as standard tips, such as the avoidance of cliché (e.g., Hathaway is not one of Shakespeare's ancestors, and money buried at the bottom of the garden is likely to be dug up long before Howard finds it) and advice on character-ization (e.g., consider how people live rather than what they say), which ties into earlier books such as *Dogsbody*, which describes people through scent, and *The Spellcoats*, in which Kankredin's features are described in bits, "a wriggly grey sheet of hair on either side of his face, and that the top of his head was bald and grey with dirt, with one or two big pink lumps on it ... the eyes thick-lidded, in folds,"[80] because features do not describe people. *Archer's Goon* can also be considered a book about editing: Howard–Venturus does not live his thirteen years in quite the same way each time. The last time around (actually Howard's third attempt at grow-ing up) has been revised—the introduction of Awful (Anthea) into the mix results in a different, less selfish Howard. But the book is perhaps most interesting because it brings into focus Jones's fondness for writing structure books, books that are not simply structured around an idea but around the way in which the very structures themselves are there to be proved.

Jones has said that the theses at the front of *Archer's Goon* came from the Dutch approach to dissertations in which the theses have to be stated at the front.[81] They are, of course, a joke: they add to the fun of the book as one sees them, one by one, come true. But they also demonstrate an approach to writing that can be seen in all of the books discussed in this chapter. Jones's work is written in such a way that structure carries as much meaning as does the plot or the language. Even as frivolous a book as *The Magicians of Caprona* follows this approach. Very early on in the novel, the children sing the words to "The Angel of Caprona." The words of the song tell us what the solution is, both to find the *right* words, and who should sing them and in what spirit. In *Archer's Goon* there are con-stant dropped hints: Suzanne Rahn has noticed that we are actually told that Howard is unusually tall, and at thirteen he is almost the size of a grown man. Hathaway mentions Venturus's interest in the future and his adoration of Archer, and Howard knows there is something he is missing, but the reader misses it too. "Howard's dislike of his family is so strong that he resists the discovery to the very end."[82] As with the Simon Says spell in *Witch Week*, if we pay attention to the structure we can work out what is happening, but the very structure forces our gaze away to all the other things that are happening. We cannot even keep our eyes on those opening thesis statements. *Archer's Goon*'s thesis structure turns a quest into a formal research project in which Howard must work out what the problem is, assemble and analyze the evidence, and finally develop and implement a solution. Each of the theses is a step on the way, and only once he has sorted out his research can he apply words (Quentin's as it happens) in ways that are powerful. If there is a thesis in *Fire and Hemlock* and *Hexwood,* it is that creativity is essentially the interaction of elements, a process of antagonism and synthesis between many different materials—it has a source. Fiction as written by Diana Wynne Jones is a critical process.

EPILOGUE

...to encourage some part of one generation at least to use their minds as minds are supposed to be used.[1]

Each novel Diana Wynne Jones has written takes children through the art of logic, the nature of story, a writing and editing course, and a discussion of ethics. She demands of them that they continually question the assumptions on which any happy ending rests. What kind of children can unravel the stories in the ways I have suggested are possible? To conclude, I want to suggest two arguments: first that Jones is actually challenging the popular construction of the Child Reader found in the literature on children reading, and second that she has done this in part by setting out to grow the readers she wishes to have.

In thinking about Jones—and some of the other authors such as William Mayne and Alan Garner, whose audience is frequently called into question—we need to get away from the idea of the Child Reader, that figure that Karin Lesnik-Oberstein described as stabilized "with the help of psychological theories of cognitive and emotional development."[2] The Child Reader has been constructed as the reader for whom adults choose books, who has to be tempted into reading because reading, we have decided, is good for him or her. Sue Walsh points out, correctly I believe, that "Appeals to 'the child reader,' are ... often used to foreclose certain kinds of reading that are thereby produced as 'adult' and therefore have no validity in the context of children's literature."[3] The Child Reader is frequently to be tempted by content, by identification. The Child Reader is, it seems, the reluctant reader. But the construction of the Child Reader

193

conflicts with what we know of someone we might call the "Reading Child".

The Reading Child is the child who can go from nonreader to reader almost overnight. This can happen at a young age, but it does not have to. The point is that for these children, it is the process of reading rather than the content of particular books that grabs them. These are the children who have to be steered around lampposts, who are reprimanded for being antisocial, and who quickly work out the maximum number of books they can borrow from the maximum number of reachable libraries (although they are not necessarily fast readers). These children, like Jones who read Malory and Burton at the age of eight, are relatively oblivious to the suitability of texts.[4] These children are absent from many of the discussions of the Child Reader but might be central to Jones's construction of her audience. *Wilkins' Tooth* seems to speak to what Mike Cadden described as the generalized child.[5] As Jones's work developed, she clearly moved away from this notion toward a more specific audience. One result is that Jones writes as if children can already read. We can see this in the intertextuality that haunts her books from the start.

Jones's use of intertextuality assumes that there is no specific age at which a text cannot be accessed at some level or another. Her justification for doing so, however, has altered as she has reflected on the audiences she has met. Discussing her use of Eliot's *Four Quartets,* Jones wrote, "I never worry about putting in things that are not within children's capacities, because I don't think this matters. I think it's very good for children to notice that there's something going on that they don't understand."[6] But later when Jones considered the process of writing *A Sudden Wild Magic*—which was commissioned as an adult novel—she concluded that children might be better at reading complex texts than are adults. "Children are used to not knowing, and therefore they make sure that they *do* know and remember ... there is that much difference, that perhaps in sheer sympathy for adults you ought to make it a bit looser, so that they can understand what's going on."[7] The reading child, Jones seems to be saying, has an unconscious awareness of intertextuality that can be extended and kept alive.

Jones's intertextuality seems aimed at the Reading Child in yet another way—Jones writes for the book-starved. The intertextuality of her books can be understood in a number of ways, but at least one element is that they seem designed to be reread and wrung dry of all possible detail, and then even the manner in which the detail is fitted together is to be considered. Her books are each many books in one. Like Edith Nesbit's children, her protagonists "occupy a book-shaped world."[8]

This book-shaped world is a creative place. Children in such worlds shape the writing of their own story. There is a term for this: Diana Wynne Jones writes *Künstlerromane,* tales that are essentially about the growing of the child into the artist. The *Künstlerroman* is traditionally about the urge to create, and, as we saw in chapter 7, many of Jones's books are also ostentatiously about the craft of creativity. Moril, Cat, Tanaqui, Tonino and Angelica, Maree, Nan Pilgrim, and Howard all are "pushed by internal and abstract forces towards regions of the mysterious and unknown, towards words, colors, and the music of inspiration."[9]

Amusingly, Jones seems to be training her readers to be what Peter Hunt described as those who "read in a deviant way";[10] that is, critically. A Jones reader will, by the time he or she has read *Witch Week, Archer's Goon,* and *Fire and Hemlock,* particularly if he or she reads it more than once, have realized that the idea of a transparent text is untenable. Brian Attebery wrote,

> The experience of someone reading a poem or a novel is a configuration … it takes place over time, involves negotiations with earlier readers and previously read texts, includes sudden shifts and dramatic transformations, and centers on the relationships between the reader and various other characters such as the authorial presence perceived in the text. How better to represent this complicated whole than by telling a story about it?[11]

This continual exchange of meanings between author, text, reader, and intertexts is how Jones constructs her metafictions. This is not coincidental on her use of intertext but a precise configuration that is intended to open up across a reader's reading lifetime. The consequences for her readership, however, extend further: Wayne C. Booth wrote, "The author makes his readers. … If he makes them well—that is, makes them see what they have never seen before, moves them into a new order of perception and experience altogether—he finds his reward in the peers he has created."[12] For Jones we can find evidence for this if we return, finally, and briefly, to the historical record of Jones criticism. For such a prolific writer, there has been very little work on Jones. In the 1980s her work was mostly either dismissed as mildly interesting or ignored. Diana Wynne Jones's name rarely crops up in indexes of the wider studies of children's fiction. Only in the 1990s do we begin to see articles by Suzanne Rahn,

Ruth Waterhouse, and Martha Hixon and mentions by C.W. Sullivan II
and Maria Nikolajeva. Yet when Teya Rosenberg, Martha Hixon, Sharon
Scapple, and Donna R. White put out their call for papers on Diana
Wynne Jones's work in 2000, they were overwhelmed with proposals.

Wilkins' Tooth was published in 1973. Many of the critics now writing
about Jones are just reaching their late thirties and early forties. They
would have been young children when *Eight Days of Luke* and *The Ogre
Downstairs* were published. It is just possible that for Jones's complexity to
be appreciated, first she had to grow her critics.

In 2005 Jones produced her forty-fifth novel, an addition to the Chrestomanci series. *Conrad's Fate* is a gothic romance complete with spooky
castle and possible ghosts; it has all of the usual Jones themes of careless
parents and obsessive and controlling adults. But this is Jones, and Jones is
always looking for one more thing to teach us about the fantastic. At the
end we are presented with a set of photographs; in each, part of a building
is shown in all of its possible manifestations. Each of these pictures resem-
bles Michael Wesley's experimentations with three-year film exposures in
which buildings visibly contain their own endoskeletons.[13] In Jones's construction these "possibility-grams" are only the start. What matters about
the fantastic is what you do with it. If we consider it as much an act of
criticism as a fashioning of fiction, then Jones's work is a thirty-year-long
argument about teaching children to read and about what reading and
reading the fantastic mean.

NOTES

Introduction

1. Nicholas Tucker, "The Child in Time," *Independent Magazine,* April 5, 2003, 16.
2. Suzanne Rahn, *Rediscoveries in Children's Literature* (New York and London: Garland, 1995), 177.
3. See Francis J. Molson, *Children's Fantasy* (Starmont Reader's Guide, 33) (San Bernardino, CA: Borgo Press, 1989), 4, for a similar assertion; and Brian Attebery, *Strategies of Fantasy* (Bloomington and Indianapolis: Indiana University Press, 1992), ix; and John Clute and John Grant, eds., *The Encyclopedia of Fantasy* (London: Orbit, 1997), passim, for a demonstration of this easy conflation.
4. Beverly Lyon Clark, *Kiddie Lit: The Cultural Construction of Children's Literature in America* (Baltimore: Johns Hopkins University Press, 2003), 48–77.
5. Peter Hunt, "The World of Children's Literature Studies," in *Understanding Children's Literature,* ed. Peter Hunt (London: Routledge, 1999), 4.
6. Jacqueline Rose, *The Case of Peter Pan or the Impossibility of Children's Fiction* (Basingstoke: Macmillan, 1984), 154.
7. Clark, "Kiddie Lit in the Academy," in *Kiddie Lit,* 48–77; Gary K. Wolfe, "Malebolge, Or the Ordnance of Genre," *Conjunctions: 39, The New Wave Fabulists* (Annandale-on-Hudson, NY: Bard College, 2002): 406–407, 409; and Robert Leeson, "To the Toyland Frontier," in *The Signal Approach to Children's Books,* ed. N. Chambers (Harmondsworth: Kestrel, 1980), 209.
8. Teya Rosenberg, "Introduction," in *Diana Wynne Jones: An Exciting and Exacting Wisdom,* ed. Teya Rosenberg et al. (New York: Peter Lang, 2002), 6.
9. Carolyn Cushman, "All Time List," *Locus: The Magazine of the Science Fiction and Fantasy Field* 52, no. 1 (January 2004): 40.

10. Diana Wynne Jones, *Yes Dear,* illustrated by Graham Philpot (New York: Greenwillow, 1992).

11. Kathryn Hume, *Fantasy and Mimesis: Responses to Reality in Western Literature* (New York and London: Methuen, 1984), 21.

12. Tzvetan Todorov, *The Fantastic: A Structural Approach to a Literary Genre* (New York: Cornell University Press, 1975), 41–57. It is a common joke among genre fantasy specialists that by the time Todorov is finished, only Henry James's *The Turn of the Screw* will count as fantasy.

13. Eric S. Rabkin, *The Fantastic in Literature* (Princeton, NJ: Princeton University Press, 1976), 8.

14. Brian Attebery, *The Fantasy Tradition in American Literature* (Bloomington: Indiana University Press, 1980), 2.

15. Gary K. Wolfe, "Evaporating Genre: Strategies of Dissolution in the Postmodern Fantastic," in *Edging into the Future: Science Fiction and Contemporary Cultural Transformation,* ed. Veronica Hollinger and Joan Gordon (Philadelphia: University of Pennsylvania Press, 2002), 16.

16. Diana Wynne Jones, "The Profession of Science Fiction, 51: Answers to Some Questions," *Foundation: The International Review of Science Fiction* 70 (Summer 1997): 12.

17. Arthur C. Clarke, *Profiles of the Future: An Inquiry into the Limits of the Possible,* 2nd ed. (London: Gollancz, 1974), 1–21.

18. Farah Mendlesohn, "Introduction," in *The Cambridge Companion to Science Fiction,* ed. Edward James and Farah Mendlesohn (Cambridge: Cambridge University Press, 2003), 1, 2.

19. Diana Wynne Jones, "Diana Wynne Jones: Writing for Children," *Locus* (April 1989): 5, 62.

20. Jack Zipes, *When Dreams Came True: Classical Fairy Tales and Their Traditions* (New York: Routledge, 1999), 133.

21. "Incomers" are people who come to live permanently in an area that has had no new settlement for decades, sometimes centuries, usually a village. The nearest U.S. equivalent seems to be "summer people," but that implies transience.

22. Diana Wynne Jones, "A Plague of Peacocks," in *Unexpected Magic* (New York: Greenwillow, 2004), 36–49.

23. "Interview with Diana Wynne Jones, conducted by Charles Butler, 22 March 2001," in *An Exciting and Exacting Wisdom,* 171.

24. Nicolette Jones, "Fantasy Matches How Our Brains Are Made," *The Times,* March 26, 2003, 17.

25. Molson, *Children's Fantasy,* 31–32

26. Natasha Walter, "The Accidental Realist," *The Guardian,* October 9, 2004 (from the Internet). We also know that *The Magician's Nephew* is Jones's favorite of the Narnia series. Diana Wynne Jones, "The Magic of Narnia," http://www.amazon.com/exec/obidos/tg/feature/-/91955/104-6380809-0505511.

27. N. Jones, "Fantasy Matches How Our Brains Are Made," 17.

28. Julia Briggs, *A Woman of Passion: The Life of E. Nesbit 1858–1924* (London: Hutchinson, 1987).
29. This title was not chosen by Diana Wynne Jones who regards the comparison between giving birth and writing a book as "bunkum" (email, Chris Bell, January 24, 2005).
30. Robert Giddings, ed., *J.R.R. Tolkien: This Far Land* (London: Vision, 1983).
31. Diane Wynne Jones, "The Shape of the Narrative in *Lord of the Rings*," in *J.R.R. Tolkien: This Far Land,* 88.
32. Ibid., 91.
33. Ibid., 104.
34. Diana Wynne Jones, "The Heroic Ideal—A Personal Odyssey," *The Lion and the Unicorn* 13 (1989): 132.
35. Ibid., 139.
36. Jones, "Answers to Some Questions," 5.
37. Ibid., 6.
38. Diana Wynne Jones, "Birthing a Book," *Horn Book Magazine,* July–August 2004, 381.
39. Jones, "Carol Oneir's Hundredth Dream," in *Dragons and Dreams,* ed. Jane Yolen, Martin H. Greenberg, and Charles G. Waugh (New York: Harper and Row, 1986), 108–35; reprinted in Jones, *Mixed Magics* (London: Harper Collins, 1984), 101–29.
40. Jones, "Answers to Some Questions," 5. Twyford is the name of a manufacturer of bathroom equipment, as well as that of a small town in Berkshire.
41. Alice Mills, "The Trials and Tribulations of Two Dogsbodies: A Jungian Reading of Diana Wynne Jones's *Dogsbody*," in *An Exciting and Exacting Wisdom,* 138–48.
42. Diana Wynne Jones, "Heroes," a lecture originally delivered in Australia, 1992; held at the "Diana Wynne Jones Fansite," http://www.leemac.freeserve.co.uk/.
43. Ibid.
44. Ibid.
45. Diana Wynne Jones, *Year of the Griffin* (London: Victor Gollancz, 2000), 42.
46. Ibid., 81; Jones, "Answers to Some Questions," 11.
47. Jones, "The Shape of the Narrative in *Lord of the Rings*," 87.
48. Jones, *Year of the Griffin,* 84.
49. Sue Walsh, "Author and Authorship, Effigies of Effie: On Kipling Biographies," in *Children's Literature: New Approaches,* ed. Karin Lesnik-Oberstein (Basingstoke: Palgrave Macmillan, 2004), 25.
50. Jones, "Answers to Some Questions," 6.
51. Interview with Maureen Kincaid Speller, "In Her Own Words, Part 2," *Charmed Lives Fanzine,* no. 2, 1998, http://www.leemac.freeserve.co.uk/cl2int.htm.
52. Jones, "The Girl Jones," in *Unexpected Magic: Collected Stories* (New York: Greenwillow, 2004), 1–12.

53. Diana Wynne Jones, "1934–," *Something about the Author,* vol. 70 (Detroit: Gale, 1993), 115–18. Internet version used.

54. Ibid.

55. Virginia Nicholson, *Among the Bohemians: Experiments in Living 1900–1939* (London: Penguin Books, 2003), particularly the story of Kitty Garman, daughter of Jacob Epstein and Kathleen Garman (p. 80), and Anna Campbell, her cousin, who recalled her mother's failing to notice that they had been staying with friends for a week (p. 81). In these stories it is noticeable how often, as in Jones's childhood and novels, it is grandmothers who come to the rescue with peace, order, and discipline.

56. Mills, "The Trials and Tribulations of Two Dogsbodies," 138.

57. Maureen Kincaid Speller, "In Her Own Words, Part 2."

58. Jones, "1934–," *Something about the Author.*

59. Jones, "Birthing a Book," 384.

60. Attebery, *The Fantasy Tradition in American Literature,* 15.

61. Suman Gupta, *Re-reading Harry Potter* (Basingstoke: Palgrave Macmillan, 2003), 97.

62. Karina Hill, "Dragons and Quantum Foam: Mythic Archetypes and Modern Physics in Selected Works by Diana Wynne Jones," in *An Exciting and Exacting Wisdom,* 40–52.

63. Sharon M. Scapple, "Transformation of Myth in *A Tale of Time City,*" in *An Exciting and Exacting Wisdom,* 119.

64. Ibid., 119.

65. "Legacy texts" are those texts that are common knowledge within a genre and enable writers to use shorthand. For example, in science fiction an author can write "FTL" and be sure that his or her readers will read this as "faster than light." See Mendlesohn, "Introduction," *The Cambridge Companion to Science Fiction,* 6, 7. The term "legacy texts" was modified from Ken MacLeod's coinage of "legacy code" in *Cosmonaut Keep* (London: Orbit, 2000), 27, to describe the old layers of code that accrete beneath modern programming.

66. Jones, "Answers to Some Questions," 10.

67. Diana Wynne Jones, "Inventing the Middle Ages"; held at the "Diana Wynne Jones Fansite," http://www.leemac.freeserve.co.uk/, 1997.

68. Daniella Caselli, "Reading Intertextuality: The Natural and the Legitimate; Intertextuality in 'Harry Potter,'" in *Children's Literature: New Approaches,* 183.

69. "Interview with Diana Wynne Jones," in *An Exciting and Exacting Wisdom,* 163.

70. Charles Butler, "Applied Archaeology," in *Four British Fantasists: The Children's Fantasy Fiction of Penelope Lively, Alan Garner, Diana Wynne Jones, and Susan Cooper* (forthcoming Scarecrow Press and Children's Literature Association).

71. "It seemed to me a bad thing to do to children, to express a deep knowledge of a place they haven't a chance of going to see"; "Interview with Diana Wynne Jones," in *An Exciting and Exacting Wisdom*, 164.

72. Jones, "Inventing the Middle Ages."

73. Ibid.

74. Jack Zipes, "Introduction," in *The Oxford Companion to Fairy Tales: The Western Fairy Tale Tradition from Medieval to Modern* (Oxford: Oxford University Press, 2000), xxxi, although Jones has produced one direct retelling, a Scholastic edition of *Puss in Boots* (London: Scholastic, 1999): "I agreed to do this retelling, mostly because the gaps in the logic of the story as it is usually told have always irritated me"; personal communication, January 10, 2005.

75. Mills, "The Trials and Tribulations of Two Dogsbodies," 142.

76. Maria Nikolajeva, "Diana Wynne Jones," in *The Oxford Companion to Fairy Tales*, 272.

77. Heidi Anne Heiner, "The Sur La Lune Fairy Tale Pages," http://www.surlalunefairytales.com/twelvedancing/.

78. Gili Bar-Hillel, December 16, 2004, on the Diana Wynne Jones mailing list, January 12, 2002, http://suberic.net/dwj/list.

79. Christine Wilkie, "Relating Texts: Intertextuality," in *Understanding Children's Literature*, ed. Peter Hunt (London: Routledge, 1999), 132.

80. Ibid.

81. Jones, "Inventing the Middle Ages."

82. Wilkie, "Relating Texts," 134.

83. Akiko Yamazaki, "*Fire and Hemlock:* A Text as Spellcoat," in *An Exciting and Exacting Wisdom*, 109.

84. Teya Rosenberg, "Introduction," in *An Exciting and Exacting Wisdom*, 1.

85. Jack Zipes, *Happily Ever After: Fairy Tales, Children and the Culture Industry* (New York: Routledge, 1997), 137.

86. Jones, "Answers to Some Questions," 12.

87. Jones, letter, December 6, 2004.

88. C.W. Sullivan III, "High Fantasy," in *International Companion Encyclopedia of Children's Literature*, ed. Peter Hunt and Sheila Ray (London and New York: Routledge, 2002), 303–13.

89. Gary K. Wolfe, *Critical Terms for Science Fiction and Fantasy: A Glossary and Guide to Scholarship* (Westport, CT: Greenwood, 1986), 52.

Chapter 1

1. John Rowe Townsend, "The Turbulent Years," in *Only Connect: Reading on Children's Literature*, 3rd ed., ed. Sheila Egoff et al. (Toronto, New York, Oxford: Oxford University Press, 1996), 332. Also see Nancy Larrick, "A Feminist Look at Children's Books," *School Library Journal* (January 1971): 19–24.

2. Jones, letter, December 6, 2004.

3. Alison Lurie, *Don't Tell the Grown-Ups: Subversive Children's Literature* (London: Bloomsbury, 1990), 12; and Nicholas Tucker and Nikki Gamble, *Family Fictions* (Contemporary Classics of Children's Literature) (London and New York: Continuum, 2001), 1–48.

4. See Lila Marz Harper's article, "Children's Literature, Science and Faith: *The Water Babies,*" in *Children's Literature: New Approaches,* ed. Karin Lesnik-Oberstein (Basingstoke: Palgrave Macmillan, 2004), 118–43. Harper discussed the complex aims of Charles Kingsley in attempting to rationalize religion and science and to present the new scientific understandings to his audience.

5. See Virginia Nicholson, "Children of the Light," in *Among the Bohemians: Experiments in Living 1900–1939* (London: Penguin Books, 2003), chapter 3, 67–98, for a discussion of the ideological discourse that lay behind the works of Ransome and Nesbit.

6. See Valerie Krips, "A Notable Irrelevance: Class and Children's Fiction," *The Lion and the Unicorn* 17 (1993): 195–209.

7. Chris Hill recalls friends who were children of farmworkers receiving pocket money in the 1970s but also that there was very little paid work for children in the area; e-mail message, September 25, 2002.

8. The U.S. first printing of *Witch's Business* rewrote some of the slang to suit an American audience but stuck to the swearing Jones created. In the recent reprints, the U.K. edition replaces "nig" with "scum," throughout, whereas the U.S. edition has chosen to replace the color slang entirely: United Kingdom: London and Basingstoke: Macmillan, 1973: "Blankety Own Back!" (p. 12), "Blankery-blue Pirie kids" (p. 12), and "crimson nig" (p. 13); United States: New York: E.P. Dutton, 1974: "Blankety Own Back!" and "Blankery-blue Pirie kids" (p. 6) and "Crimson nig" (p. 7); United Kingdom 2001: "That orange scum" or "Those blankety-blue Piries"; United States 2001: "Degutted Own Back" (p. 7), "Eyeballs-in-salsa Pirie kids" (p. 7), and "that slimy maggot scum" (p. 9).

9. In 1973 ten pence would have bought a child two comics and some candy. *The Beano* and *The Dandy* (the two mass-market favorites) retailed at four pence each. In 2004 equivalent purchasing power would be in the region of £1 or $2 (U.S.).

10. Jones, *Wilkins' Tooth,* 50.

11. Ibid., 13, 69. The multiculturalism is not just surface here. Vernon's color has been a matter mostly of implication, apart from the insult of "Nig," we first learn that he is black obliquely, from Jess's comment that he has two black eyes. Charles Butler pointed out that although he is "addressed as 'darkie' by one of the adult characters, ... this is not a book in which race or racial prejudice are sustained themes. ... *Wilkins' Tooth* thus deals with the problem of race ... by declining to define its eponymous character in terms of his colour. In speech–act terms it is a book that challenges prejudice performatively, simply by refusing to make the book be *about* race at the level of content"; Butler, "Longing and Belonging," in *Four British Fantasists: The*

Children's Fantasy Fiction of Penelope Lively, Alan Garner, Diana Wynne Jones, and Susan Cooper (forthcoming).

12. Donnarae MacCann, "Editor's Introduction: Racism and Antiracism: Forty Years of Theories and Debates," *The Lion and the Unicorn* 25 (2001): 337–52. Wilkins is one of only four obviously nonwhite characters in Jones's books (Jonathan in *A Tale of Time City,* Nirupam in *Witch Week,* Abdullah in *Castle in the Air*). Vernon Wilkins is presented entirely from the outside; we do not see what might be different about him. This is a complex issue because the very presentation of Vernon's sameness is a specific statement in the context of 1970s United Kingdom (and the rise of the National Front and British Nationalist Party), but in current terms it might be seen as a denial of his ethnicity. We have to contrast this with the portrayal of the other children and the ways in which they are classed. Although not wholly satisfactory, Jones does pull off a sense that the children have different backgrounds, and Vernon's is different enough that, despite living in much the same sort of area as do the member's of Buster's gang, he is not "of them."

13. Jones, *Wilkins' Tooth,* 30–31.

14. *Yaga;* retold in Arthur Ransome, *Old Peter's Russian Tales* (London: Nelson, 1916, and Puffin, 1974).

15. Philip Pullman noted in an interview with Edward James at the 2004 East-ercon (*Concourse*), that he now has to explain "Cinderella" to child audiences when he reads from *My Life as a Rat.*

16. Jones, *Wilkins' Tooth,* 33.

17. Ibid., 34.

18. Vigen Guroian, *Tending the Heart of Virtue: How Classic Stories Awaken a Child's Moral Imagination* (Oxford: Oxford University Press, 1998), 4.

19. Jones, *Wilkins' Tooth,* 78. The lady then goes on to explain that for five years she has been paying for having done precisely this: "I did someone a favour once for a half-crown bus fare, and it's taken me all this time to work it off." But as it turns out—according to Biddy—that her crime was to marry Mr. Adams, it is all a bit unclear. One suspects an editing problem.

20. Jones, *Wilkins' Tooth,* 154.

21. Suzanne Rahn, *Rediscoveries in Children's Literature* (New York and London: Garland, 1995), 150.

22. John Clute, in "Canaries in the Coal Mine," pointed to Patricia McKillip's *In the Forests of Serre* as using a similar device—a knowing hero, and a witch who is imbued with an understanding of story. (Address given at SUNY, New Palz, April 2004.) Terry Pratchett's *Witches Abroad* is centered on the idea that if you know how story works you can rework it from the inside.

23. Deborah Stevenson, "Sentiment and Significance: The Impossibility of Recovery in the Children's Literature Canon or, the Drowning of *The Water Babies,*" *The Lion and the Unicorn* 21 (1997): 112–30.

24. Lurie, *Don't Tell the Grown-Ups,* 26.

25. Diana Wynne Jones, "The Heroic Ideal—A Personal Odyssey," *The Lion and the Unicorn* 13 (1989): 133.

26. Ibid., 134.

27. Jones, *Wilkins' Tooth*, 52.
28. Although Lurie pointed out that fairy tales actually have many resourceful heroines, it is the more passive ones who have been popularized by commercial culture: *Don't Tell the Grown-Ups*, 18. The notion of intelligence as heroic is still denied in children's fiction; see Hermione's declaration to Harry in *Harry Potter and the Chamber of Secrets* that his bravery matters more than her intelligence. Lemony Snicket's Klaus and Violet Baudelaire, the first knowledgeable, the second ingenious, are a rare and refreshing exception (see *An Awfully Bad Beginning*).

Chapter 2

1. John Stephens, *Language and Ideology in Children's Fiction* (London: Longman, 1992), 3.
2. Caroline Hunt, "Form as Fantasy—Fantasy as Form," *Children's Literature Quarterly* 12, no. 1. (Spring 1987): 8.
3. Plot Coupons—see Diana Wynne Jones, *The Tough Guide to Fantasyland* (London: Vista, 1996). The term was coined by critic Nick Lowe: see David Langford, "Plot Coupons, in *The Encyclopedia of Fantasy*, ed. John Clute and John Grant (New York: St Martins Griffin, 1999), 767.
4. Fred Inglis, *The Promise of Happiness: Value and Meaning in Children's Fiction* (Cambridge: Cambridge University Press, 1981), 240. For a discussion of the construction of this situation in the Harry Potter novels, see Farah Mendlesohn, "Crowning the King: Harry Potter and the Construction of Authority," in *The Ivory Tower and Harry Potter: Perspectives on a Literary Phenomenon*, ed. Lana A. Whited (Columbia and London: University of Missouri Press, 2003), 159–81.
5. Gillian Spraggs, "A Lawless World: The Fantasy Novels of Susan Cooper," *The Lion and the Unicorn* 33, no. 2 (Spring 1982): 27.
6. Margaret Rumbold, "Taking the Subject Further," *Places* 7 (1997): 16–18.
7. In Margaret Mahy's *The Changeover*, for example, it seems unlikely that Laura would let her brother die if she could possibly save him through magic, however scary. Harry Potter seems unlikely to follow Voldemort when Voldemort is trying to kill him. Garth Nix's New Days series, beginning with *Mr. Monday*, is entirely structured around making obvious moral choices.
8. Vigen Guroian, *Tending the Heart of Virtue: How Classic Stories Awaken a Child's Moral Imagination* (Oxford: Oxford University Press, 1998), 24.
9. See Mahy, Almond, Hallam, Potter, and Cooper for other examples of why the intrusion narrative is particularly successful in this.
10. Diana Wynne Jones, *The Ogre Downstairs* (London and Basingstoke: Macmillan, 1974), 48–49.
11. Diana Wynne Jones, "The Magic of Narnia," http://www.amazon.com/exec/obidos/tg/feature/-/91955/104-6380809-0505511, and "Answers to Some Questions," *Foundation: The International Review of Science Fiction* 70 (Summer 1997): 13.

12. Ibid., 125.

13. Alice Mills, "The Trials and Tribulations of Two Dogsbodies: A Jungian Reading of Diana Wynne Jones's *Dogsbody*," in *Diana Wynne Jones: An Exciting and Exacting Wisdom*, ed. Teya Rosenberg et al. (New York: Peter Lang, 2002), 140.

14. Diana Wynne Jones, *Eight Days of Luke* (London and Basingstoke: Macmillan, 1975), 50.

15. Jones mentions the Three Formed Goddess and Lorelie, but, this being Jones, she probably functions as other avatars as well; Diana the huntress is one possibility. Jones, "The Heroic Ideal—A Personal Odyssey," *The Lion and the Unicorn* 13 (1989): 137.

16. Ibid., 134.

17. Stephens, *Language and Ideology in Children's Fiction*, 41–42.

18. Jones, "The Heroic Ideal," 136.

19. Elizabeth Kedge discussed the role of the Rhymer poems in a paper at the SFRA conference in July 2002, New Lanark, Scotland.

20. Suzanne Rahn, *Rediscoveries in Children's Literature* (New York and London: Garland, 1995), 150.

21. Diana Wynne Jones, *Witch Week* (London and Basingstoke: Macmillan, 1982), 38.

22. An aside: in Jewish tradition the duty of the parent is precisely to explain the world to the child. This is behind the four questions ritual at Passover. In Jones's work, it seems to be precisely in this area of parental duty that the older generation fails.

23. Deborah Kaplan, "Diana Wynne Jones and the World-Shaping Power of Language," in *An Exciting and Exacting Wisdom*, 57.

24. Jones, *Witch Week*, 25.

25. Ibid., 196.

26. Ibid., 129.

27. In Bohemia, "The more 'enlightened' the parent, the fewer the toys provided"; Virginia Nicholson, *Among the Bohemians: Experiments in Living 1900–1939* (London: Penguin Books, 2003), 72.

28. See Attebery, *Strategies of Fantasy*, 75–78.

29. Diana Wynne Jones, *Cart and Cwidder* (London and Basingstoke: Macmillan, 1975), 155–58.

30. Ibid., 192.

31. In *The Homeward Bounders* the gamers promise the pieces that they can stop wandering if they can get home, without explaining that time slippage will ensure that they never can return to a place that feels like home.

32. Margaret Rumbold, "Taking the Subject Further," *Places* 7 (1997): 21.

33. Diana Wynne Jones, *Archer's Goon* (London: Methuen, 1984), 177.

34. Rahn, *Rediscoveries in Children's Literature*, 172.

35. Diana Wynne Jones, *Howl's Moving Castle* (Methuen: London, 1986), 1.

36. Jones, "The Heroic Ideal," 129–31, for the process of resistance in which Jones engaged.

37. Diana Wynne Jones, *Hexwood* (London: Methuen, 1993), 139.

38. John Stephens and Robyn McCallum, *Retelling Stories, Framing Culture: Traditional Story and Metanarratives in Children's Literature* (New York and London: Garland, 1998), 121–22.

39. In this book all of the characters have some problems with their magic. On page 198 the students (trapped in a misdirected moon capsule) discuss how their jinxes—the appearance of holes, constantly losing their way—are linked with their unhappiness—kingship as a hole, two residences equally disliked. This scene is uncharacteristically direct for Jones. Jones, *Year of the Griffin* (London: Victor Gollancz, 2000), 198.

40. Diana Wynne Jones, *Minor Arcana* (London: Victor Gollancz, 1996), 13.

41. Ibid., 27.

42. Dr. Edward Kessler of the Centre for Jewish–Christian Relations, Cambridge, and his lecture, "Reading Violent Scripture" the week ending May 22, 2004; cited in Paul Vallely, "When the Scriptures Are Violent, It's Time to Argue with God," *The Independent*, May 22, 2004.

43. John Clute, in John Clute and John Grant, eds., *The Encyclopedia of Fantasy* (London: Orbit, 1997), 804–805.

44. Diana Wynne Jones, *Fire and Hemlock* (London: Methuen, 1985), 144.

45. Terry Pratchett, *The Wee Free Men* (London and New York: Doubleday, 2003), 62–63.

46. Diana Wynne Jones, *Power of Three* (London and Basingstoke: Macmillan, 1976), 252.

47. Clute and Grant, *The Encyclopedia of Fantasy*, 466, 848.

48. Nicki Humble, "The Rewards of Intertextuality: The Mythic Dimensions of the Work of Diana Wynne Jones" (paper presented at the CLISS day conference, Roehampton, November 13, 2004).

49. Clute and Grant, *The Encyclopedia of Fantasy*, 414.

50. Ibid., 414.

51. Humble, "The Rewards of Intertextuality."

Chapter 3

1. Paul J. Nahin, *Time Machines: Time Travel in Physics, Metaphysics, and Science Fiction* (New York: American Institute of Physics, 1993).

2. Heather Dyke, "McTaggart and the Truth about Time," in *Time, Reality and Experience*, ed. Craig Callender (Cambridge: Cambridge University Press, 2002), 137–52, at 138.

3. Ibid., 139.

4. Dorrit Cohn, cited in Maria Nikolajeva, "Imprints of the Mind: The Depiction of Consciousness in Children's Fiction," *Children's Literature Association Quarterly* 26 (2002): 180–82.

5. Diana Wynne Jones, *The Time of the Ghost* (London and Basingstoke: Macmillan, 1981), 109.

6. Nahin, *Time Machines*, 39.

7. Michael Friedman, *Foundations of Space-Time Theories: Relativistic Physics and Philosophy of Science* (Princeton, NJ: Princeton University Press, 1983), 7.

8. Jones, *The Time of the Ghost*, 109.
9. Ibid., 177.
10. Maria Nikolajeva, *The Magic Code* (Stockholm: Almquist and Wiskell International, 1988), 96.
11. Tess Cosslett, " 'History from Below': Time Slip Narratives and National Identity," *The Lion and the Unicorn* 26 (2002): 244, 247.
12. Jones, letter, December 6, 2004.
13. Diana Wynne Jones, *A Tale of Time City* (London: Methuen, 1987), 140.
14. Ibid., 37.
15. Ibid., 147.
16. Ibid., 148.
17. Ibid., 170.
18. Frank Sadler, *The Unified Ring: Narrative Art and the Science Fiction Novel* (Ann Arbor: University of Michigan Research Press, 1984).
19. Werner Heisenberg, "The Representation of Nature in Contemporary Physics," 126–27, cited in Frank Sadler, *The Unified Ring*, 15.
20. Christopher Ray, *Time, Space and Philosophy* (London and New York: Routledge, 1991), 156.
21. David Carr, *Time, Narrative, and History* (Bloomington/Indianapolis: Indiana University Press, 1991), 49–50.

> One way in which the separation is often made between the lived reality and the literary artifice is to say that the narrative arrangement of events departs altogether from the *temporal* order to install itself in the *logical* domain. Louis Mink speaks of the configurational aspect of narrative as if it were *atemporal* ... in the sense that the multiplicity of events is seized all at once by an authorial overview. This idea of transcending the temporal is especially favoured by the structuralists, though they, unlike Mink, want to avoid altogether the appeal to an authorial act of creation. ... Greimas, Bremond, and others tend to dechronologize narrative, taking its temporal features as a mere surface aspect, mere sequences, and analyzing anything beyond pure sequentiallity as atemporal, quasi-logical structures and relations.

One idea that this triggers is the notion of the Aristotelian unities. Quite obviously, Jones is not trying to accomplish this but there is a sense in *Hexwood* that it is our expectation of unity that is being manipulated.

> The most fundamental configurational relation we have pointed to, that of beginning, middle, and end, is a strictly temporal ordering principle, and it is a serious confusion to describe it as if it resided in a non-temporal domain. Other ordering principles may resemble it superficially and are indeed timeless: an argument has its premises (including a "middle term") and its conclusion; the alphabet has its

first and last letters; a hierarchy may have a highest and lowest instance of authority; and a design may have a middle point between its top and bottom. But none of these features become beginnings, middles, and ends unless the order in question is deployed in time, run through in sequence, whether in thought or action. (51)

22. Derived from Nahin, *Time Machines*, notes, fig. 4.3.
23. I am indebted to N.M. Browne for this visualization. N.M. Browne (talk at the British Science Fiction Association, the Star Tavern, Kensington, October 27, 2004). The diagram also nicely illuminates what Todorov described as the structure of the crime story, in which there are two tales, the story of the crime, and the story of the investigation, and *The Merlin Conspiracy* is, of course, a crime narrative.
24. Donald Williams, "Physics and Flux: Comment on Professor Capek's Essay," in *Boston Studies in the Philosophy of Science*, vol. 2 (Humanities Press, 1965), 465–66.
25. Diana Wynne Jones, *The Merlin Conspiracy* (London: HarperCollins, 2003), 300.
26. Ibid., 390.
27. The whole lecture series on time travel can be found at http://www.utas.edu.au/docs/humsoc/philosophy/Time_Travel/lectures.htm.
28. Jones, *The Merlin Conspiracy*, 148.
29. Ibid., 302.
30. Ibid., 199.
31. Ibid., part 11, chapter 2, 424.
32. Ibid., 472.
33. Ibid., 127.
34. Clifford A. Pickover, *Time: A Traveller's Guide* (New York, Oxford: Oxford University Press, 1998), 41.
35. See Terry Pratchett, *Equal Rites* (London: Corgi, 1987), 13. I am indebted to David Langford (e-mail, 22 December 2004) for the comment that "this may be an Pratchettian echo—conscious or unconscious—of the similar view of a human life that appeared many years previously in Charles Harness's sf novel *The Paradox Men* (1953), Chapter VIII, which features an endless-seeming column whose cross-section, the disentimed hero realizes, "would resemble very closely the vertical cross section of a human being." In fact it is, or represents, his own extension through time.
36. Jones, *The Merlin Conspiracy*, 66.
37. Eleanor Cameron pointed to the writing of William Mayne: "He works the phases of development of a paragraph toward the final effect by gradual release, with full attention to timing, to pace. Mayne is a master of the art of exquisite control, of the disciplined paying out of his line ... the mounting tension of movement conveyed fully as much through sentence structure as through the tightening of action"; Eleanor Cameron, "Of Style and the Stylist" (c. 1962), in *Only Connect: Reading on Children's Literature*, 3rd ed.,

ed. Sheila Egoff et al. (Toronto, New York, Oxford: Oxford University Press, 1996), 93.

38. Diana Wynne Jones, *The Magicians of Caprona* (London and Basingstoke: Macmillan, 1980), 29.

39. Jones, *The Magicians of Caprona*, 32.

40. Ibid., 186.

41. Ibid., 187.

42. Ibid., 192.

43. John Stephens, "Modernism to Postmodernism, or the Line from Insk to Onsk: William Mayne's *Tiger's Railway*," *Papers: Explorations into Children's Literature* 3 (1993): 52; Robyn McCallum, "Very Advanced Texts: Metafictions and Experimental Work," in *Understanding Children's Literature*, ed. Peter Hunt (London: Routledge, 1999), 145, cited *Witch Week* as a temporal heterotopia, but although time, and the splitting of spatio-temporal time is central to the book, there is no sense in the narrative of coexisting possible time zones.

44. Diana Wynne Jones, *Hexwood* (London: Methuen, 1993), 209.

45. Alan Garner, interviewed by Justin Wintle in *The Pied Pipers: Interviews with the Influential Creators of Children's Literature* (London: Paddington Press, 1975).

46. Jones, *Hexwood*, 16.

47. Ibid., 17.

48. Ibid., 17–18.

49. Given that the Bannus turns out to be a computer, the choice of a virus is probably metaphoric and practical.

50. Jones, *Hexwood*, 46.

51. Ibid., 47.

52. Ibid., 61.

53. Ibid., 196.

54. Ibid., 259.

55. Ibid., 146.

56. Ibid., 227.

Chapter 4

1. Geoffrey Trease, *Tales out of School: A Survey of Children's Fiction* (London: New Education Book Club, 1948), 108.

2. John Clute, "Crosshatch," in *The Encyclopedia of Fantasy*, ed. John Clute and John Grant (London: Orbit, 1997), 237.

3. Farah Mendlesohn, "Towards a Taxonomy of Fantasy," *Journal of the Fantastic in the Arts* 13 (2002): 173–87, discussed this problematic in detail.

4. The first *Oz* book might more usually be thought of as a fantastical journey in that the portal is patterned after the incredible journeys of the nineteenth century in which the whirlwind might be seen as a facilitator rather than a portal and the actual adventures are incidental rather than developmental.

5. K.C. Dyer, *Seeds of Time* (Toronto and Oxford: Dundurn, 2002).

6. Christopher Chant's nighttime walks start remarkably similarly to Garner's adventures in the ceiling when he was bed bound as a boy; Alan Garner, *The Voice That Thunders: Essays and Lectures* (London: Harvill Press, 1997): "The sensation was that of sliding out of phase with the boy in the bed ... to find that I had crossed the neutralised zone from the best into the ceiling. I did not sleep. There was no relaxing of consciousness. It was the opposite. I had to think harder, relatively, than at any previous time of my life" (p. 10) and "Although the way to the ceiling was along the same road in the ceiling, the land beyond the road, from visit to visit, was inconsistent. ... Sooner or later I would stop whatever I was doing in the ceiling, turn around, and always be facing the same road-forest-cloud-hill picture that I saw from my bed" (p. 12).

7. "My favorite is *The Magician's Nephew*. This is how to write a prequel. I admire the way Lewis contrives an explanation of that solitary streetlight in Narnia by shamelessly borrowing from E. Nesbit—and improving on her—to do it. I am utterly overwhelmed by The Wood Between the Worlds, including the way the kids nearly forget to mark their home pool;" Jones, "The Magic of Narnia," http://www.amazon.com/exec/obidos/tg/feature/-/91955/104-6380809-0505511.

8. Diana Wynne Jones, *The Merlin Conspiracy* (London: HarperCollins, 2003), 37.

9. Diana Wynne Jones, *The Lives of Christopher Chant* (London: Methuen, 1988), 8.

10. Ibid., 390.

11. Ibid., 119.

12. Peter Hunt, "Landscape and Journeys, Metaphors and Maps: The Distinctive Feature of English Fantasy," *Children's Literature Quarterly* 12 (1987): 13.

13. Ibid., 11.

14. Interestingly this is also true of migrants. Voluntary migrants tend to find it much easier to settle and succeed than do the displaced and to experience better health, beyond the effect of variable such as skills and education.

15. "*It probably comes of not having a proper head to keep my thoughts in, she decided. I shall have to be very careful*"; Jones, *The Time of the Ghost* (London and Basingstoke: Macmillan, 1981), 9.

16. Charles Butler, *The Fetch of Mardy Watt* (London: HarperCollins, 2003), 149–50.

17. Jones, *The Lives of Christopher Chant*, 9.

18. Jones, *The Merlin Conspiracy*, 37.

19. Ibid., 39.

20. This proved a problem in the first one hundred pages of J.K. Rowling's *Harry Potter and the Order of the Phoenix* (London: Bloomsbury, 2003), in which Harry is confined to a house. It lacks the joie de vivre of the later parts of the novel.

21. Diana Wynne Jones, *The Tough Guide to Fantasyland* (London: Vista, 1996), 121.

22. Diana Wynne Jones, *Archer's Goon* (London: Methuen, 1984), 63–64.
23. Ibid., 64.
24. Ibid., 193.
25. Diana Wynne Jones, *Howl's Moving Castle* (London: Methuen, 1986), 100.
26. Ibid.
27. Ibid., 105.
28. Diana Wynne Jones, "What the Cat Told Me," in *Fantasy Stories*, ed. D.W. Jones (London: Kingfisher, 1994), 236.
29. John Clute, "Beyond the Pale," in *Conjunctions: 39, The New Wave Fabulists* (Annandale-on-Hudson, NY: Bard College, 2003)), 421–22.
30. "Autonomous monologue" is from Dorrit Cohn, cited by Maria Nikolajeva, "Imprints of the Mind: The Depiction of Consciousness in Children's Fiction," *Children's Literature Association Quarterly* 26 (2002): 176–77.
31. Strictly speaking, "His Majesty Rudolph IX, King of Trenjen, Frinjen, and Corriarden, Protector of Leathe and Overlord of the Fiveir of the Orthe."
32. Maureen Kincaid Speller pointed out that the gods are Norse, rather than unique to Dalemark; "Diana Wynne Jones in Her Own Words: Part 2," *Charmed Lives Fanzine*, no. 2 (Midsummer, 1998).
33. Diana Wynne Jones, *Minor Arcana* (London: Victor Gollancz, 1996), 11.
34. Jones, "The True State of Affairs," in *Minor Arcana*, 153.
35. Ibid., 154.
36. Ibid., 153.
37. Ibid., 158.
38. Ibid., 160.
39. Ibid., 164.
40. Far too often, occupation becomes shorthand for character, a tradition Terry Pratchett mocked mercilessly in *Small Gods*. Torturers are really very nice men who have mugs that say "World's Greatest Dad" and go home to be loving fathers and husbands.
41. Jones, "The True State of Affairs," 178.
42. Ibid., 171.
43. Ibid., 188.
44. Ibid., 199.
45. Ibid., 220.
46. Ibid., 272.
47. Ibid., 286.
48. Ibid., 247.
49. Jeff Noon's *Vurt* (1993) and Michael Swanwick's *The Iron Dragon's Daughter* (1994), in which the quest is for the portal.

Chapter 5

1. W.R. Irwin, *The Game of the Impossible: A Rhetoric of Fantasy* (Urbana, Chicago, London: University of Illinois, 1976), 60.

2. Diana Wynne Jones, *The Dark Lord of Derkholm* (London: Victor Gollancz, 1998), 7.
3. Ibid., 8.
4. Ibid., 9.
5. Diana Wynne Jones, *Howl's Moving Castle* (London: Methuen, 1986), 85.
6. Ibid., 1.
7. Ibid., 21.
8. "Storyable" is a term used and developed in the criticism of John Clute, e.g. in *The Cambridge Companion to Science Fiction*, ed. Edward James and Farah Mendlesohn (Cambridge: Cambridge University Press, 71.
9. "Interview with Diana Wynne Jones, conducted by Charles Butler, 22 March 2001," in *Diana Wynne Jones: An Exciting and Exacting Wisdom*, ed. Teya Rosenberg et al. (New York: Peter Lang, 2002), 167.
10. Jones, *Howl's Moving Castle*, 112.
11. Diana Wynne Jones, *Dogsbody* (London and Basingstoke: Macmillan, 1975), 12–13.
12. Fred Inglis, *The Promise of Happiness: Value and Meaning in Children's Fiction* (Cambridge: Cambridge University Press, 1981), 13.
13. Jones, *Dogsbody*, 186.
14. Jones, *Howl's Moving Castle*, 28–29.
15. Ibid., 29.
16. Ibid., 45.
17. John Stephens (*Language and Ideology in Children's Fiction* [London: Longman, 1992], 156) wrote of Leon Garfield,

> The principal effect of the interrogative text is to foreground the processes of signification whereby signs are related to things, and thence to draw attention to the social forces which determine what that relationship will be. Readers are thus constantly reminded that what is socially desirable and socially undesirable are cultural and linguistic constructs. By making the familiar strange and over-turning some conventional aspects of narrative and picture book modes, these books are available to see the world differently. … The most notable effect of these strategies is to discourage unquestioning empathy or identification with the main characters as subjects and to situate the reader as a separately constructed subject firmly outside the text, sometimes as a subject position in opposition to society's official structures of authority.

18. In both *Cart and Cwidder* and *Dogsbody*, intention is vital. Moril's remorse is because he committed murder for the loss of his horse. Kathleen is remorseful because she destroyed Duffie's pots not because her Daddy died but because she had always wanted to (158). Doing things for the wrong reasons matters.

19. For her nonfiction comments, see *The Tough Guide to Fantasyland* and "Inventing the Middle Ages"; held at the "Diana Wynne Jones Fansite," http://www.leemac.freeserve.co.uk/.

20. Diana Wynne Jones, *Cart and Cwidder* (London and Basingstoke: Macmillan, 1975), 32.

21. Ibid., 33.

22. Gillian Spraggs, "True Dreams: The Fantasy Fiction of Diana Wynne Jones," *The Lion and the Unicorn* 34 (1983): 18.

23. Jones, *Cart and Cwidder*, 2.

24. Ibid., 1.

25. Ibid., 55. An interesting comparison is to be found in *Dogsbody*, written in the same year. Here Jones tells, rather than shows. Hearing her father is dead, Katherine tells Sirius, "I'd no idea what a muddle being sad is. ... I almost keep forgetting my Daddy's dead. And then I wonder if it hurt, and hope it didn't, and I hope he wasn't horribly frightened. Then, in the middle, I remember how annoying he could be sometimes" (*Dogsbody*, 149). Katherine is moving between the layers of her memory.

26. Jones, *Cart and Cwidder*, 13.

27. Diana Wynne Jones, *The Spellcoats* (London and Basingstoke: Macmillan, 1979), 9.

28. I owe this realization to two incidents: I am an Eastern European Jew who has not lived in a Jewish community since the age of eleven. In June 2004 I got off the bus in the London Jewish community of Stamford Hill, to see endless reworkings of my own face. Later in the year I moved to Dublin, to find that, with the high number of red-heads in the population, my own toffee-colored hair was unremarkable. The sense of dissonance in both contexts drew my attention to the degree to which my internal narrative was headed: "the one who looks like an outsider."

29. Jones, *The Spellcoats*, 82.

30. Ibid., 165.

31. The nature of their souls might also give a clue. Kankredin looks at Tanaqui and Duck's souls and says, "Empty things they are. Suspiciously empty"; Jones, *The Spellcoats*, 136.

32. Jones, *The Spellcoats*, 173.

33. Ibid., 13–14.

34. Ibid., 46.

35. Ibid., 50.

36. Diana Wynne Jones, *Drowned Ammet* (London and Basingstoke: Macmillan, 1977), 5.

37. Ibid., 11.

38. Ibid., 32–33.

39. Ibid., 87–88.

40. Ibid., 88.

41. Ibid., 61–62.

42. Ibid., 62–63.

43. Ibid., 63. The scene is very strongly reminiscent of a scene in the nineteenth-century novel *The Fairchild Family* (three parts, 1818, 1842, 1847). Here the children are made to watch a hanging to warn them of the dreadful consequences of theft. Their father lectures them on the road to the gallows:

> Whilst Mr. Fairchild was speaking, the wind blew strong and shook the body upon the gibbet, rattling the chains by which it hung.

> "Oh! Let us go Papa!" said the children, pulling Mr. Fairchild's coat. "*Not yet*," *said Mr. Fairchild* : "first I must tell you the history of that wretched man before we go from this place."

Quoted by Nicholas Tucker and Nikki Gamble, *Family Fictions* (Contemporary Classics of Children's Literature) (London and New York: Continuum, 2001), 8. Jones's version reads as a devastating parody, an unveiling of the brutality behind fatherly concern.

44. Jones, *Drowned Ammet*, 206.
45. Ibid., 146.
46. Ibid., 28.
47. Ibid., 70.
48. In John Rowe Townsend, *A Sounding of Storytellers: New and Revised Essays on Contemporary Writers for Children* (Harmondsworth: Kestrel Books, 1979), 29.
49. Jones, *Drowned Ammet*, 24.
50. Ibid., 116.
51. Ibid., 90.
52. Ibid., 156.
53. Diana Wynne Jones, *The Crown of Dalemark* (London: Mandarin, 1993), 15.
54. Ibid., 195.
55. Penelope Lively, *A Stitch in Time* (Harmondsworth: Puffin, 1986), 77.
56. In *A Sudden Wild Magic*, Jones reversed this, while continuing to insist that people are made by places. Maureen discovers Joe's duplicity, "And she realized what the odd thing was about his face. There were all sorts of foreign thoughts in it. She could see the alien consciousness behind his face pushing the features she had thought she knew well into a completely new shape" (98).
57. Patrick O'Donovan, "Between Politics and Literature: The Case of Constant" (paper presented at the Todorov conference, Sheffield, June 27–29, 2004).
58. Teya Rosenberg, "Magical Realism and Children's Literature: Diana Wynne Jones's *Black Maria* and Salman Rushdie's *Midnight's Children* as a Test Case," *Papers* 11, no. 1 (2001): 17.
59. Jones, *The Spellcoats*, 71.

60. Ibid., 77.
61. Ibid., 88.
62. Ibid., 96.
63. Ibid., 123–24.
64. Ibid., 139.
65. Ibid., 240.
66. Ibid., 246.
67. Jones, *Drowned Ammet*, 182.
68. Ibid., 159.
69. Ibid., 160.
70. Ibid., 163.
71. Jones, *The Crown of Dalemark*, 31.
72. Ibid., 33.
73. Ibid., 171.
74. Ibid., 175.
75. Ibid., 255–56.
76. By convention, Singers are observers not participants, so that Moril cannot regard himself as at the center of the tale. This leaves Mitt, who has the constant sense that it is not his story, that he is there only to accompany others; the discovery that Noreth has disappeared consequently shakes his foundations and brings him closer to the center.
77. Jones, *The Crown of Dalemark*, 346.
78. Ibid., 349.

Chapter 6

1. See Catherine Storr, "Things That Go Bump in the Night," in *The Cool Web: The Pattern of Children's Reading*, ed. Margaret Meek, Aidan Warlow, and Griselda Barton (London, Sydney, Toronto: Bodley Head, 1977), 120–28.
2. See Elizabeth Hammill, " 'Real' Stories or 'Pretty' Stories: A Question of Criteria," in *Voices Off: Texts, Contexts and Readers*, ed. Morag Styles, Eve Bearne, and Victor Watson (London: Cassell, 1996), 20–21. Charles Butler pointed to Polly's awareness of Mr. Leroy's surveillance, but "makes little distinction between his keeping watch by traditional methods … and by magical ones"; Charles Butler, "Now Here: Where Now? Magic as Metaphor and as Reality in the Writing of Diana Wynne Jones," in *Diana Wynne Jones: An Exciting and Exacting Wisdom*, ed. Teya Rosenberg et al. (New York: Peter Lang, 2002), 70. (Butler's article should, if possible, be read alongside this chapter.)
3. Butler, "Now Here: Where Now?" 77.
4. Ibid., 76.
5. Farah Mendlesohn, "*Conjunctions 39* and Liminal Fantasy," *Journal of the Fantastic in the Arts* 15 (2005).

6. For a discussion of equipoise, see John Clute, "Beyond the Pale," in *Conjunctions: 39, The New Wave Fabulists* (Annandale-on-Hudson, NY: Bard College, 2003), 423–25.
7. See Tzvetan Todorov, *The Fantastic: A Structural Approach to a Literary Genre* (Ithaca, NY: Cornell University Press, 1975).
8. Butler, "Now Here: Where Now?" 71–74.
9. Brian Attebery, *Strategies of Fantasy* (Bloomington and Indianapolis: Indiana University Press, 1992), 126.
10. Of all the major series of children's adventure stories, only the *Famous Five* follows a similar pattern, and in Enid Blyton's stories the children use the home to congregate before departing elsewhere for their adventure. At the conclusion of *Eight Days of Luke,* David is told he will be living at Alan's house where a portal into a fantasy world has also been located. This circularity might well be significant. The rejection of home is one reason *Lady, My Life as a Bitch* caused so much controversy. See also Farah Mendlesohn, "Is There Any Such Thing as Children's SF?: A Position Piece," *The Lion and the Unicorn* 28 (2004): 284–313.
11. One of the portals is located in the house that might become David's home with Astrid. The relationship between this house and the portal it contains might be one indication of the safety of the house—that it welcomes rather than despises magic.
12. Diana Wynne Jones, *Eight Days of Luke* (London and Basingstoke: Macmillan, 1975), 1.
13. Ibid., 14.
14. A term introduced and defined in *The Encyclopedia of Fantasy*, ed. John Clute and John Grant (New York: St Martins Griffin, 1998), 772.
15. Ibid., 21.
16. Ibid., 22.
17. Ibid., 23.
18. Ibid., 23.
19. Ibid., 24.
20. Ibid., 27.
21. Ibid., 2.
22. Ibid., 62.
23. Ibid., 42.
24. Karen Sands O'Connor, "Nowhere to Go, No One to Be: Diana Wynne Jones and the Concepts of Englishness and Self-Image," in *An Exciting and Exacting Wisdom*, 16.
25. Jones, *Eight Days of Luke*, 73.
26. Ibid., 74.
27. Francis Spufford, *The Child That Books Built: A Memoir of Childhood and Reading* (London: Faber and Faber, 2002), 86.
28. Jones, *Eight Days of Luke*, 75.
29. Ibid., 75.
30. Spufford, *The Child That Books Built*, 86.

31. Jones, *Eight Days of Luke*, 82 and 74.

32. Ibid., 114.

33. Ibid., 140–49.

34. Ibid., 143.

35. Ibid., 143.

36. Butler, "Now Here: Where Now?" 74.

37. Fred Inglis placed Diana Wynne Jones in a very long tradition: "It is no accident that so many of these writers [Hodgson-Burnett, Nesbit, et al.] were women (or self-consciously separate and 'impractical' men …). The women saw the separation of manly and feminine virtues as deadly, and attempted to free children from the results of this split. The children … have to work out their lives away from parents and placed in the space between home and work"; *The Promise of Happiness: Value and Meaning in Children's Fiction* (Cambridge: Cambridge University Press, 1981), 114.

38. Diana Wynne Jones, *Black Maria* (London: Methuen, 1991), 183.

39. Excerpted from Jones, *Black Maria*, 94.

40. Suzanne Rahn, *Rediscoveries in Children's Literature* (New York and London: Garland, 1995), 145–75.

41. Adrienne E. Gavin and Christopher Routledge, "Introduction," in *Mystery in Children's Literature: From the Rational to the Supernatural*, ed. Gavin and Routledge (Basingstoke: Palgrave, 2001), 2.

42. Rahn, *Rediscoveries in Children's Literature*, 145–75.

43. Attebery, *Strategies of Fantasy*, 58.

44. Rahn, *Rediscoveries in Children's Literature*, 159.

45. Jones, letter, December 6, 2004.

46. It is always tricky to decide what is actually a thread in Jones's work and what is just coincidence, but it is perhaps worth noting that in *The Merlin Conspiracy* Roddy's father uses a model of Blest on a table to focus his weather magic.

47. Rahn, *Rediscoveries in Children's Literature*, 169.

48. Ibid., 145–48.

49. Diana Wynne Jones, *Archer's Goon* (London: Methuen, 1984), 3.

50. Ibid., 6.

51. "The air of her city rings with unwanted noise that is the direct result of the aliens abusing the inhabitants: jackhammers from pointless construction projects, ear splitting factories … the din of entertainment gone awry"; Marilynn S. Olson, "Cats and Aliens in the Unreal City: T.S. Eliot, Diana Wynne Jones, and the Urban Experience," in *An Exciting and Exacting Wisdom*, 153.

52. Rahn, *Rediscoveries in Children's Literature*, 161.

53. Ibid., 7.

54. Maria Nikolajeva, *The Magic Code* (Stockholm: Almquist and Wiskell International, 1988), 11.

55. Jones, *Archer's Goon*, 28.

56. Ibid., 40.

57. Ibid., 44.

58. Ibid., 46.
59. Ibid., 147.
60. A picture Jones owned: Diana Wynne Jones, "The Heroic Ideal—A Personal Odyssey," *The Lion and the Unicorn* 13 (1989): 135.
61. Ibid.
62. Martha P. Hixon, "The Importance of Being Nowhere: Narrative Dimensions and Their Interplay in *Fire and Hemlock*," in *An Exciting and Exacting Wisdom*, 103.
63. Ibid., 101.
64. Ibid., 102.
65. Diana Wynne Jones, *Fire and Hemlock* (London: Methuen, 1985), 151.
66. Butler, "Now Here: Where Now?" 66–78.
67. Butler, "Magic as Metaphor," 76.
68. Diana Wynne Jones, "The Shape of Narrative in *Lord of the Rings*," in *J.R.R. Tolkien: This Far Land*, ed. Robert Giddings (London: Vision, 1983), 87–107.
69. Jones, *Fire and Hemlock*, 31.
70. Ibid., 89.
71. Ibid., 204.
72. Ibid., 207.
73. Ibid.; "Despite the similarity of names, it was not Tam Lin but Thomas the Rhymer whom Thomas Lynn most resembled. He had been turned out too, also with a gift. And Laurel had been furious with Thomas Lynn at the time. She was still furious at the funeral. So the gift had been given with a twist. Anything he made up would prove to be true, and then come back and hit him. ... But this was where Polly herself had come in. She had become connected to the gift because she had helped Mr. Lynn make up Tan Coul. And she rather thought that the gift had been intended to be conveyed through the pictures ... until Polly had stepped in there too and mixed the pictures up" (307).
74. Jones, letter, December 6, 2004.
75. Jones, *Fire and Hemlock*, 19.
76. Posted by Sally Odgers, on the Diana Wynne Jones mailing list, January 12, 2002, http://suberic.net/dwj/list.
77. Nicki Humble, "The Rewards of Intertextuality: The Mythic Dimensions of the Work of Diana Wynne Jones" (paper presented at the IBBY day conference, Roehampton, November 13, 2004).
78. Jones, "The Heroic Ideal," 139.
79. Jones, *Fire and Hemlock*, 341.

Chapter 7

1. John Clute, "Instauration Fantasy," in *The Encyclopedia of Fantasy*, ed. John Clute and John Grant (New York: St. Martin's Griffin, 1999), 501.
2. Maria Nikolajeva, "Heterotopia as a Reflection of Postmodern Consciousness in the Works of Diana Wynne Jones," in in *Diana Wynne Jones: An*

Exciting and Exacting Wisdom, ed. Teya Rosenberg et al. (New York: Peter Lang, 2002), 27.

3. Charles Butler, "Now Here: Where Now? Magic as Metaphor and as Reality in the Writing of Diana Wynne Jones," in *Diana Wynne Jones: An Exciting and Exacting Wisdom,* ed. Teya Rosenberg et al. (New York: Peter Lang, 2002), 66.

4. "Diana Wynne Jones's power lies in the unconventional solutions, sharp observations and deep examinations of human nature in her works. Magic adventures are not there for their own sake, and the struggle between good and evil is merely background for the protagonists' struggle with themselves"; Maria Nikolajeva, *Children's Literature Comes of Age: Toward a New Aesthetic* (London and New York: Garland, 1996), 74.

5. Clare Bradford, "Possessed by the Beast: Subjectivity and Agency in *Pictures in the Dark and Foxspell,*" in *Mystery in Children's Literature: From the Rational to the Supernatural,* ed. Adrienne Gavin and Christopher Routledge (Basingstoke: Palgrave, 2001), 150.

6. Butler, "Now Here: Where Now?" 68.

7. Diana Wynne Jones, *Deep Secret* (London: Victor Gollancz, 1997), 18.

8. Ibid., 271.

9. Ibid.

How many miles to Babylon?
Three score miles and ten.
Can I get there by candle-light?
Yes, and back again.
If your feet are speedy and light
You can get there by candle-light. (271)

Then Rupert's verse again, extended:

Where is the road to Babylon?
Right beside your door.
Can I walk that road whenever I want?
No, three times and no more.
If you mark the road and measure it right
You can go there by candle-light. (271)

Then Stan's verse:

How do I go to Babylon?
Outside of here and there.
Am I crossing a bridge or climbing a hill?
Yes, both before you're there.
If you follow outside of day and night
You can be there by candle-light. (271)

Then Will's verse:

> How hard is the road to Babylon?
> As hard as grief or greed.
> What do I ask for when I get there?
> Only for what you need.
> If you travel in need and travel light
> You can get there by candle-light. (272)

Then a public verse that Rob knows also:

> How long is the way to Babylon?
> Three score years and ten.
> Many have gone to Babylon
> But few come back again.
> If your feet are nimble and light
> You can be back by candle-light. (272)

And then later, when Rob returns without Maree, desperate to know what he should carry, Zinka gives them another verse:

> What shall I take to Babylon?
> A handful of salt and some grain,
> Water, some wool for warmth on the way,
> And a candle to make the road plain.
> If you carry three things and use them right
> You can be there by candle-light. (284)

10. There are very real differences between Tolkien and his emulators. The most significant is that the heroes of the Tolkienistas are almost always in search of power. All the heroes of *The Lord of the Rings* were anxious to divest themselves of power.
11. Jones, *Deep Secret*, 126.
12. Ibid., 150.
13. Chris Bell, personal communication, December 29, 2004, and January 10, 2005. The hotel with five sides was the Victoria Park Hotel: "Hotel on a five-sided square—walk for miles and end up at your room just outside the door on the other side of the main hall from where you were." The lifts "are both Fannish Legend, as are the lifts at the Adelphi and the lifts at the Harrogate hotel in which a Mexicon was held. DWJ was not actually at the Glasgow convention nor the Mexicon, but knows the Adelphi and the Hotel de France on Jersey." "The invasion of the kitchens to find whole grain at midnight happened in a hotel in Milton Keynes (another filk con, and just don't ask why whole grain was essential at that point) and was made easy because the stairs from the bedrooms at one end of the hotel went straight down into the kitchens rather than to the foyer." But "DWJ was not

implicated in this action, but was told about it," while "at a previous Fantasycon, in a different London hotel, and the Finnish receptionist and the hotel computer between them conflated Terry Pratchett and Alex Stewart really comprehensively, such that their names were mixed in several combinations in different rooms."

14. Teya Rosenberg, "Magical Realism and Children's Literature: Diana Wynne Jones's *Black Maria* and Salman Rushdie's *Midnight's Children* as a Test Case," *Papers* 11 (2001): 19.

15. Margery Fisher, *Intent upon Reading: A Critical Appraisal of Modern Fiction for Children* (London: Hodder and Stoughton, 1976), 154.

16. Diana Wynne Jones, "Heroes," a lecture originally delivered in Australia, 1992; held at the "Diana Wynne Jones Fansite," http://www.leemac.freeserve.co.uk/.

17. Diana Wynne Jones, "The Heroic Ideal—A Personal Odyssey," *The Lion and the Unicorn* 13 (1989): 129–44.

18. Mary Norton, "Paul's Tale," in *The Last Borrower's Story: Poor Stainless* (London: Viking, 1994), 55–80; cited by Elizabeth Hammill, " 'Real' Stories or 'Pretty' Stories: A Question of Criteria," in *Voices Off: Texts, Contexts and Readers*, ed. Morag Styles, Eve Bearne, and Victor Watson (London: Cassell, 1996), 20–21.

19. Diana Wynne Jones, "Birthing a Book," *Horn Book Magazine*, July–August 2004, 393. Some years after writing *The Magicians of Caprona*, Jones received a letter from a real Count of Caprona; e-mail, January 10, 2005.

20. Deborah Kaplan, "Diana Wynne Jones and the World-Shaping Power of Language," in *An Exciting and Exacting Wisdom*, 57.

21. Diana Wynne Jones, *Fire and Hemlock* (London: Methuen, 1985), 227.

22. Diana Wynne Jones, Dogsbody (London and Basingstoke: Macmillan, 1975), 161.

23. Diana Wynne Jones, *Witch Week* (London and Basingstoke: Macmillan, 1982), 94.

24. Ibid., 106.

25. Ibid., 126.

26. This ability to slide in material that later becomes crucial is noted by John Stephens, who pointed to the number of times we are alerted to the ring in Hasruel's nose in *Castle in the Air;* Stephens, *Language and Ideology in Children's Fiction* (London: Longman, 1992), 274. It should be noted, however, that Stephens seems to miss what is under his nose. One of *Castle in the Air*'s taproot tales is *The Twelve Dancing Princesses,* and much that Stephens described as "inversion"—such as the character of Princess Beatrice—can be found there.

27. Ibid., 272.

28. Diana Wynne Jones, *Castle in the Air* (London: Methuen, 1990), 155.

29. Stephens, *Language and Ideology*, 272.

30. As in the polite heavy man of the crime novel. Ibid., 272.

31. Jones, *Witch Week*, 196.

32. Ibid., 37.

33. Kaplan, "Diana Wynne Jones and the World-Shaping Power of Language," in *An Exciting and Exacting Wisdom*, 54.
34. Ibid., 55.
35. Diana Wynne Jones, *Black Maria* (London: Methuen, 1991), 17.
36. Rosemary Ross Johnson pointed to something similar in Susan Price's *The Ghost Drum:* a cat tells of a czar who convinces his people that dying in war is glorious and that accepting starvation a sign of their nobility; "The Special Magic of the Eighties: Shaping Words and Shape-Shifting Words," *Children's Literature in Education* 26 (1995): 214.
37. Jones, *Black Maria*, 110.
38. The tendency of her mother to decide her daughters' futures to indicate love; Diana Wynne Jones, "1934–," *Something about the Author*, vol. 70 (Detroit: Gale, 1993).
39. Jones, *Black Maria*, 138.
40. Ibid., 200.
41. Margaret Mahy, "A Dissolving Ghost," in *Only Connect: Reading on Children's Literature*, ed. Sheila Egoff et al., 3rd ed. (Toronto, New York, Oxford: Oxford University Press, 1996), 137.
42. Jones, *Black Maria*, 95.
43. Ibid., 183.
44. Jones, *Witch Week*, 24.
45. Ibid., 183.
46. Ibid., 203.
47. Diana Wynne Jones, *A Sudden Wild Magic* (New York: Avon Books, 1992), 19–20.
48. Sue Walsh, " 'Irony?—But Children Don't Get It, Do They?' The Idea of Appropriate Language in Narratives for Children," *Children's Literature Quarterly* 28 (2003): 26–36.
49. Jones, *A Sudden Wild Magic*, 13–14.
50. Ibid., 62.
51. Ibid., 132.
52. Jones, *Deep Secret*, 61.
53. Ibid., 81.
54. Ibid.
55. Ibid., 82.
56. Ibid., 153.
57. Jones, "Birthing a Book," 381.
58. Ibid.
59. One of the more unnerving developments at science fiction conventions is for panelists discussing the problems with J.K. Rowling's work to be brought up short by a child's standing up and declaring, "But I think Harry Potter is the best ever." Most critics cannot bring themselves to respond, and the panel grinds to a halt.
60. Diana Wynne Jones, "Carol Oneir's Hundreth Dream," in *Mixed Magics* (London: HarperCollins, 1984), 111.

61. Ibid., 116.
62. Ibid., 123.
63. Ibid., 126.
64. Jones, *Fire and Hemlock*, 17.
65. Ibid., 20.
66. Ibid., 61, 62.
67. Ibid., 229.
68. Brian Attebery, "Metafictions: Stories of Reading, Introduction," *Paradoxa* 4, no. 10 (1988): 185.
69. Diana Wynne Jones, *The Spellcoats* (London and Basingstoke: Macmillan, 1979), 65.
70. Ibid., 9.
71. Ibid., 143.
72. Ibid., 139.
73. Ibid., 156.
74. Ibid., 165.
75. A number of different editions were used at different stages in the research and writing of this book, starting with my old Puffins, moving to the new Collins editions, and eventually securing the first editions. Each new layout attracted the eye to different elements of Jones's writing.
76. Jones, *The Spellcoats*, 78.
77. Ibid., 82.
78. See Diana Wynne Jones, "Hints about Writing a Story"; held at the "Diana Wynne Jones Fansite," http://www.leemac.freeserve.co.uk/.
79. Diana Wynne Jones, *Hexwood* (London: Methuen, 1993), 275.
80. Jones, *The Spellcoats*, 129.
81. Suzanne Rahn, *Rediscoveries in Children's Literature* (New York and London: Garland, 1995), 171.
82. Ibid., 167, 168.

Epilogue

1. Diana Wynne Jones, "The Profession of Science Fiction, 51: Answers to Some Questions," *Foundation: The International Review of Science Fiction* 70 (Summer 1997): 14.
2. Karin Lesnik-Oberstein, *Children's Literature: Criticism and the Fictional Child* (Oxford: Clarendon, 1994), 104.
3. Sue Walsh, " 'Irony?—But Children Don't Get It, Do They?' The Idea of Appropriate Language in Narratives for Children," *Children's Literature Quarterly* 28 (2003): 27.
4. Diana Wynne Jones, "1934–," *Something about the Author*, vol. 70 (Detroit: Gale, 1993).
5. Mike Cadden, "Speaking to Both Children and Genre: Le Guin's Ethics of Audience," *The Lion and the Unicorn* 24 (2000): 128–42.

6. "Interview with Diana Wynne Jones, conducted by Charles Butler, 22 March 2001," in *Diana Wynne Jones: An Exciting and Exacting Wisdom,* ed. Teya Rosenberg et al. (New York: Peter Lang, 2002), 172.
7. Ibid., 168.
8. Julia Briggs, *A Woman of Passion: The Life of E. Nesbit 1858–1924* (London: Hutchinson, 1987), 402.
9. Roberta Seret, *Voyage into Creativity: The Modern Künstlerroman,* Studies in European Thought 4 (New York: Peter Lang, 1992), 3.
10. Peter Hunt, *Criticism, Theory and Children's Literature* (Oxford: Blackwell, 1991), 4.
11. Brian Attebery, "Metafictions: Stories of Reading, Introduction," *Paradoxa* 4, no. 10 (1988): 188.
12. Wayne C. Booth, *The Rhetoric of Fiction,* 2nd ed. (Chicago: University of Chicago Press, 1983), 397–98.
13. Michael Wesley, *The Walrus,* December–January 2005, 27.

BIBLIOGRAPHIES

Bibliography 1: Books by Diana Wynne Jones (in chronological order of publication)

Diana Wynne Jones noted (letter, December 6, 2004) that *Eight Days of Luke* was written at least two years before *Wilkins' Tooth; Power of Three* was begun several years before *Cart and Cwidder* but finished after it; *Dogsbody* was written while *Eight Days of Luke, Cart and Cwidder,* and *Power of Three* were in press but was published in the same year as the first two, with *Power of Three* being postponed. Finally, *Fire and Hemlock* was completed before *Archer's Goon,* but the latter was offered to the new publisher (Methuen) first, before *Fire and Hemlock.*

Changeover. London and Basingstoke: Macmillan, 1970. Reprinted London: Moondust, 2004.

Wilkins' Tooth. London and Basingstoke: Macmillan, 1973. Reprinted New York: E.P. Dutton, 1974, as *Witch's Business.* U.K. title reprinted London: Collins, 2002; U.S. title reprinted New York: Greenwillow, 2002.

The Ogre Downstairs. London and Basingstoke: Macmillan, 1974.

Cart and Cwidder. London and Basingstoke: Macmillan, 1975.

Eight Days of Luke. London and Basingstoke: Macmillan, 1975.

Dogsbody. London and Basingstoke: Macmillan, 1975.—this is correct, which mean the ff are not.

Power of Three. London and Basingstoke: Macmillan, 1976.

Charmed Life. London and Basingstoke: Macmillan, 1977.

Drowned Ammet. London and Basingstoke: Macmillan, 1977.

Who Got Rid of Angus Flint? London: Evans Brothers, 1979. (Retitling of "The Fearsome Friend," 1975). Reprinted in Jones, *Stopping for a Spell,* 111–48.

The Spellcoats. London and Basingstoke: Macmillan, 1979.

The Four Grannies. London: Hamish Hamilton, 1980. Reprinted in Jones, *Stopping for a Spell,* 65–110.

The Magicians of Caprona. London and Basingstoke: Macmillan, 1980.

The Homeward Bounders. London and Basingstoke: Macmillan, 1981.

The Time of the Ghost. London and Basingstoke: Macmillan, 1981.

Witch Week. London and Basingstoke: Macmillan, 1982.

Archer's Goon. London: Methuen, 1984.

The Skiver's Guide. Sevenoaks: Knight, 1984.

The Warlock at the Wheel and Other Stories. London and Basingstoke: Macmillan, 1984.

Fire and Hemlock. London: Methuen, 1985.

Howl's Moving Castle. London: Methuen, 1986.

A Tale of Time City. London: Methuen, 1987.

The Lives of Christopher Chant: The Childhood of Chrestomanci. London: Methuen, 1988.

Chair Person. London: Hamilton Children's, 1989.

Hidden Turnings, ed. Jones. London: Methuen, 1989.

Wild Robert. London: Methuen, 1990.

Castle in the Air. London: Methuen, 1990.

Black Maria. London: Methuen, 1991. (In United States, *Aunt Maria*.)

A Sudden Wild Magic. New York: Morrow/AvoNova, 1992.

Yes, Dear, illustrated by Graham Philpot. London: HarperCollins, 1992.

Hexwood. London: Methuen, 1993.

The Crown of Dalemark. London: Mandarin, 1993.

Stopping for a Spell. New York: Morrow Greenwillow, 1993.

Fantasy Stories, ed. Jones. London: Kingfisher, 1994.

Everard's Ride. Framingham, MA: NESFA Press, 1995.

Minor Arcana. London: Victor Gollancz, 1996.

The Tough Guide to Fantasyland. London: Vista, 1996.

Deep Secret. London: Victor Gollancz, 1997.

The Dark Lord of Derkholm. London: Victor Gollancz, 1998.

Puss in Boots. London: Scholastic Children's Books, 1999.

Believing Is Seeing. New York: Greenwillow, 1999.

Year of the Griffin. London: Victor Gollancz, 2000.

Mixed Magics: The Worlds of Chrestomanci. London: Collins, 2000.

The Merlin Conspiracy. London: Collins, 2003.

Unexpected Magic: Collected Stories. New York: Greenwillow, 2004.

Conrad's Fate. London: HarperCollins, 2005.

Bibliography 2: Stories by Diana Wynne Jones (in chronological order of publication)

"The Fearsome Friend," in *Young Winter's Tales 6*. London and Basingstoke: Macmillan, 1975. Reprinted as *Who Got Rid of Angus Flint?* London: Evans Bros, 1979. Reprinted in Jones, *Stopping for a Spell*, 111–48.

"Carruthers," in *Young Winter's Tales 8*. London and Basingstoke: Macmillan, 1978. Reprinted in Jones, *Warlock and the Wheel*, 54–74, and Jones, *Unexpected Magic*, 131–55.

"Auntie Bea's Day Out," in *The Cat Flap and the Apple Pie and Other Funny Stories*. London: W.H. Allen, 1979. Reprinted in Jones, *Warlock at the Wheel*, 43–53, and Jones, *Unexpected Magic*, 118–30.

"The Fluffy Pink Toadstool," in *Puffin Post* 13, no. 4 (1979). Reprinted in Jones, *Warlock at the Wheel*, 35–42, and Jones, *Unexpected Magic*, 109–17.

"The Sage of Theare," in *Hecate's Cauldron*, ed. Susan Shwartz, 76–101. New York: DAW, 1982. Reprinted in Jones, *Mixed Magics*, 131–72, and Jones, *Minor Arcana*, 13–42.

"Dragon Reserve, Home Eight," in Jones, *The Warlock at the Wheel and Other Stories*, 100–28. London and Basingstoke: Macmillan, 1984. Reprinted in Jones, *Minor Arcana*, 80–109, and Jones, *Unexpected Magic*, 233–65.

"No One," in Jones, *The Warlock at the Wheel and Other Stories*, 75–99. London and Basingstoke: Macmillan, 1984. Reprinted in Jones, *Unexpected Magic*, 203–32.

"The Plague of Peacocks," in Jones, *The Warlock at the Wheel and Other Stories*, 23–34. London and Basingstoke: Macmillan, 1984. Reprinted in Jones, *Unexpected Magic*, 36–50.

"Warlock at the Wheel," in Jones, *The Warlock at the Wheel and Other Stories*, 7–22. London and Basingstoke: Macmillan, 1984. Reprinted in Jones, *Mixed Magics*, 9–32.

"Carol Oneir's Hundredth Dream," in *Dragons and Dreams*, ed. Jane Yolen, Martin H. Greenberg, and Charles G. Waugh, 108–35. New York: Harper and Row, 1986. Reprinted in Jones, *Mixed Magics*, 101–29.

"Enna Hittims," in *The Methuen Book of Humorous Stories*. London: Methuen, 1987. Reprinted in Jones, *Unexpected Magic*, 71–88.

"The Fat Wizard," in *Guardian Angels*, ed. Stephanie Nuttell. London: Viking Kestrel, 1987. Reprinted in Jones, *Unexpected Magic*, 188–202.

"The Green Stone," in *Gaslight and Ghosts*, ed. Stephen Jones and Jo Fletcher, 21–27. London: Robinson and World Fantasy Convention, 1988. Reprinted in Jones, *Unexpected Magic*, 181–87.

"The Master," in *Hidden Turnings*, ed. Jones, 63–81. London: Methuen, 1989. Reprinted in Jones, *Minor Arcana*, 43–61, and Jones, *Unexpected Magic*, 50–70.

"Chair Person," in *Things That Go Bump in the Night*, ed. Jane Yolen and Martin H. Greenberg, 122–63. New York: Harper and Row, 1989. Published in book form, 1989. Reprinted in *Stopping for a Spell*, 1–64.

"Mela Worms," in *Arrows of Eros*, ed. Alex Stewart, 221–40. London: NEL, 1989.

"The Girl Who Loved the Sun," in *Heartache*, ed. Miriam Hodgson. London: Methuen, 1990. Reprinted in Jones, *Minor Arcana*, 62–79, and Jones, *Unexpected Magic*, 89–108.

"nad and Dan adn Quaffy," in *Digital Dreams*, ed. David V. Barrett, 259–80. London: NEL, 1990. Reprinted in Jones, *Minor Arcana*, 133–52, and Jones, *Unexpected Magic*, 13–35.

"What the Cat Told Me," in *Fantasy Stories*, ed. Jones, 230–55. London: Kingfisher, 1994. Reprinted in Jones, *Minor Arcana*, 110–32, and Jones, *Unexpected Magic*, 156–80.

"Everard's Ride," in *Everard's Ride*, 1–114. Framingham, MA: NESFA Press, 1995. Reprinted Jones, *Unexpected Magic*, 303–497.

"The True State of Affairs," in *Everard's Ride*, 213–303. Framingham, MA: NESFA Press, 1995. Reprinted Jones, *Minor Arcana*, 153–287.

"Stealer of Souls," first published in Jones, *Mixed Magics*, 33–99.

"Little Dot," in *Firebirds: An Anthology of Original Fantasy and Science Fiction*, ed. Sharyn November, 297–335. New York: Firebird, 2003. Reprinted Jones, *Unexpected Magic*, 266–302.

Bibliography 3: Other Fictional Works Cited

Aiken, Joan. *The Wolves of Willoughby Chase*. London: Jonathan Cape, 1962.

Alexander, Lloyd. *The High King*. New York: Holt, Rinehart and Winston, 1968.

Applegate, K.A. *Everworld*. New York: Scholastic, 1999. Twelve volumes starting with *Search for Sena*.

Barber, Antonia. *The Ghosts*. London: Jonathan Cape, 1969.

Barrie, J.M. *Peter Pan, or The Boy Who Would Not Grow Up* (first produced 1904), in J.M. Barrie, *The Plays of J.M. Barrie*, 1–91. London: Hodder and Stoughton, 1928.

Baum, L. Frank. *The Wonderful Wizard of Oz*. Chicago and New York: George M. Hill, 1900.

The Beano. Dundee, UK: D.C. Thomson.

Bunyan, John. *Pilgrim's Progress*. London, 1678.

Burgess, Melvin. *Junk*. London: Andersen, 1996.

Burgess, Melvin. *Lady, My Life as a Bitch*. London: Andersen, 2001.

Butler, Charles. *The Fetch of Mardy Watt*. London: HarperCollins, 2003.

Christie, Agatha. *The Murder of Roger Ackroyd*. London: Collins, 1926.

Cockayne, Steve. *Wanderers and Islanders*. London: Orbit, 2002.

Cooper, Susan, *The Dark Is Rising*. London: Chatto and Windus, 1973.

Cooper, Susan. *Greenwitch*. London: Chatto and Windus, 1974.

Cooper, Susan. *The Grey King*. London: Chatto and Windus, 1975.

Cooper, Susan. *Silver on the Tree*. London: Chatto and Windus, 1977.

Crowley, John. *Little, Big*. Toronto and New York: Bantam, 1981.

Delany, Samuel R. *Dhalgren*. New York: Bantam, 1975.

Dyer, K.C. *Seeds of Time*. Toronto, Oxford: Dundurn, 2002.

Farmer, Penelope. *Charlotte Sometimes*. London: Chatto and Windus, 1969.

Garner, Alan. *The Owl Service*. London: Collins, 1967.

Garner, Alan. *Thursbitch*. London: Harvill, 2003.

Garnett, Eve. *The Family from One End Street*. London: Frederick Muller, 1937.

Goudge, Elizabeth. *Henrietta's House*. London: Hodder and Stoughton, 1945.

Heinlein, Robert A. *Beyond This Horizon*. Reading, PA: Fantasy Press, 1948.

Kingsley, Charles. *The Water-Babies*. London: Macmillan, 1863.

Lewis, C.S. *The Lion, the Witch and the Wardrobe*. London: Bles, 1950.

Lewis, C.S. *The Magician's Nephew*. London: J. Lane, 1955.

Lewis, C.S. *The Voyage of the Dawn Treader*. London: Bles, 1952.

Lindsay, David A. *Voyage to Arcturus*. London: Methuen, 1920.

Lively, Penelope. *A Stitch in Time*. Harmondsworth: Penguin, 1986. (Orig. pub. 1976.)

MacDonald, George. *Lilith*. London: Chatto and Windus, 1895.

MacLeod, Ken. *Cosmonaut Keep*. London: Orbit, 2000.

Mahy, Margaret. *The Changeover*. London: Dent, 1984.

McKillip, Patricia A. *In the Forests of Serre*. New York: Ace, 2003.

Miéville, China. *The Scar*. London and Basingstoke: Macmillan, 2002.

Nesbit, Edith. *Five Children and It*. London: T. Fisher Unwin, 1902.

Nix, Garth. *Mister Monday*. London: HarperCollins, 2003.

Noon, Jeff. *Vurt*. Manchester: Ringpull, 1993.

Parker, K.J. *The Fencer* trilogy: *Colours in the Steel* (1998); *The Belly of the Bow* (1999); and *The Proof House* (2000). London: Orbit.

Peake, Mervyn. *Titus Groan*. London: Eyre and Spottiswood, 1946.

Pearce, Philippa. *Minnow on the Say*. London: Oxford University Press, 1955.

Pratchett, Terry. *The Colour of Magic*. Gerrards Cross: Colin Smythe, 1983.

Pratchett, Terry. *Small Gods*. London: Victor Gollancz, 1992.

Pratchett, Terry. *The Wee Free Men*. London and New York: Doubleday, 2003.

Pratchett, Terry. *Witches Abroad*. London: Victor Gollancz, 1991.

Pullman, Philip. *His Dark Materials* trilogy: *Northern Lights* (1995); *The Subtle Knife* (1997); and *The Amber Spyglass* (2001). London: Scholastic.

Ransome, Arthur. *Swallows and Amazons*. London: Cape, 1930.

Rowling, J.K. *Harry Potter and the Chamber of Secrets*. London: Bloomsbury, 1998.

Rowling, J.K. *Harry Potter and the Order of the Phoenix*. London: Bloomsbury, 2003.

Smith, Dodie. *The Hundred and One Dalmatians*. London: Heinemann, 1956.

Smith, Dodie. *The Starlight Barking*. London: Heinemann, 1967.

Snickett, Lemony. *A Bad Beginning* (A Series of Unfortunate Events, 1). New York: Harper-Collins, 1999.

Swanwick, Michael. *The Iron Dragon's Daughter*. New York: William Morrow, 1994.

Tolkien, J.R.R. *The Lord of the Rings*. London: Allen and Unwin, 1954–55.

Travers, P.L. *Mary Poppins Comes Back*. London: Dickson and Thompson, 1935.
Trease, Geoffrey. *Bows against the Barons*. London: Martin Lawrence, 1934.

Bibliography 4: Critical Works

Appleyard, J.A. *Becoming a Reader: The Experience of Fiction from Childhood to Adulthood*. Cambridge: Cambridge University Press, 1990.

Attebery, Brian. *The Fantasy Tradition in American Literature*. Bloomington: Indiana University Press, 1980.

Attebery, Brian. "Metafictions: Stories of Reading, Introduction," *Paradoxa* 4, no. 10 (1988): 185–92.

Attebery, Brian. *Strategies of Fantasy*. Bloomington and Indianapolis: Indiana University Press, 1992.

Booth, Wayne C. *The Rhetoric of Fiction*. 2nd ed. Chicago: University of Chicago Press, 1983.

Bottigheimer, Ruth G., ed. *Fairy Tales and Society: Illusion, Allusion, and Paradigm*. Philadelphia: University of Pennsylvania Press, 1986.

Briggs, Julia. *A Woman of Passion: The Life of E. Nesbit 1858–1924*. London: Hutchinson, 1987.

Browne, N.M. Talk at the British Science Fiction Association, the Star Tavern, Kensington, October 27, 2004.

Butler, Charles. *Four British Fantasists: The Children's Fantasy Fiction of Penelope Lively, Alan Garner, Diana Wynne Jones, and Susan Cooper* (forthcoming, Scarecrow Press and Children's Literature Association).

Callender, Craig, ed. *Time, Reality and Experience*. Cambridge: Cambridge University Press, 2002.

Cameron, Eleanor. *The Green and Burning Tree: On the Writing and Enjoyment of Children's Books*. Boston and Toronto: Little, Brown, 1969.

Campbell, Joseph. *The Hero with a Thousand Faces*. Princeton, NJ: Princeton University Press, 1949.

Carr, David. *Time, Narrative, and History*. Bloomington and Indianapolis: Indiana University Press, 1991.

Chambers, N., ed. *The Signal Approach to Children's Books*. Harmondsworth: Kestrel, 1980.

Clark, Beverly Lyon. *Kiddie Lit: The Cultural Construction of Children's Literature in America*. Baltimore: Johns Hopkins University Press, 2003.

Clarke, Arthur C. *Profiles of the Future: An Inquiry into the Limits of the Possible*. Rev. ed. London: Victor Gollancz, 1974.

Clute, John. "Beyond the Pale," in *Conjunctions: 39*, 420–34. Annandale-on-Hudson, NY: Bard College, 2003.

Clute, John. "Canaries in the Coalmine." Address given at SUNY, New Palz, April 2004.

Clute, John, and John Grant, eds. *The Encyclopedia of Fantasy*. London: Orbit, 1997; corrected edition, New York: St Martins Griffin, 1999

Clute, John, and Peter Nicholls, eds. *The Encyclopedia of Science Fiction*. New York: St. Martin's Griffin, 1995.

Cosslett, Tess. "'History from Below': Time Slip Narratives and National Identity," *The Lion and the Unicorn* 26 (2002): 243–53.

Cushman, Carolyn. "All Time List," *Locus: The Magazine of the Science Fiction and Fantasy Field* 52, no. 1 (issue 516, 2004): 40.

Donovan, John. "American Dispatch," *Signal*, January 28, 1979, 3–8.

Dyke, Heather. "McTaggart and the Truth about Time," in *Time, Reality and Experience*, ed. Craig Callender, 137–52. Cambridge: Cambridge University Press, 2002.

Egoff, Sheila, Gordon Stubbs, Ralph Ashley, and Wendy Sutton, eds. *Only Connect: Reading on Children's Literature*. 3rd ed. Toronto, New York, Oxford: Oxford University Press, 1996.

Fisher, Margery. *Intent upon Reading: A Critical Appraisal of Modern Fiction for Children.* London: Hodder and Stoughton, 1976.

Friedman, Michael. *Foundations of Space-Time Theories: Relativistic Physics and Philosophy of Science.* Princeton, NJ: Princeton University Press, 1983.

Garner, Alan. "Part 1: Some Influences and Inspirations," *Swing* 51, no. 7: 16–21, 28.

Garner, Alan. "Part 2: The Lad of the Gad, the Guizer, Red Shift and Others," *Swing* 51, no. 8: 20–27.

Garner, Alan. *The Voice That Thunders: Essays and Lectures.* London: Harvill Press, 1997.

Gavin, Adrienne, and Christopher Routledge, eds. *Mystery in Children's Literature: From the Rational to the Supernatural.* Basingstoke: Palgrave, 2001.

Gödel, Kurt. "Spacetime with Closed Time-like Curves." From Gödel, "An Example of a New Type of Cosmological Solution to Einstein's Field Equations of Gravitation," *Review of Modern Physics* 21 (July 1949): 447–50; http://www.utas.edu.au/docs/humsoc/philosophy/Time_Travel/lectures/10a.htm.

Grey, Dorian E. Posted by Sally Odgers, on the Diana Wynne Jones mailing list, January 12, 2002, http://suberic.net/dwj/list.

Gupta, Suman. *Re-reading Harry Potter.* Basingstoke: Palgrave Macmillan, 2003.

Guroian, Vigen. *Tending the Heart of Virtue: How Classic Stories Awaken a Child's Moral Imagination.* Oxford: Oxford University Press, 1998.

Heiner, Heidi Anne. *The SurLaLune Fairy Tale Pages,* http://www.surlalunefairytales.com/twelvedancing/.

Hollindale, Peter. *An Interview with Anne Fine.* London: Egmont Press, 2000. (© 1999)

Hollinger, Veronica, and Joan Gordon, eds. *Edging into the Future: Science Fiction and Contemporary Cultural Transformation.* Philadelphia: University of Pennsylvania Press, 2002.

Hooper, Walter. *Past Watchful Dragons.* London: Collins, 1971.

Humble, Nicki. "The Rewards of Intertextuality: The Mythic Dimensions of the Work of Diana Wynne Jones." Delivered at the IBBY day conference November 13, 2004, Roehampton, to be published by Pied Piper Press, Lichfield, 2005.

Hume, Kathryn. *Fantasy and Mimesis: Responses to Reality in Western Literature.* New York and London: Methuen, 1984.

Hunt, Caroline. "Form as Fantasy—Fantasy as Form," *Children's Literature Quarterly* 12 (Spring 1987): 7–10.

Hunt, Peter. *Criticism, Theory and Children's Literature.* Oxford: Blackwell, 1991.

Hunt, Peter. "Landscape and Journeys, Metaphors and Maps: The Distinctive Feature of English Fantasy," *Children's Literature Quarterly* 12 (1987): 11–14.

Hunt, Peter, ed. *Literature for Children: Contemporary Criticism.* London and New York: Routledge, 1990.

Hunt, Peter. "The Mayne Game: An Experiment in Response," *Signal* 28 (1979): 9–25.

Hunt, Peter, ed. *Understanding Children's Literature.* London: Routledge, 1999.

Hunt, Peter, and Sheila Ray, eds. *International Companion Encyclopedia of Children's Literature.* London and New York: Routledge, 2002.

Inglis, Fred. *The Promise of Happiness: Value and Meaning in Children's Fiction.* Cambridge: Cambridge University Press, 1981.

Irwin, W.R. *The Game of the Impossible: A Rhetoric of Fantasy.* Urbana, Chicago, London: University of Illinois, 1976.

Jackson, Rosemary. *Fantasy: The Literature of Subversion.* London and New York: Routledge, 1984.

James, Edward, and Farah Mendlesohn, eds. *The Cambridge Companion to Science Fiction.* Cambridge: Cambridge University Press, 2003.

Johnson, Rosemary Ross. "The Special Magic of the Eighties: Shaping Words and Shape-Shifting Words," *Children's Literature in Education* 26 (1995): 211–17.

Jones, Diana Wynne. "1934–," in *Something about the Author.* Vol. 70, 115–18. Detroit: Gale, 1993.

Jones, Diana Wynne. "Article from the Medusa," reprinted at http://suberic.net/dwj/medusa.html with the permission of Will Shetterly (an article about writing for children as opposed to adults).

Jones, Diana Wynne. "Birthing a Book," *Horn Book Magazine,* July–August 2004, 379–93.

Jones, Diana Wynne. "Diana Wynne Jones: Writing for Children," *Locus* (April 1989): 5, 62.

Jones, Diana Wynne. "Heroes," a lecture originally delivered in Australia, 1992; held at the "Diana Wynne Jones Fansite," http://www.leemac.freeserve.co.uk/.

Jones, Diana Wynne. "The Heroic Ideal—A Personal Odyssey," *The Lion and the Unicorn,* 13 (1989): 129–40.

Jones, Diana Wynne. "Hints about Writing a Story"; held at the "Diana Wynne Jones Fansite," http://www.leemac.freeserve.co.uk/.

Jones, Diana Wynne. "Inventing the Middle Ages"; held at the "Diana Wynne Jones Fansite," http://www.leemac.freeserve.co.uk/, from a talk given at the University of Nottingham, 1997.

Jones, Diana Wynne. "The Magic of Narnia," http://www.amazon.com/exec/obidos/tg/feature/-/91955/104-6380809-0505511.

Jones, Diana Wynne. "Old Irish Hymn"; held at the "Diana Wynne Jones Fansite," http://www.leemac.freeserve.co.uk/, 1998.

Jones, Diana Wynne. "The Profession of Science Fiction, 51: Answers to Some Questions," *Foundation: The International Review of Science Fiction* 70 (Summer 1997): 5–14.

Jones, Diane Wynne. "The Shape of the Narrative in *Lord of the Rings*," in *J.R.R. Tolkien: This Far Land,* ed. R. Giddings, 87–107. London: Vista, 1983.

Jones, Nicolette. "Fantasy Matches How Our Brains Are Made," *The Times,* March 26, 2003, 17.

Kedge, Elizabeth. Paper given at the Science Fiction Research Conference, New Lanark, Scotland, July 2002.

Larrick, Nancy. "A Feminist Look at Children's Books," *School Library Journal* (January 1971): 19–24.

Lesnik-Oberstein, Karín. *Children's Literature: Criticism and the Fictional Child.* Oxford: Clarendon, 1994.

Lesnik-Oberstein, Karín, ed. *Children's Literature: New Approaches.* Basingstoke: Palgrave Macmillan, 2004.

Locherbie-Cameron, M.A.L. "Journeys through the Amulet: Time-Travel in Children's Fiction," *Signal* 79 (January 1996): 45–61.

Lucas, Ann Lawson, ed. *The Presence of the Past in Children's Literature.* Westport, CT, and London: Praeger, 2003.

Lurie, Alison. *Don't Tell the Grown-Ups: Subversive Children's Literature.* London: Bloomsbury, 1990.

Meek, Margaret, Aidan Warlow, and Griselda Barton, eds. *The Cool Web: The Pattern of Children's Reading.* London, Sydney, Toronto: Bodley Head, 1977.

Mendlesohn, Farah. "*Conjunctions 39* and Liminal Fantasy," *Journal of the Fantastic in the Arts* 15.3 (2005).

Mendlesohn, Farah. "Crowning the King: Harry Potter and the Construction of Authority," in *The Ivory Tower and Harry Potter: Perspectives on a Literary Phenomenon,* ed. Lana A. Whited, 159–81. Columbia and London: University of Missouri Press, 2002.

Mendlesohn, Farah. "Is There Any Such Thing as Children's SF? A Position Piece," *The Lion and the Unicorn* 28 (2004): 284–313.

Mendlesohn, Farah. "Towards a Taxonomy of Fantasy," *Journal of the Fantastic in the Arts* 13 (2002): 173–87.

Molson, Francis J. *Children's Fantasy* (Starmont Reader's Guide, 33). San Bernardino, CA: Borgo Press, 1989.

Moorcock, Michael. *Wizardry and Wild Romance*. London: Victor Gollancz, 1987.

Nahin, Paul J. *Time Machines: Time Travel in Physics, Metaphysics, and Science Fiction*. New York: American Institute of Physics, 1993.

Nicholson, Virginia. *Among the Bohemians: Experiments in Living 1900–1939*. London: Penguin, 2003.

Nikolajeva, Maria. *Children's Literature Comes of Age: Toward a New Aesthetic*. London and New York: Garland, 1996.

Nikolajeva, Maria. "Imprints of the Mind: The Depiction of Consciousness in Children's Fiction," *Children's Literature Association Quarterly* 26 (2002): 173–87.

Nikolajeva, Maria. *The Magic Code: The Use of Magical Patterns in Fantasy for Children*. Stockholm: Almquist and Wiskell International, 1988.

Olendorf, Donna, and Diane Telgen. *Something about the Author: Facts and Pictures about Authors and Illustrators of Books for Young People*. Vol. 70, 115–18. Detroit and London: Gale Research, 1993.

Philip, Neil. "England's Dreaming," *Signal* 82 (January 1997): 14–30.

Pickover, Clifford A. *Time: A Traveller's Guide*. New York and Oxford: Oxford University Press, 1998.

Popp, V. *Morphology of the Folktale*. Austin: University of Texas Press, 1968.

Rabkin, Eric S. *The Fantastic in Literature*. Princeton, NJ: Princeton University Press, 1976.

Rahn, Suzanne, " 'It Would Be Awful Not to Know Greek': Rediscovering Geoffrey Trease," *The Lion and the Unicorn* 14 (1990): 23–53.

Rahn, Suzanne. *Rediscoveries in Children's Literature*. New York and London: Garland, 1995.

Ray, Christopher. *Time, Space and Philosophy*. London and New York: Routledge, 1991.

Rose, Jacqueline. *The Case of Peter Pan or the Impossibility of Children's Fiction*. Basingstoke: Macmillan, 1984.

Rosenberg, Teya. "Magical Realism and Children's Literature: Diana Wynne Jones's *Black Maria* and Salman Rushdie's *Midnight's Children* as a Test Case," *Papers: Explorations into Children's Literature* 11 (2001): 14–25.

Rosenberg, Teya, Martha P. Hixon, Sharon M. Scapple, and Donna R. White, eds. *Diana Wynne Jones: An Exciting and Exacting Wisdom*. New York: Peter Lang, 2002.

Rumbold, Margaret. "Taking the Subject Further," *Places* 7 (1997): 16–28.

Sadler, Frank. *The Unified Ring: Narrative Art and the Science Fiction Novel*. Ann Arbor: University of Michigan Research Press, 1984.

Seret, Roberta. *Voyage into Creativity: The Modern Künstlerroman* (Studies in European Thought, 4). New York: Peter Lang, 1992.

Speller, Maureen Kincaid. "Diana Wynne Jones in Her Own Words: Part 2," *Charmed Lives Fanzine*, issue 2 (Midsummer, 1998), http://wwww.leemac.freeserve.co.uk/cl2int.htm.

Spraggs, Gillian. "A Lawless World: The Fantasy Novels of Susan Cooper," *The Lion and the Unicorn* 33 (1982): 23–31.

Spraggs, Gillian. "True Dreams: The Fantasy Fiction of Diana Wynne Jones," *The Lion and the Unicorn* 34 (1983): 17–22.

Spufford, Francis. *The Child That Books Built: A Memoir of Childhood and Reading*. London: Faber and Faber, 2002.

Stephens, John. *Language and Ideology in Children's Fiction*. London: Longman, 1992.

Stephens, John. "Modernism to Postmodernism, or the Line from Insk to Onsk: William Mayne's Tiger's Railway," *Papers: Explorations into Children's Literature* 3 (1993): 51–59.

Stephens, John, and Robyn McCallum. *Retelling Stories, Framing Culture: Traditional Story and Metanarratives in Children's Literature*. New York and London: Garland, 1998.

Styles, Morag, Eve Bearne, and Victor Watson, eds. *Voices Off: Texts, Contexts and Readers*. London: Cassell, 1996.

Todorov, Tzvetan. *The Fantastic: A Structural Approach to a Literary Genre*. Ithaca, NY: Cornell University Press, 1975.

Townsend, John Rowe. *A Sounding of Storytellers: New and Revised Essays on Contemporary Writers for Children*. Harmondsworth: Kestrel Books, 1979.

Trease, Geoffrey. *Tales out of School: A Survey of Children's Fiction*. London: New Education Book Club, 1948.

Tucker, Nicholas. "The Child in Time," *Independent Magazine,* April 5, 2003, 16.

Tucker, Nicholas, and Nikki Gamble. *Family Fictions* (Contemporary Classics of Children's Literature). London and New York: Continuum, 2001.

Varsamopoulou, Evy. *The Poetics of the Künstlerinroman and the Aesthetics of the Sublime* (Studies in European Cultural Transition, 11). Aldershot: Ashgate, 2002.

Wall, Barbara. *The Narrator's Voice: The Dilemma of Children's Fiction*. London: Macmillan, 1991.

Walsh, Sue. " 'Irony?—But Children Don't Get It, Do They?' The Idea of Appropriate Language in Narratives for Children," *Children's Literature Quarterly* 28 (2003): 26–36.

Walter, Natasha. "The Accidental Realist," *The Guardian,* October 9, 2004. (From the Internet.)

Warner, Marina. *From the Beast to the Blonde: On Fairy Tales and Their Tellers*. London: Vintage, 1995.

Wesley, Michael. *The Walrus,* December–January 2005, 27.

White, Frances P. "Between the Lines: A Study of the Themes and Techniques in the Work of William Mayne." MA diss., Loughborough, September 1987.

Wintle, Justin, and Emma Fisher, eds. *The Pied Pipers: Interviews with the Influential Creators of Children's Literature*. London: Paddington Press, 1975.

Wolfe, Gary K. *Critical Terms for Fantasy and Science Fiction: A Glossary and Guide to Scholarship*. Westport, CT: Greenwood, 1986.

Wolfe, Gary K. "Malebolge, Or the Ordnance of Genre," in *Conjunctions: 39,* 405–19. Annandale-on-Hudson, NY: Bard College, 2002.

Zipes, Jack. *Breaking the Magic Spell: Radical Theories of Folk and Fairy Tales*. Rev. ed. Lexington: University Press of Kentucky, 2002. (Orig. pub. 1984.)

Zipes, Jack. *Happily Ever After: Fairy Tales, Children and the Culture Industry*. New York: Routledge, 1997.

Zipes, Jack, ed. *The Oxford Companion to Fairy Tales: The Western Fairy Tale Tradition from Medieval to Modern*. Oxford: Oxford University Press, 2000.

Zipes, Jack. *When Dreams Came True: Classical Fairy Tales and Their Traditions*. New York: Routledge, 1999.

Index